Safety Symbols

These symbols appear in laboratory activities.
They alert you to possible dangers and remind
you to work carefully.

General Safety Awareness Read all directions for an experiment several times. Follow the directions exactly as they are written. If you are in doubt, ask your teacher for assistance.

Physical Safety If the lab includes physical activity, use caution to avoid injuring yourself or others. Tell your teacher if there is a reason that you should not participate.

Safety Goggles Always wear safety goggles to protect your eyes in any activity involving chemicals, heating, or the possibility of broken glassware.

Lab Apron Wear a laboratory apron to protect your skin and clothing from harmful chemicals or hot materials.

Plastic Gloves Wear disposable plastic gloves to protect yourself from contact with chemicals that can be harmful. Keep your hands away from your face. Dispose of gloves according to your teacher's instructions.

Heating Use a clamp or tongs to hold hot objects. Test an object by first holding the back of your hand near it. If you feel heat, the object may be too hot to handle.

Heat-Resistant Gloves Hot plates, hot water, and hot glassware can cause burns. Never touch hot objects with your bare hands. Use an oven mitt or other hand protection.

Flames Tie back long hair and loose clothing, and put on safety goggles before using a burner. Follow instructions from your teacher for lighting and extinguishing burners.

No Flames If flammable materials are present, make sure there are no flames, sparks, or exposed sources of heat.

Electric Shock To avoid an electric shock, never use electrical equipment near water, or when the equipment or your hands are wet. Use only sockets that accept a three-prong plug. Be sure cords are untangled and cannot trip anyone. Disconnect equipment that is not in use.

Fragile Glassware Handle fragile glassware, such as thermometers, test tubes, and beakers, with care. Do not touch broken glass. Notify your teacher if glassware breaks. Never use chipped or cracked glassware.

Corrosive Chemical Avoid getting corrosive chemicals on your skin or clothing, or in your eyes. Do not inhale the vapors. Wash your hands after completing the activity.

Poison Do not let any poisonous chemical get on your skin, and do not inhale its vapor. Wash your hands after completing the activity.

Fumes When working with poisonous or irritating vapors, work in a well-ventilated area. Never test for an odor unless instructed to do so by your teacher. Avoid inhaling a vapor directly. Use a wafting motion to direct vapor toward your nose.

Sharp Object Use sharp instruments only as directed. Scissors, scalpels, pins, and knives are sharp and can cut or puncture your skin. Always direct sharp edges and points away from yourself and others.

Disposal All chemicals and other materials used in the laboratory must be disposed of safely. Follow your teacher's instructions.

Hand Washing Before leaving the lab, wash your hands thoroughly with soap or detergent, and warm water. Lather both sides of your hands and between your fingers. Rinse well.

Cells and Heredity

PRENTICE HALL Science Explorer

PEARSON

Prentice Hall

Boston, Massachusetts
Upper Saddle River, New Jersey

Cells and Heredity

Book-Specific Resources

Student Edition
StudentExpress™ with Interactive Textbook
Teacher's Edition
All-in-One Teaching Resources
Color Transparencies
Guided Reading and Study Workbook
Student Edition on Audio CD
Discovery Channel School® Video
Lab Activity Video
Consumable and Nonconsumable Materials Kits

Program Print Resources

Integrated Science Laboratory Manual
Computer Microscope Lab Manual
Inquiry Skills Activity Books
Progress Monitoring Assessments
Test Preparation Workbook
Test-Taking Tips With Transparencies
Teacher's ELL Handbook
Reading Strategies for Science Content

Differentiated Instruction Resources

Adapted Reading and Study Workbook
Adapted Tests
Differentiated Instruction Guide for Labs and Activities

Program Technology Resources

TeacherExpress™ CD-ROM
Interactive Textbooks Online
PresentationExpress™ CD-ROM
ExamView®, Computer Test Bank CD-ROM
Lab zone™ Easy Planner CD-ROM
Probeware Lab Manual With CD-ROM
Computer Microscope and Lab Manual
Materials Ordering CD-ROM
Discovery Channel School® DVD Library
Lab Activity DVD Library
Web Site at PHSchool.com

Spanish Print Resources

Spanish Student Edition
Spanish Guided Reading and Study Workbook
Spanish Teaching Guide With Tests

Acknowledgments appear on page 210, which constitutes an extension of this copyright page.

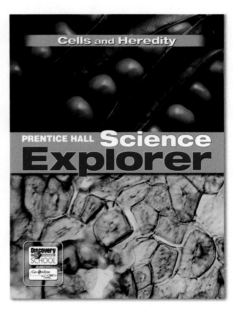

Cover
Ripe peas represent both the end and the beginning of a reproductive cycle (top). The thick walls of pea seed cells protect the cells' contents (bottom).

PEARSON

Prentice Hall

ISBN 0-13-115088-X

5 6 7 8 9 10   09 08 07 06

Program Authors

Michael J. Padilla, Ph.D.
Professor of Science Education
University of Georgia
Athens, Georgia

Michael Padilla is a leader in middle school science education. He has served as an author and elected officer for the National Science Teachers Association and as a writer of the National Science Education Standards. As lead author of Science Explorer, Mike has inspired the team in developing a program that meets the needs of middle grades students, promotes science inquiry, and is aligned with the National Science Education Standards.

Ioannis Miaoulis, Ph.D.
President
Museum of Science
Boston, Massachusetts

Originally trained as a mechanical engineer, Ioannis Miaoulis is in the forefront of the national movement to increase technological literacy. As dean of the Tufts University School of Engineering, Dr. Miaoulis spearheaded the introduction of engineering into the Massachusetts curriculum. Currently he is working with school systems across the country to engage students in engineering activities and to foster discussions on the impact of science and technology on society.

Martha Cyr, Ph.D.
Director of K–12 Outreach
Worcester Polytechnic Institute
Worcester, Massachusetts

Martha Cyr is a noted expert in engineering outreach. She has over nine years of experience with programs and activities that emphasize the use of engineering principles, through hands-on projects, to excite and motivate students and teachers of mathematics and science in grades K–12. Her goal is to stimulate a continued interest in science and mathematics through engineering.

Book Author

Donald Cronkite, Ph.D.
Professor of Biology
Hope College
Holland, Michigan

Contributing Writer

Thomas R. Wellnitz
Science Instructor
The Paideia School
Atlanta, Georgia

Consultants

Reading Consultant

Nancy Romance, Ph.D.
Professor of Science
    Education
Florida Atlantic University
Fort Lauderdale, Florida

Mathematics Consultant

William Tate, Ph.D.
Professor of Education and
    Applied Statistics and
    Computation
Washington University
St. Louis, Missouri

Reviewers

Teacher Reviewers

David R. Blakely
Arlington High School
Arlington, Massachusetts

Jane E. Callery
Two Rivers Magnet Middle
School
East Hartford, Connecticut

Melissa Lynn Cook
Oakland Mills High School
Columbia, Maryland

James Fattic
Southside Middle School
Anderson, Indiana

Dan Gabel
Hoover Middle School
Rockville, Maryland

Wayne Goates
Eisenhower Middle School
Goddard, Kansas

Katherine Bobay Graser
Mint Hill Middle School
Charlotte, North Carolina

Darcy Hampton
Deal Junior High School
Washington, D.C.

Karen Kelly
Pierce Middle School
Waterford, Michigan

David Kelso
Manchester High School Central
Manchester, New Hampshire

Benigno Lopez, Jr.
Sleepy Hill Middle School
Lakeland, Florida

Angie L. Matamoros, Ph.D.
ALM Consulting, INC.
Weston, Florida

Tim McCollum
Charleston Middle School
Charleston, Illinois

Bruce A. Mellin
Brooks School
North Andover, Massachusetts

Ella Jay Parfitt
Southeast Middle School
Baltimore, Maryland

Evelyn A. Pizzarello
Louis M. Klein Middle School
Harrison, New York

Kathleen M. Poe
Fletcher Middle School
Jacksonville, Florida

Shirley Rose
Lewis and Clark Middle School
Tulsa, Oklahoma

Linda Sandersen
Greenfield Middle School
Greenfield, Wisconsin

Mary E. Solan
Southwest Middle School
Charlotte, North Carolina

Mary Stewart
University of Tulsa
Tulsa, Oklahoma

Paul Swenson
Billings West High School
Billings, Montana

Thomas Vaughn
Arlington High School
Arlington, Massachusetts

Susan C. Zibell
Central Elementary
Simsbury, Connecticut

Safety Reviewers

W. H. Breazeale, Ph.D.
Department of Chemistry
College of Charleston
Charleston, South Carolina

Ruth Hathaway, Ph.D.
Hathaway Consulting
Cape Girardeau, Missouri

Douglas Mandt, M.S.
Science Education Consultant
Edgewood, Washington

Activity Field Testers

Nicki Bibbo
Witchcraft Heights School
Salem, Massachusetts

Rose-Marie Botting
Broward County Schools
Fort Lauderdale, Florida

Colleen Campos
Laredo Middle School
Aurora, Colorado

Elizabeth Chait
W. L. Chenery Middle School
Belmont, Massachusetts

Holly Estes
Hale Middle School
Stow, Massachusetts

Laura Hapgood
Plymouth Community
Intermediate School
Plymouth, Massachusetts

Mary F. Lavin
Plymouth Community
Intermediate School
Plymouth, Massachusetts

James MacNeil, Ph.D.
Cambridge, Massachusetts

Lauren Magruder
St. Michael's Country
Day School
Newport, Rhode Island

Jeanne Maurand
Austin Preparatory School
Reading, Massachusetts

Joanne Jackson-Pelletier
Winman Junior High School
Warwick, Rhode Island

Warren Phillips
Plymouth Public Schools
Plymouth, Massachusetts

Carol Pirtle
Hale Middle School
Stow, Massachusetts

Kathleen M. Poe
Fletcher Middle School
Jacksonville, Florida

Cynthia B. Pope
Norfolk Public Schools
Norfolk, Virginia

Anne Scammell
Geneva Middle School
Geneva, New York

Karen Riley Sievers
Callanan Middle School
Des Moines, Iowa

David M. Smith
Eyer Middle School
Allentown, Pennsylvania

Gene Vitale
Parkland School
McHenry, Illinois

Contents

Cells and Heredity

Reference Section

VIDEO

Enhance understanding through dynamic video.

Preview Get motivated with this introduction to the chapter content.

Field Trip Explore a real-world story related to the chapter content.

Assessment Review content and take an assessment.

Web Links

Get connected to exciting Web resources in every lesson.

*SCi*LINKS™ **NSTA** Find Web links on topics relating to every section.

Active Art Interact with selected visuals from every chapter online.

Planet Diary® Explore news and natural phenomena through weekly reports.

Science News® Keep up to date with the latest science discoveries.

Experience the complete text-book online and on CD-ROM.

Activities Practice skills and learn content.

Videos Explore content and learn important lab skills.

Audio Support Hear key terms spoken and defined.

Self-Assessment Use instant feedback to help you track your progress.

Activities

FIGURE 12
Plant and Animal Cells
These illustrations show typical structures found in plant and animal cells. *Comparing and Contrasting* Identify one structure found in plant cells but not animal cells.

Endoplasmic Reticulum This network of passageways carries materials from one part of the cell to another.

Nucleus The nucleus directs all of the cell's activities, including reproduction.

Cytoplasm

Ribosomes

Cell Wall In a plant cell, a stiff wall surrounds the membrane, giving the cell a rigid, boxlike shape.

Chloroplasts These organelles capture energy from sunlight and use it to produce food for the cell.

Vacuole Most mature plant cells have one large vacuole. This sac within the cytoplasm stores water, food, waste products, and other materials.

Golgi Body

Mitochondrion

Cell Membrane The cell membrane protects the cell and regulates what substances enter and leave the cell.

Plant Cell

20 ◆ C

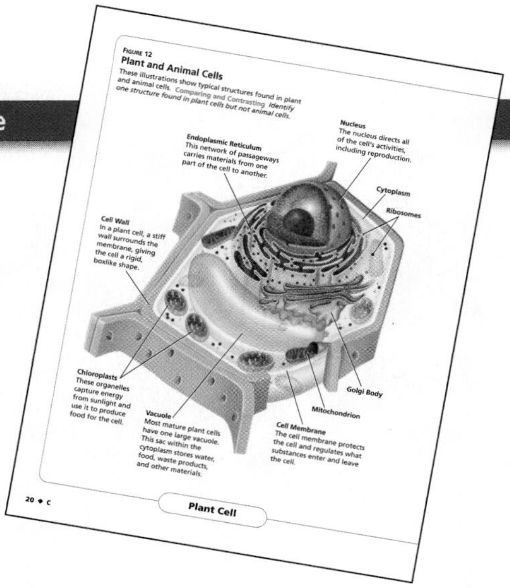

An Unfolding Mystery

Understanding the cause of a disease is the first step toward finding a cure. Dr. Wilfredo Colón searches for the causes of certain human diseases. But he is not a physician working in a hospital. Dr. Colón, who likes to be called "Freddie," is a biochemist who works in a laboratory. He uses microscopes, computers, and other equipment to find out how proteins can cause disease.

Proteins are an essential part of every living cell. "Proteins are the building blocks of cells," Dr. Colón explains. "You know that your body is made mostly of water. If you took all of the water out of your body, most of what would be left would be proteins."

Proteins are made up of chains of chemicals called amino acids. The amino acids are chemically strung together like beads on a string. Each protein has its own unique series of amino acids, and there are tens of thousands of different proteins in the human body. If a protein chain does not form correctly, it can mean big trouble for the cell.

Freddie Colón is working to solve the mystery of folding and misfolding proteins.

Scientists created this computer model of protein folding.

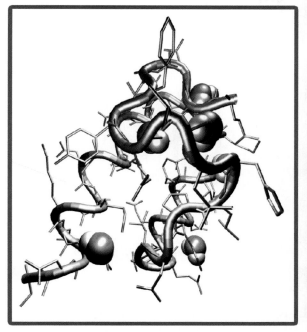

Freddie Colón uses a spectrophotometer to set up samples for a protein folding experiment.

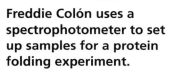

Career Path

Wilfredo Colón was born in New York City and moved with his family to Puerto Rico when he was 10 years old. He received his bachelor's degree at the University of Puerto Rico at Mayagüez. Now he is an associate professor of chemistry at Rensselaer Polytechnic Institute, in Troy, New York. In 2000, Freddie received the Presidential Early Career Award for Scientists and Engineers. In 2002, he received a federal grant for one million dollars to fund his research into ALS.

Talking with **Wilfredo Colón**

? **W**hy is protein shape important?

As a protein chain forms inside the cell, it folds into a shape particular to that protein. The shape of a protein is sometimes compared to a key that fits into a lock. If the shape of the lock is incorrect, the key will no longer work. If the shape of a protein is wrong, it won't function properly. Disease may result. "No one knows exactly what makes normal proteins fold the way they do," says Freddie. "Until we know that, we won't fully understand how to cure diseases that occur when the folding goes wrong."

? **W**hat happens when proteins misfold?

Misfolded proteins tend to stick together in clumps that are useless to the cell. The clumping of improperly folded, or misfolded, proteins is similar to what happens to an egg white when an egg is boiled. An egg white is mainly water and protein. When you first crack open an uncooked egg, the white is clear and runny. But when you cook an egg, the proteins it contains change shape, and the egg white becomes hard and is no longer clear. These changes are like the changes that occur when a protein folds incorrectly.

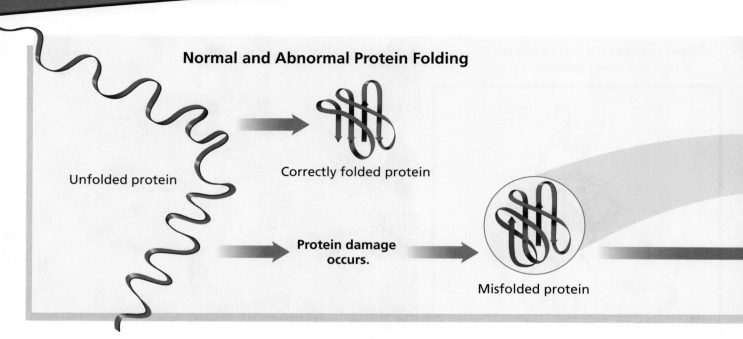

Normal and Abnormal Protein Folding

Unfolded protein

Correctly folded protein

Protein damage occurs.

Misfolded protein

? **W**hat diseases are caused by misfolding?

Diseases that may be caused by improperly folded proteins include Parkinson's disease, type II diabetes, and Alzheimer's disease. Dr. Colón is especially interested in finding out how misfolded proteins may cause a disease called amyotrophic lateral sclerosis (ALS), which is also known as Lou Gehrig's disease.

Lou Gehrig, who played first base for the New York Yankees, was one of baseball's greatest players. He died at age 38. The disease that took his life was named after him.

? **W**hat is ALS?

"ALS is a disease of the nerve cells that tell your muscles to move," Freddie explains. "A person with ALS slowly loses the ability to move. The disease is always fatal. Many scientists hypothesize that ALS may be caused by proteins that do not fold correctly." On average, ALS strikes people who are around 50 years of age.

? **W**hat causes ALS?

In ALS, the misfolded proteins appear to poison nerve cells, the cells that control movement. Misfolded proteins are too large for the cell to get rid of, so they build up inside the cell. Nerve cells that contain too many protein clumps can no longer receive signals from the brain. Without instruction from the brain, muscles cannot move. Over time, as more and more nerve cells die, the muscles completely lose their ability to move.

? **H**ow do you research proteins?

"We are researching two areas," Freddie explains. "First, we are trying to understand how proteins fold correctly.

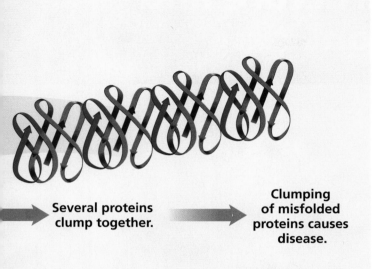

Several proteins clump together. → Clumping of misfolded proteins causes disease.

"I can think of four things that make a good scientist," says Freddie. "First, scientists need to be hardworking. In my job, I do whatever my work requires. Often that means long hours. Second, scientists need to have perseverance. You have to realize that many of your experiments won't work! Perseverance means to keep going even when nothing is going right. Third, I think scientists have to be able to see many aspects of a problem and put them together toward a possible solution. Finally, and most important, a scientist needs confidence. If you want to be a scientist, go for it!"

"Second, we are testing the hypothesis that certain ALS cases are caused by the misfolding of a particular protein. Since we can't see protein molecules with our eyes, we use a machine called a spectrophotometer.

"The spectrophotometer can tell us when the protein is folded correctly or when it misfolds and clumps up. We use an atomic force microscope to look at the shape of the clumped protein.

"If we can unlock the mystery of how the ALS protein behaves, we may begin to understand how it causes disease. We could begin to look for medicines that would slow the progress of this disease. This information would help us better understand other diseases that seem to be caused by protein misfolding."

? **D**id you always want to be a scientist?

"No!" Freddie exclaims. "I always wanted to be a physician, to cure diseases. But, when I took a chemistry class in my second year of college, that subject really came alive for me. Then I saw an ad for an undergraduate research assistant in a laboratory and applied for the job. This opportunity to do research was a turning point for me, and I decided on a career in chemistry. Now I work on chains of amino acids that make up proteins. So, instead of a physician, now I'm a scientist!"

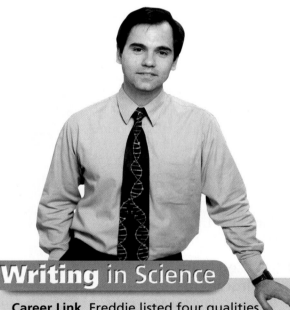

Writing in Science

Career Link Freddie listed four qualities that make a good scientist. One of those qualities is perseverance. Someone with perseverance doesn't give up when faced with difficulties. In a paragraph, describe how perseverance might help in a science career.

Go Online
PHSchool.com

For: More on this career
Visit: PHSchool.com
Web Code: ceb-3000

Chapter 1

Cell Structure and Function

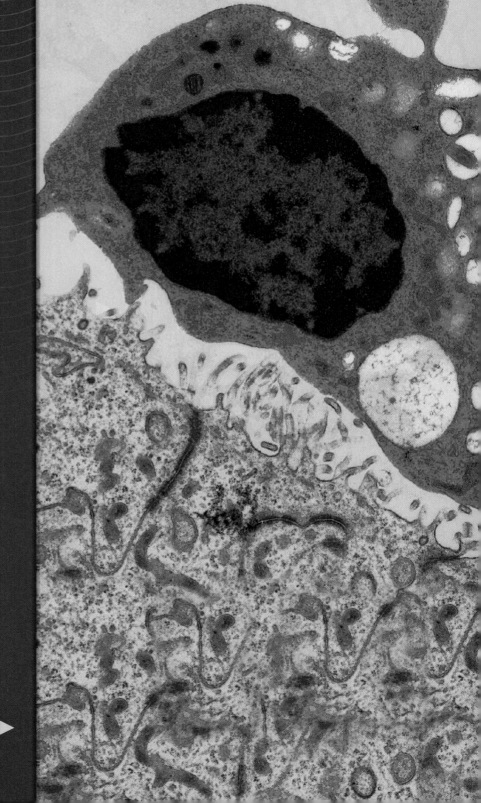

The cell that has been colored red is found in blood. This kind of cell destroys bacteria. ▶

◢Lab zone™ Chapter **Project**

Egg-speriment With a Cell

In this chapter, you'll learn that all living things are made of cells—sometimes just one cell, sometimes trillions! You can study an everyday object that can serve as a model of a cell: an uncooked egg.

Your Goal To observe how various materials enter or leave a cell, using an egg as a model of the cell

To complete this project, you will

● observe what happens when you soak an uncooked egg in vinegar, then in water, food coloring, salt water, and finally in a liquid of your choice

● measure the circumference of the egg every day, and graph your results

● explain the changes that you observe in your egg

● follow the safety guidelines in Appendix A

Plan It! Predict what might happen when you put an uncooked egg in vinegar for two days. How might other liquids affect an egg? Find a place where you can leave your egg undisturbed. Then begin your egg-speriment!

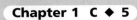

Discovering Cells

Reading Preview

Key Concepts
- What are cells?
- How did the invention of the microscope contribute to knowledge about living things?
- What is the cell theory?
- How do microscopes produce magnified images?

Key Terms
- cell • microscope • cell theory

Target Reading Skill
Sequencing A sequence is the order in which a series of events occurs. As you read, construct a flowchart showing how the work of Hooke, Leeuwenhoek, Schleiden, Schwann, and Virchow contributed to scientific understanding of cells.

Discovering Cells

Hooke sees cells in cork.

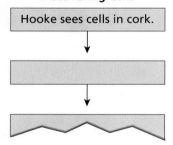

Lab zone Discover **Activity**

Is Seeing Believing?

1. ✂ Cut a black-and-white photograph out of a page in a newspaper. With only your eyes, closely examine the photo. Record your observations.
2. Examine the same photo with a hand lens. Again, record your observations.
3. Place the photo on the stage of a microscope. Use the clips to hold the photo in place. Shine a light down on the photo. Focus the microscope on part of the photo. (See Appendix B for instructions on using the microscope.) Record your observations.

Think It Over
Observing What did you see in the photo with the hand lens that you could not see with only your eyes? What additional details could you see with the microscope?

A forest is filled with an amazing variety of living things. Some are easy to see, but you have to look closely to find others. If you look carefully at the floor of a forest, you can often find spots of bright color. A beautiful pink coral fungus grows beneath tall trees. Beside the pink fungus, a tiny red newt perches on a fallen leaf.

What do you think a fungus, a tree, and a red newt have in common? They are all living things, or organisms, and, like all organisms, they are made of cells.

FIGURE 1
Newt and Coral Fungus
All living things are made of cells, including this pink fungus and the red newt that perches next to it.

An Overview of Cells

You are made of cells. **Cells are the basic units of structure and function in living things.** This means that **cells** form the parts of an organism and carry out all of an organism's processes, or functions.

Cells and Structure When you describe the structure of an object, you describe what it is made of and how its parts are put together. The structures of many buildings, for example, are determined by the way in which bricks, steel beams, and other materials are arranged. The structures of living things are determined by the amazing variety of ways in which cells are put together. A tall tree, for example, consists of cells arranged to form a high trunk and leafy branches. A red newt's cells form a body with a head and four legs.

Cells and Function An organism's functions are the processes that enable it to stay alive and reproduce. Some functions in organisms include obtaining oxygen, getting rid of wastes, obtaining food, and growing. Cells are involved in all these functions. For example, cells in your digestive system absorb food. The food provides your body with energy and materials needed for growth.

Many and Small Figure 2 shows human skin cells. One square centimeter of your skin's surface contains more than 100,000 cells. But no matter how closely you look with your eyes alone, you won't be able to see individual skin cells. That is because, like most cells, those of your skin are very small. Until the late 1600s, no one knew cells existed because there was no way to see them.

 **What are some functions that cells perform in living things?**

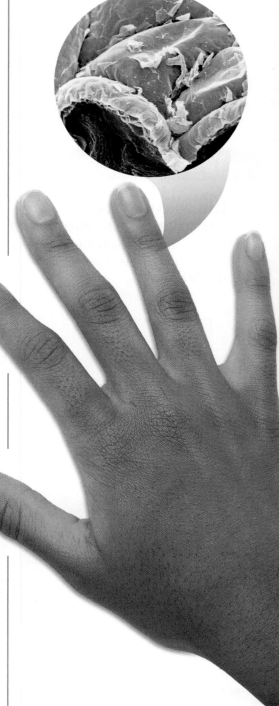

FIGURE 2
Skin Cells
Your skin is made of cells such as these. **Applying Concepts** *What are cells?*

First Observations of Cells

Around 1590, the invention of the microscope enabled people to look at very small objects. **The invention of the microscope made it possible for people to discover and learn about cells.** A **microscope** is an instrument that makes small objects look larger. Some microscopes do this by using lenses to focus light. The lenses used in light microscopes are similar to the clear, curved pieces of glass or plastic used in eyeglasses. A simple microscope contains only one lens. A light microscope that has more than one lens is called a compound microscope.

Robert Hooke One of the first people to observe cells was the English scientist and inventor Robert Hooke. Hooke built his own compound microscope, which was one of the best microscopes of his time. In 1663, Hooke used his microscope to observe the structure of a thin slice of cork. Cork, the bark of the cork oak tree, is made up of cells that are no longer alive. To Hooke, the empty spaces in the cork looked like tiny rectangular rooms. Therefore, Hooke called the empty spaces *cells*, which is a word meaning "small rooms."

Hooke described his observations this way: "These pores, or cells, were not very deep, but consisted of a great many little boxes. . . ." What most amazed Hooke was how many cells the cork contained. He calculated that in a cubic inch there were about twelve hundred million cells—a number he described as "almost incredible."

• Tech & Design in History •

The Microscope: Improvements Over Time

The microscope made the discovery of cells possible. Microscopes have improved in many ways over the last 400 years.

1590 First Compound Microscope
Dutch eyeglass makers Zacharias and Hans Janssen made one of the first compound microscopes. It was a tube with a lens at each end.

1674 Leeuwenhoek's Simple Microscope
Although Anton Von Leeuwenhoek's simple microscope used only one tiny lens, it could magnify a specimen up to 266 times.

1660 Hooke's Compound Microscope
Robert Hooke's compound microscope included an oil lamp for lighting. A lens focuses light from the flame onto the specimen.

1500	1600	1700

Anton van Leeuwenhoek At about the same time that Robert Hooke made his discovery, Anton van Leeuwenhoek (LAY vun hook) also began to observe tiny objects with microscopes. Leeuwenhoek was a Dutch businessman who sold cloth. In his spare time, he built simple microscopes.

Leeuwenhoek looked at drops of lake water, scrapings from teeth and gums, and water from rain gutters. In many materials, Leeuwenhoek was surprised to find a variety of one-celled organisms. Leeuwenhoek noted that many of these tiny organisms moved. Some whirled, some hopped, and some shot through water like fast fish. He called these moving organisms *animalcules* (an ih MAL kyoolz), meaning "little animals."

 **Reading Checkpoint** **Which type of microscope—simple or compound— did Leeuwenhoek make and use?**

Writing in Science

Research and Write Find out more about one of the microscopes. Then write an advertisement for it that might appear in a popular science magazine. Be creative. Emphasize the microscope's usefulness or describe the wonders that can be seen with it.

1965 Scanning Electron Microscope (SEM)
An SEM sends electrons over the surface of a specimen, rather than through it. The result is a three-dimensional image of the specimen's surface. SEMs can magnify a specimen up to 150,000 times.

1981 Scanning Tunneling Microscope (STM)
An STM measures electrons that leak, or "tunnel," from the surface of a specimen. STMs can magnify a specimen up to 1,000,000 times.

1886 Modern Compound Light Microscope
German scientists Ernst Abbé and Carl Zeiss made a compound light microscope with complex lenses that greatly improved the image. A mirror focuses light up through the specimen. Modern compound microscopes can effectively magnify a specimen up to 1,000 times.

1933 Transmission Electron Microscope (TEM)
German physicist Ernst Ruska created the first electron microscope. TEMs send electrons through a very thinly sliced specimen. TEMs can magnify a specimen up to 500,000 times.

| 1800 | 1900 | 2000 |

FIGURE 3
Monarch and Milkweed
The monarch butterfly caterpillar and the milkweed leaf that the caterpillar nibbles on are both made of cells.

Plant Cells

Animal Cells

Development of the Cell Theory

Leeuwenhoek's exciting discoveries caught the attention of other researchers. Like Hooke, Leeuwenhoek, and all good scientists, these other researchers were curious about the world around them, including things they couldn't normally see. Many other people began to use microscopes to discover what secrets they could learn about cells.

Schleiden, Schwann, and Virchow Three German scientists made especially important contributions to people's knowledge about cells. These scientists were Matthias Schleiden (SHLY dun), Theodor Schwann, and Rudolf Virchow (FUR koh). In 1838, Schleiden concluded that all plants are made of cells. He based this conclusion on his own research and on the research of others before him. The next year, Theodor Schwann concluded that all animals are also made up of cells. Thus, stated Schwann, all living things are made up of cells.

Schleiden and Schwann had made an important discovery about living things. However, they didn't explain where cells came from. Until their time, most people thought that living things could come from nonliving matter. In 1855, Virchow proposed that new cells are formed only from cells that already exist. "All cells come from cells," wrote Virchow.

What the Cell Theory Says Schleiden, Schwann, Virchow, and others helped develop the cell theory. The **cell theory** is a widely accepted explanation of the relationship between cells and living things. **The cell theory states the following:**

- **All living things are composed of cells.**

- **Cells are the basic units of structure and function in living things.**

- **All cells are produced from other cells.**

Go Online
SCi**LINKS** NSTA

For: Links on cell theory
Visit: www.SciLinks.org
Web Code: scn-0311

The cell theory holds true for all living things, no matter how big or how small. Since cells are common to all living things, they can provide information about the functions that living things perform. Because all cells come from other cells, scientists can study cells to learn about growth and reproduction.

 **Reading Checkpoint** **What did Schleiden and Schwann conclude about cells?**

Light and Electron Microscopes

The cell theory could not have been developed without microscopes. For a microscope to be useful, it must combine two important properties—magnification and resolution. Scientists today use two kinds of microscopes: light microscopes and electron microscopes.

Magnification and Lenses The first property, magnification, is the ability to make things look larger than they are. **The lenses in light microscopes magnify an object by bending the light that passes through them.** If you examine a hand lens, such as the one in Figure 4, you will see that the lens is curved, not flat. The center of the lens is thicker than the edge. A lens with this curved shape is called a convex lens. The light passing through the sides of the lens bends inward. When this light hits the eye, the eye sees the object as larger than it really is.

Lab zone Skills Activity

Observing

1. Read about using the microscope (Appendix B) before beginning this activity.

2. Place a prepared slide of a thin slice of cork on the stage of a microscope.

3. Observe the slide under low power. Draw what you see.

4. Place a few drops of pond water on another slide and cover it with a coverslip.

5. Observe the slide under low power. Draw what you see. Wash your hands after handling pond water.

How does your drawing in Step 3 compare to Hooke's description of cells on page 8? Based on your observations in Step 5, why did Leeuwenhoek call the organisms he saw "little animals"?

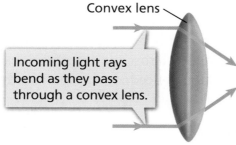

Convex lens

Incoming light rays bend as they pass through a convex lens.

FIGURE 4
A Convex Lens
A magnifying glass is a convex lens. The lines in the diagram represent rays of light, and the arrows show the direction in which the light travels.
Interpreting Diagrams *Describe what happens to light rays as they pass through a convex lens.*

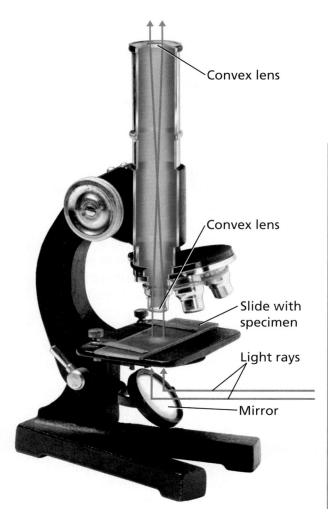

Convex lens

Convex lens

Slide with specimen

Light rays

Mirror

FIGURE 5

A Compound Microscope

A compound microscope has two convex lenses.

Calculating *If one lens has a magnification of 10, and the other lens has a magnification of 50, what is the total magnification?*

Compound Microscope Magnification Since a compound microscope uses more than one lens, it can magnify an object more than one lens by itself. Light passes through a specimen and then through two lenses, as shown in Figure 5. The first lens, near the specimen, magnifies the object. Then a second lens, near the eye, further magnifies the enlarged image. The total magnification of the microscope is equal to the magnifications of the two lenses multiplied together. For example, suppose the first lens makes an object look 10 times bigger than it actually is, and the second lens makes the object look 40 times bigger than it actually is. The total magnification of the microscope is 10×40, or 400.

Resolution To create a useful image, a microscope must also help you see individual parts clearly. The ability to clearly distinguish the individual parts of an object is called resolution. Resolution is another term for the sharpness of an image. For example, a photograph in a newspaper is really made up of a collection of small dots. If you put the photo under a microscope, you can see the dots. You see the dots not only because they are magnified but also because the microscope improves resolution. Good resolution is needed when you study cells.

FIGURE 6

Light Microscope Photos

The pictures of the water flea and the threadlike *Spirogyra* were both taken with a light microscope.

Water flea
40 times actual size

Spirogyra
300 times actual size

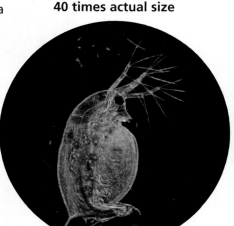

FIGURE 7
Electron Microscope Picture
A head louse clings to a human hair. This picture was taken with a scanning electron microscope. The louse has been magnified to more than 100 times its actual size.

Electron Microscopes The microscopes used by Hooke, Leeuwenhoek, and other early researchers were all light microscopes. Since the 1930s, scientists have developed different types of electron microscopes. **Electron microscopes use a beam of electrons instead of light to produce a magnified image.** Electrons are tiny particles that are smaller than atoms. Electron microscopes can obtain pictures of extremely small objects—much smaller than those that can be seen with light microscopes. The resolution of electron microscopes is much better than the resolution of light microscopes.

 **Reading Checkpoint** **What do electron microscopes use to produce magnified images?**

Section 1 Assessment

Target Reading Skill Sequencing Review your flowchart and use it to answer Questions 2 and 3 below.

Reviewing Key Concepts

1. **a. Defining** Define *structure* and *function*.
   b. Explaining Explain this statement: Cells are the basic units of structure and function in organisms.
   c. Applying Concepts In what important function are the cells in your eyes involved?
2. **a. Reviewing** What does a microscope enable people to do?
   b. Summarizing Summarize Hooke's observations of cork under a microscope.
   c. Relating Cause and Effect Why would Hooke's discovery have been impossible without a microscope?
3. **a. Reviewing** What are the main ideas of the cell theory?
   b. Explaining What did Virchow contribute to the cell theory?

   c. Applying Concepts Use the ideas of Virchow to explain why plastic plants and stuffed animals are not alive.
4. **a. Defining** What is magnification?
   b. Comparing and Contrasting Contrast the way light microscopes and electron microscopes magnify objects.

Writing in Science

Writing an Award Speech Suppose you are a member of a scientific society that is giving an award to one of the early cell scientists. Choose the scientist, and write a speech that you might give at the award ceremony. Your speech should describe the scientist's accomplishments.

Technology Lab
· Tech & Design ·

Design and Build a Microscope

Problem
How can you design and build a compound microscope?

Design Skills
building a prototype, evaluating design constraints

Materials
- book
- 2 dual magnifying glasses, each with one high-power and one low-power lens
- metric ruler
- 2 cardboard tubes from paper towels, or black construction paper
- tape

Procedure

PART 1 Research and Investigate

1. Work with a partner. Using only your eyes, examine words in a book. Then use the high-power lens to examine the same words. In your notebook, contrast what you saw with and without the magnifying lens.

2. Hold the high-power lens about 5–6 cm above the words in the book. When you look at the words through the lens, they will look blurry.

3. Keep the high-power lens about 5–6 cm above the words. Hold the low-power lens above the high-power lens, as shown in the photograph on the right.

4. Move the low-power lens up and down until the image is in focus and upside down. (*Hint:* You may have to move the high-power lens up or down slightly too.)

5. Once the image is in focus, experiment with raising and lowering both lenses. Your goal is to produce the highest magnification while keeping the image in clear focus.

6. When the image is in focus at the position of highest magnification, have your lab partner measure and record the distance between the book and the high-power lens. Your lab partner should also measure and record the distance between the two lenses.

7. Write a description of how the magnified words viewed through two lenses compares with the words seen without magnification.

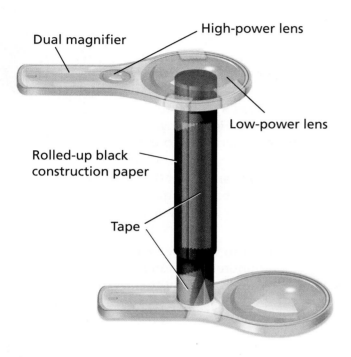

Dual magnifier

High-power lens

Low-power lens

Rolled-up black construction paper

Tape

PART 2

Design and Build

8. Based on what you learned in Part 1, work with a partner to design your own two-lens (compound) microscope. Your microscope should
   - consist of one high-power lens and one low-power lens, each attached to a tube of paper or rolled-up cardboard
   - allow one tube to fit snugly inside the other tube so the distance between the two lenses can be easily adjusted
   - focus to produce a clear, enlarged, upside-down image of the object
   - be made from dual magnifying glasses, cardboard tubes, and tape

9. Sketch your design on a sheet of paper. Obtain your teacher's approval for your design. Then construct your microscope.

PART 3 **Evaluate and Redesign**

10. Test your microscope by examining printed words or a printed photograph. Then, examine other objects such as a leaf or your skin. Record your observations. Did your microscope meet the criteria listed in Step 8?

11. Examine microscopes made by other students. Based on your tests and your examination of other microscopes, list ways you could improve your microscope.

Analyze and Conclude

1. **Observing** Compare the images you observed using one lens with the image from two lenses.

2. **Evaluating** When you used two lenses, how did moving the top lens up and down affect the image? What was the effect of moving the bottom lens up and down?

3. **Building a Prototype** Describe how you built your microscope and explain why you built it that way.

4. **Evaluating the Impact on Society** Describe some of the ways that microscopes have aided scientists in their work.

Communicate

Imagine it is 1675. Write an explanation that will convince scientists to use your new microscope rather than the single-lens variety used by Leeuwenhoek.

Looking Inside Cells

Reading Preview

Key Concepts
- What role do the cell wall and cell membrane play in the cell?
- What are the functions of cell organelles?
- How are cells organized in many-celled organisms?
- How do bacterial cells differ from plant and animal cells?

Key Terms
- organelle • cell wall
- cell membrane • nucleus
- cytoplasm • mitochondria
- endoplasmic reticulum
- ribosome • Golgi body
- chloroplast • vacuole
- lysosome

Target Reading Skill
Previewing Visuals Before you read, preview Figure 12. Then write two questions that you have about the illustrations in a graphic organizer like the one below. As you read, answer your questions.

Plant and Animal Cells

Q.	How are animal cells different from plant cells?
A.	
Q.	

Discover Activity

How Large Are Cells?

1. Look at the organism in the photo. The organism is an amoeba (uh MEE buh), a large single-celled organism. This type of amoeba is about 1 mm long.
2. Multiply your height in meters by 1,000 to get your height in millimeters. How many amoebas would you have to stack end-to-end to equal your height?
3. Many of the cells in your body are about 0.01 mm long—one hundredth the size of an amoeba. How many body cells would you have to stack end-to-end to equal your height?

Think It Over
Inferring Look at a metric ruler to see how small 1 mm is. Now imagine a distance one one-hundredth as long, or 0.01 mm. Why can't you see your body's cells without the aid of a microscope?

Nasturtiums brighten up many gardens with green leaves and colorful flowers. How do nasturtiums carry out all the functions necessary to stay alive? To answer this question, you are about to take an imaginary journey. You will travel inside a nasturtium leaf, visiting its tiny cells. You will observe some of the structures found in plant cells. You will also learn some differences between plant and animal cells.

As you will discover on your journey, there are even smaller structures inside a cell. These tiny cell structures, called **organelles,** carry out specific functions within the cell. Just as your stomach, lungs, and heart have different functions in your body, each organelle has a different function within the cell. Now it's time to hop aboard your imaginary ship and sail into a typical plant cell.

Nasturtiums ▶

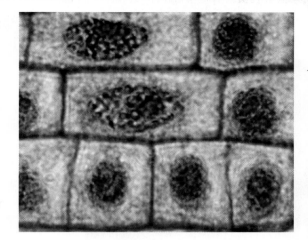

◄ Onion root cells

Paramecium ▼

Enter the Cell

Your ship doesn't have an easy time getting inside the cell. It has to pass through the cell wall and the cell membrane.

Cell Wall As you travel through the plant cell, refer to Figure 12. First, you must slip through the cell wall. The **cell wall** is a rigid layer of nonliving material that surrounds the cells of plants and some other organisms. The cells of animals, in contrast, do not have cell walls. **A plant's cell wall helps to protect and support the cell.** The cell wall is made mostly of a strong material called cellulose. Although the cell wall is tough, many materials, including water and oxygen, can pass through easily.

Cell Membrane After you sail through the cell wall, the next barrier you must cross is the **cell membrane**. All cells have cell membranes. In cells with cell walls, the cell membrane is located just inside the cell wall. In other cells, the cell membrane forms the outside boundary that separates the cell from its environment.

The cell membrane controls what substances come into and out of a cell. Everything the cell needs, from food to oxygen, enters the cell through the cell membrane. Fortunately, your ship can slip through, too. Harmful waste products leave the cell through the cell membrane. For a cell to survive, the cell membrane must allow these materials to pass in and out. In addition, the cell membrane prevents harmful materials from entering the cell. In a sense, the cell membrane is like a window screen. The screen allows air to enter and leave a room, but it keeps insects out.

FIGURE 8
Cell Wall and Cell Membrane
The onion root cells have both a cell wall and a cell membrane. The single-celled paramecium has only a cell membrane.
Interpreting Photographs *What shape do the cell walls give to the onion root cells?*

 **Reading Checkpoint** **What is the function of the cell wall?**

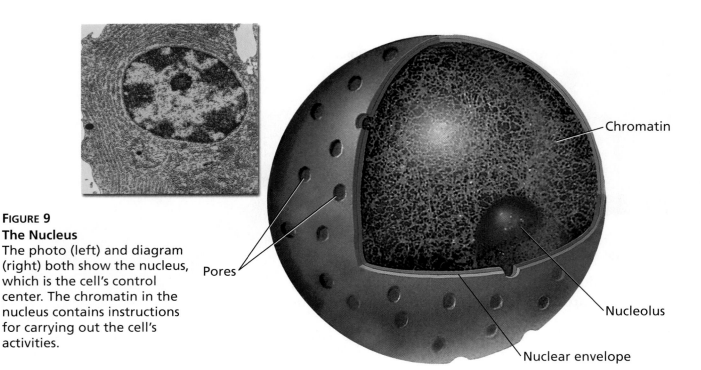

FIGURE 9
The Nucleus
The photo (left) and diagram (right) both show the nucleus, which is the cell's control center. The chromatin in the nucleus contains instructions for carrying out the cell's activities.

Chromatin

Pores

Nucleolus

Nuclear envelope

Sail on to the Nucleus

As you sail inside the cell, a large, oval structure comes into view. This structure, called the **nucleus** (NOO klee us), acts as the "brain" of the cell. **You can think of the nucleus as the cell's control center, directing all of the cell's activities.**

Nuclear Envelope Notice in Figure 9 that the nucleus is surrounded by a membrane called the nuclear envelope. Just as a mailing envelope protects the letter inside it, the nuclear envelope protects the nucleus. Materials pass in and out of the nucleus through pores in the nuclear envelope. So aim for that pore just ahead and carefully glide into the nucleus.

Chromatin You might wonder how the nucleus "knows" how to direct the cell. The answer lies in those thin strands floating directly ahead in the nucleus. These strands, called chromatin, contain genetic material, the instructions for directing the cell's functions. For example, the instructions in the chromatin ensure that leaf cells grow and divide to form more leaf cells.

Nucleolus As you prepare to leave the nucleus, you spot a small object floating by. This structure, a nucleolus, is where ribosomes are made. Ribosomes are the organelles where proteins are produced. Proteins are important chemicals in cells.

 Reading Checkpoint **Where in the nucleus is genetic material found?**

FIGURE 10
Mitochondrion
The mitochondria produce most of the cell's energy. *Inferring In what types of cells would you expect to find a lot of mitochondria?*

Organelles in the Cytoplasm

As you leave the nucleus, you find yourself in the **cytoplasm,** the region between the cell membrane and the nucleus. Your ship floats in a clear, thick, gel-like fluid. The fluid in the cytoplasm is constantly moving, so your ship does not need to propel itself. Many cell organelles are found in the cytoplasm.

Mitochondria Suddenly, rod-shaped structures loom ahead. These organelles are **mitochondria** (my tuh KAHN dree uh) (singular *mitochondrion*). **Mitochondria are known as the "powerhouses" of the cell because they convert energy in food molecules to energy the cell can use to carry out its functions.** Figure 10 shows a mitochondrion up close.

Endoplasmic Reticulum As you sail farther into the cytoplasm, you find yourself in a maze of passageways called the **endoplasmic reticulum** (en duh PLAZ mik rih TIK yuh lum). **The endoplasmic reticulum's passageways carry proteins and other materials from one part of the cell to another.**

Ribosomes Attached to some surfaces of the endoplasmic reticulum are small, grainlike bodies called **ribosomes.** Other ribosomes float in the cytoplasm. **Ribosomes function as factories to produce proteins.** Some newly made proteins are released through the wall of the endoplasmic reticulum. From the interior of the endoplasmic reticulum, the proteins will be transported to the Golgi bodies.

FIGURE 11
Endoplasmic Reticulum
The endoplasmic reticulum is similar to the system of hallways in a building. Proteins and other materials move throughout the cell by way of the endoplasmic reticulum. The spots on this organelle are ribosomes, which produce proteins.

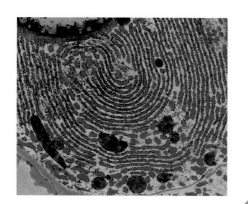

Ribosomes

FIGURE 12
Plant and Animal Cells

These illustrations show typical structures found in plant and animal cells. **Comparing and Contrasting** *Identify one structure found in plant cells but not animal cells.*

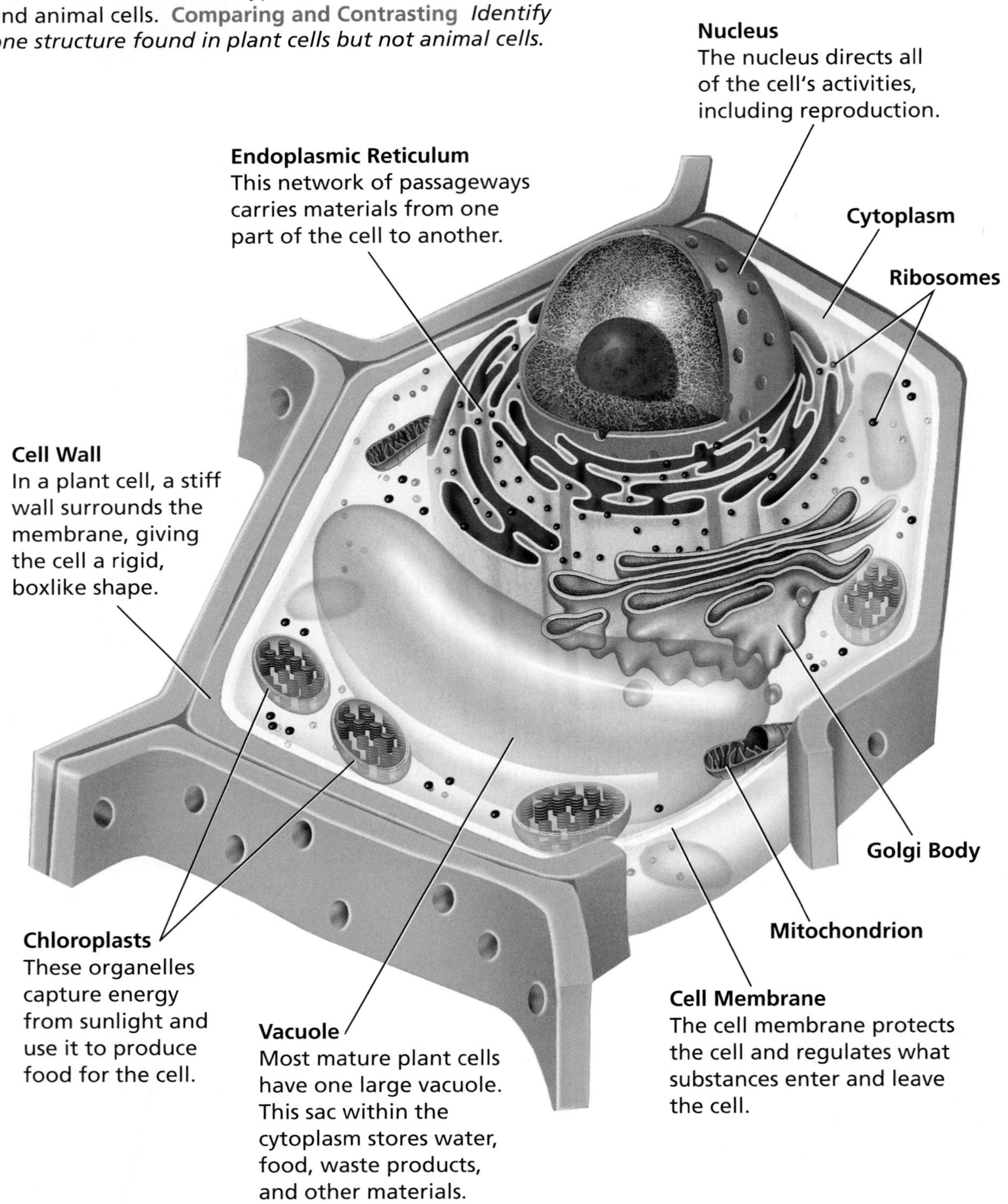

Nucleus
The nucleus directs all of the cell's activities, including reproduction.

Endoplasmic Reticulum
This network of passageways carries materials from one part of the cell to another.

Cytoplasm

Ribosomes

Cell Wall
In a plant cell, a stiff wall surrounds the membrane, giving the cell a rigid, boxlike shape.

Chloroplasts
These organelles capture energy from sunlight and use it to produce food for the cell.

Vacuole
Most mature plant cells have one large vacuole. This sac within the cytoplasm stores water, food, waste products, and other materials.

Cell Membrane
The cell membrane protects the cell and regulates what substances enter and leave the cell.

Golgi Body

Mitochondrion

Plant Cell

Ribosomes
These small structures function as factories to produce proteins. Ribosomes may be attached to the endoplasmic reticulum, or they may float in the cytoplasm.

Cytoplasm
The cytoplasm includes a gel-like fluid in which many different organelles are found.

Nucleus
The nucleus directs all of the cell's activities, including reproduction.

Mitochondria
Most of the cell's energy is produced within these rod-shaped organelles.

Endoplasmic Reticulum

Golgi Body
The Golgi bodies receive materials from the endoplasmic reticulum and send them to other parts of the cell. They also release materials outside the cell.

Lysosomes
These small organelles contain chemicals that break down food particles and worn-out cell parts.

Vacuole
Some animal cells have vacuoles that store food, water, waste, and other materials.

Cell Membrane
Since an animal cell does not have a cell wall, the cell membrane forms a barrier between the cytoplasm and the environment outside the cell.

Animal Cell

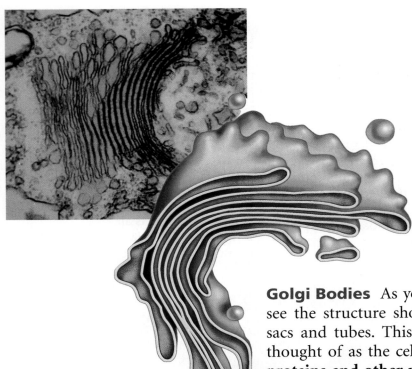

FIGURE 13
A Golgi Body
Golgi bodies are organelles that transport materials.

Golgi Bodies As you leave the endoplasmic reticulum, you see the structure shown in Figure 13. It looks like flattened sacs and tubes. This structure, called a **Golgi body,** can be thought of as the cell's mail room. **The Golgi bodies receive proteins and other newly formed materials from the endo- plasmic reticulum, package them, and distribute them to other parts of the cell.** The Golgi bodies also release materials outside the cell.

Chloroplasts Have you noticed the many large green struc- tures floating in the cytoplasm? Only the cells of plants and some other organisms have these green organelles called **chloroplasts. Chloroplasts capture energy from sunlight and use it to produce food for the cell.** Chloroplasts make leaves green.

Vacuoles Steer past the chloroplasts and head for that large, water-filled sac, called a **vacuole** (VAK yoo ohl), floating in the cytoplasm. **Vacuoles are the storage areas of cells.** Most plant cells have one large vacuole. Some animal cells do not have vacuoles; others do. Vacuoles store food and other materials needed by the cell. Vacuoles can also store waste products.

Lysosomes Your journey through the cell is almost over. Before you leave, take another look around you. If you carefully swing your ship around the vacuole, you may be lucky enough to see a **lysosome** (LY suh sohm). **Lysosomes are small, round structures containing chemicals that break down certain materials in the cell.** Some chemicals break down large food particles into smaller ones. Lysosomes also break down old cell parts and release the substances so they can be used again. In this sense, you can think of lysosomes as the cell's cleanup crew.

Reading Checkpoint What organelle captures the energy of sunlight and uses it to make food for the cell?

Specialized Cells

Plants and animals (including yourself) contain many cells. In a many-celled organism, the cells are often quite different from each other and are specialized to perform specific functions. Contrast, for example, the nerve cell and red blood cells in Figure 14. Nerve cells are specialized to transmit information from one part of your body to another, and red blood cells carry oxygen throughout your body.

In many-celled organisms, cells are often organized into tissues, organs, and organ systems. A tissue is a group of similar cells that work together to perform a specific function. For example, your brain is made mostly of nervous tissue, which consists of nerve cells. An organ, such as your brain, is made of different kinds of tissues that function together. In addition to nervous tissue, the brain contains other kinds of tissue that support and protect it. Your brain is part of your nervous system, which is an organ system that directs body activities and processes. An organ system is a group of organs that work together to perform a major function.

Reading Checkpoint — What is an organ system? Give an example.

Discovery CHANNEL SCHOOL

Cell Structure and Function

Video Preview
▶ Video Field Trip
Video Assessment

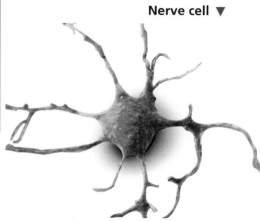

Nerve cell ▼

FIGURE 14
Specialized Cells
Nerve cells carry information throughout the human body. Red blood cells carry oxygen. Bone cells produce chemicals that strengthen bone.
Comparing and Contrasting
Compare the structures of these three types of cells.

Red blood cells in a ▼ blood vessel

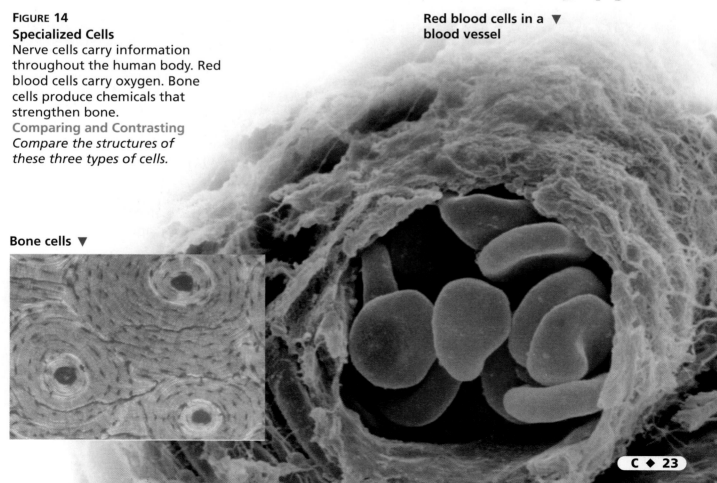

Bone cells ▼

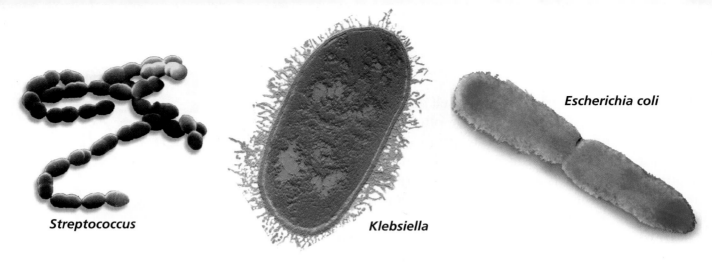

Escherichia coli

Streptococcus   *Klebsiella*

FIGURE 15
Bacterial Cells
Bacterial cells have no nuclei.

Bacterial Cells

The plant and animal cells that you just learned about are very different from the bacterial cells you see in Figure 15. First, bacterial cells are usually much smaller than plant or animal cells. A human skin cell, for example, is about ten times as large as an average bacterial cell. **While a bacterial cell does have a cell wall and a cell membrane, it does not contain a nucleus. The bacterial cell's genetic material, which looks like a thick, tangled string, is found in the cytoplasm.** Bacterial cells contain ribosomes, but none of the other organelles found in plant or animal cells.

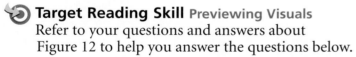

Section 2 Assessment

Target Reading Skill Previewing Visuals
Refer to your questions and answers about Figure 12 to help you answer the questions below.

Reviewing Key Concepts

1. a. **Comparing and Contrasting** Compare the functions of the cell wall and the cell membrane.
   b. **Describing** What is a characteristic of cellulose?
   c. **Inferring** How does cellulose help with the functions of the cell wall?
2. a. **Identifying** Identify the functions of ribosomes and Golgi bodies.
   b. **Describing** Describe the characteristics of the endoplasmic reticulum.
   c. **Applying Concepts** How are the functions of ribosomes, Golgi bodies, and the endoplasmic reticulum related to one another?

3. a. **Reviewing** What is a tissue? What is an organ?
   b. **Explaining** What is the relationship among cells, tissues, and organs?
   c. **Inferring** Would a tissue or an organ have more kinds of specialized cells? Explain.
4. a. **Reviewing** Where is the genetic material in a bacterial cell?
   b. **Comparing and Contrasting** Contrast the location of genetic material in bacterial cells to its location in plant and animal cells.

Writing in Science

Writing a Description Write a paragraph describing a typical animal cell. Your paragraph should include all the structures generally found in animal cells and a brief explanation of the functions of those structures.

Chemical Compounds in Cells

Reading Preview

Key Concepts
- What are elements and compounds?
- What are the main kinds of organic molecules in living things?
- How is water important to the function of cells?

Key Terms
- element • compound
- carbohydrate • lipid
- protein • amino acid
- enzyme • nucleic acid
- DNA • RNA

🎯 Target Reading Skill
Comparing and Contrasting
As you read, compare and contrast carbohydrates, lipids, and proteins in a table like the one below.

Type of Compound	Elements	Functions
Carbo-hydrate	Carbon, hydrogen, oxygen	
Lipid		
Protein		

Lab zone Discover **Activity**

WATER
hydrogen and oxygen
SALT
sodium and chlorine

What Is a Compound?

1. Your teacher will provide you with containers filled with various substances. All of the substances are chemical compounds.
2. Examine each substance. Read the label on each container to learn what each substance is made of.

Think It Over
Forming Operational Definitions Write a definition of what you think a chemical compound is.

Watch out—you are surrounded by particles that you can't see! Air is made up of millions of tiny particles. They bump into your skin, hide in the folds of your clothes, and whoosh into your nose every time you take a breath. In fact, you and the world around you, including the cells in your body, are composed of tiny particles. Some of these particles are elements, and others are compounds.

Elements and Compounds

You may not realize it, but air is a mixture of gases. These gases include both elements and compounds. Three gases in the air are oxygen, nitrogen, and carbon dioxide.

Elements Oxygen and nitrogen are examples of **elements. An element is any substance that cannot be broken down into simpler substances.** The smallest unit of an element is called an atom. An element is made up of only one kind of atom. The elements found in living things include carbon, hydrogen, oxygen, nitrogen, phosphorus, and sulfur.

FIGURE 16
An Element
Sulfur is an element. In its pure form, it sometimes forms crystals.

Compounds Carbon dioxide is a **compound** made up of the elements carbon and oxygen. **When two or more elements combine chemically, they form a compound.** Most elements in living things occur in the form of compounds.

The smallest unit of many compounds is called a molecule. A molecule of carbon dioxide consists of one carbon atom and two oxygen atoms. Water is another compound. Each water molecule is made up of two hydrogen atoms and one oxygen atom. In Figure 17, notice the diagrams of carbon dioxide and water molecules.

Organic and Inorganic Compounds Many of the compounds found in living things contain the element carbon. Most compounds that contain carbon are called organic compounds. **Some important groups of organic compounds found in living things are carbohydrates, lipids, proteins, and nucleic acids.** As you may know, many of these compounds are found in the foods you eat. This is not surprising, since the foods you eat come from living things.

Compounds that don't contain the element carbon are called inorganic compounds. Water and sodium chloride, or table salt, are familiar examples of inorganic compounds. Organisms contain many inorganic compounds as well as organic compounds.

 **Reading Checkpoint** How are inorganic compounds different from organic compounds?

FIGURE 17
Molecules and Compounds
Carbon dioxide, which is found in the gas bubbles, is a chemical compound. So is water.
Applying Concepts *What is a compound?*

Carbon Dioxide Molecule
The air bubbles contain carbon dioxide. A carbon dioxide molecule has one atom of carbon and two atoms of oxygen.

Carbon
Oxygen

Water Molecule
A water molecule is made up of one atom of oxygen and two atoms of hydrogen.

Oxygen
Hydrogen

Carbohydrates

A **carbohydrate** is an energy-rich organic compound made of the elements carbon, hydrogen, and oxygen. Sugars and starches are examples of carbohydrates.

Sugars are produced during the food-making process that takes place in plants. Foods such as fruits and some vegetables have a high sugar content. Sugar molecules can combine, forming large molecules called starches, or complex carbohydrates. Plant cells store excess energy in molecules of starch. Many foods that come from plants contain starch. These foods include potatoes, pasta, rice, and bread. When you eat these foods, your body breaks down the starch into glucose, a sugar that your cells can use to produce energy.

Carbohydrates are important components of some cell parts. For example, the cellulose found in the cell walls of plants is a type of carbohydrate. Carbohydrates are also found in cell membranes.

 **Reading Checkpoint** What is the difference between sugar and starch?

Lipids

Have you ever seen a cook trim the fat from a piece of meat before cooking it? The cook is trimming away a lipid. Fats, oils, and waxes are all lipids. Like carbohydrates, **lipids** are energy-rich organic compounds made of carbon, hydrogen, and oxygen. Lipids contain even more energy than carbohydrates. Cells store energy in lipids for later use. For example, during winter, a dormant bear lives on the energy stored in fat within its cells. In addition, cell membranes are made mainly of lipids.

FIGURE 18
Starch
These potatoes contain a large amount of starch. Starch is a carbohydrate. The blue grains in the close-up are starch granules in a potato. The grains have been colored blue to make them easier to see.

FIGURE 19
Lipids
Olive oil, which comes from olives such as those shown here, is made mostly of lipids.
Making Generalizations
What elements are lipids composed of?

Lab
zone Try This **Activity**

What's That Taste?
Use this activity to discover one role that enzymes play in your body.

1. Put an unsalted soda cracker in your mouth. Chew it, but do not swallow. Note what the cracker tastes like.

2. Continue to chew the cracker for a few minutes, mixing it well with your saliva. Note how the taste of the cracker changes.

Inferring Soda crackers are made up mainly of starch, with little sugar. How can you account for the change in taste after you chewed the cracker for a few minutes?

FIGURE 20
Feathers Made of Protein
The feathers of this peacock are made mainly of protein.
Applying Concepts *What smaller molecules make up protein molecules?*

Proteins

What do a bird's feathers, a spider's web, and your fingernails have in common? All of these substances are made mainly of proteins. **Proteins** are large organic molecules made of carbon, hydrogen, oxygen, nitrogen, and, in some cases, sulfur. Foods that are high in protein include meat, eggs, fish, nuts, and beans.

Structure of Proteins Protein molecules are made up of smaller molecules called **amino acids.** Although there are only 20 common amino acids, cells can combine them in different ways to form thousands of different proteins. The kinds of amino acids and the order in which they link together determine the type of protein that forms. You can think of the 20 amino acids as being like the 26 letters of the alphabet. Those 26 letters can form thousands of words. The letters you use and their order determine the words you form. Even a change in one letter, for example, from *rice* to *mice,* creates a new word. Similarly, a change in the type or order of amino acids can result in a different protein.

Functions of Proteins Much of the structure of cells is made up of proteins. Proteins form parts of cell membranes. Proteins also make up many of the organelles within the cell.

The proteins known as enzymes perform important functions in the chemical reactions that take place in cells. An **enzyme** is a type of protein that speeds up a chemical reaction in a living thing. Without enzymes, many chemical reactions that are necessary for life would either take too long or not occur at all. For example, enzymes in your saliva speed up the digestion of food by breaking down starches into sugars in your mouth.

✓ Reading Checkpoint **What is the role of enzymes in cells?**

Nucleic Acids

Nucleic acids are very long organic molecules made of carbon, oxygen, hydrogen, nitrogen, and phosphorus. Nucleic acids contain the instructions that cells need to carry out all the functions of life.

There are two kinds of nucleic acids. Deoxyribonucleic acid (dee ahk see ry boh noo KLEE ik), or **DNA,** is the genetic material that carries information about an organism and is passed from parent to offspring. The information in DNA also directs all of the cell's functions. Most of the DNA in a cell is found in the chromatin in the nucleus. Ribonucleic acid (ry boh noo KLEE ik), or **RNA,** plays an important role in the production of proteins. RNA is found in the cytoplasm as well as in the nucleus.

 **Reading Checkpoint** What are the two kinds of nucleic acids? What are their functions?

 **Math** **Analyzing Data**

Compounds in Bacteria and Mammals

All cells contain carbohydrates, lipids, proteins, and nucleic acids, as well as water and other inorganic compounds. But do all cells contain the same percentages of these compounds? The graph compares the percentages of some kinds of compounds found in a bacterial cell and a cell from a mammal.

1. **Reading Graphs** What do the red bars represent? What do the blue bars represent?

2. **Interpreting Data** What percentage of a mammalian cell is made up of water? How does this compare to the percentage of water in a bacterial cell?

3. **Interpreting Data** Which kind of compound—proteins or nucleic acids—makes up the larger percentage of a mammalian cell?

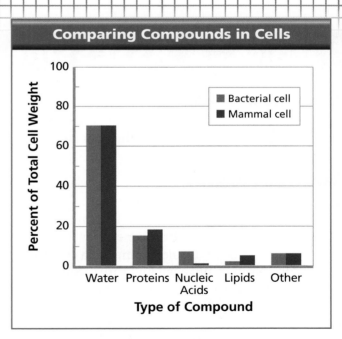

Comparing Compounds in Cells

4. **Drawing Conclusions** In general, how do a bacterial cell and a mammalian cell compare in their chemical composition?

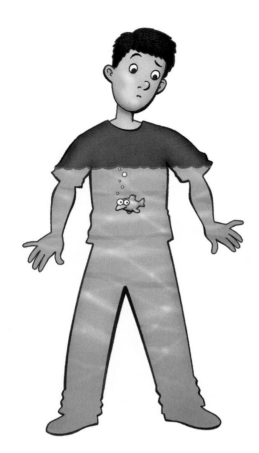

Water and Living Things

Did you know that water makes up about two thirds of your body? Water plays many important roles in cells. For example, most chemical reactions in cells involve substances that are dissolved in water. Also, water molecules themselves take part in many chemical reactions in cells. **Most chemical reactions within cells could not take place without water.**

Water also helps cells keep their size and shape. In fact, a cell without water would be like a balloon without air. In addition, because water changes temperature slowly, it helps keep the temperature of cells from changing rapidly. In the next section, you'll learn about the role that water plays in carrying substances into and out of cells.

 **What compound is needed for most chemical reactions to take place in cells?**

FIGURE 21
Mostly Water
About two-thirds of the human body is water.
Relating Cause and Effect *How does water help regulate body temperature?*

Section 3 Assessment

Target Reading Skill

Comparing and Contrasting Use the information in your table to help you answer the questions below.

Reviewing Key Concepts

1. a. Defining What is an element?
   b. Comparing and Contrasting How is a compound different from an element?
   c. Classifying A molecule of ammonia consists of one atom of nitrogen and three atoms of hydrogen. Is ammonia an element or a compound? Explain.

2. a. Reviewing What are four types of organic molecules found in living things?
   b. Classifying Which of the four types of organic molecules contain the element nitrogen?
   c. Inferring An organic compound contains only the elements carbon, hydrogen, and oxygen. Could this compound be a carbohydrate? Could it be a protein? Explain.

3. a. Reviewing What three important functions does water perform in cells?
   b. Relating Cause and Effect Suppose a cell is seriously deprived of water. How might this lack of water affect the cell's enzymes? Explain.

Lab zone **At-Home Activity**

Compounds in Food With family members, look at the "Nutrition Facts" labels on a variety of food products. Identify foods that contain large amounts of the following organic compounds: carbohydrates, proteins, and fats. Discuss with your family what elements make up each of these compounds and what roles they play in cells and in your body.

Consumer Lab

Which Foods Are Fat-Free?

Problem

Some people want to limit their intake of fats, or lipids. How can you determine whether information about fats on a food label is accurate?

Skills Focus

interpreting data, inferring

Materials

- permanent marker • 5 cotton swabs
- 5 different snack dips in their containers, including nutrition labels
- 5 fat-testing strips with color key
- watch or clock
- 5 small squares of paper towel

Procedure

1. Copy the data table on a sheet of paper. Record the brand names of the five snack dips in the table. **CAUTION:** *Do not taste the dips at any time.*

2. Examine the nutrition label on the container of each dip. Record the percentage of the Daily Value (% DV) of fat that the dip contains.

3. Look at other information on the container to see whether the dip is labeled "fat-free." Record this information in the table.

4. Obtain five fat-testing strips. Label each strip with the name of one of the dips.

5. Use a cotton swab to smear a bit of one dip onto the test square of the corresponding testing strip. After 30 seconds, gently wipe the dip from the strip with a paper towel.

6. To determine whether the sample contains fat, compare the test square with the color key. Record your observation in the table.

7. Repeat Steps 5–6 for each of the sample dips.

Analyze and Conclude

1. **Observing** According to the information on the containers, which dips had 0% fat? Which dips were labeled "fat-free"?

2. **Interpreting Data** Did the result shown on the test square always agree with the information on the dip's container?

3. **Inferring** Based on your results, what can you conclude about the accuracy of labels indicating that foods are fat-free?

4. **Communicating** Write a report for consumers that summarizes your results. Summarize the processes you used.

Design an Experiment

Protein test strips indicate *how much* protein is present in a food sample. Design an experiment to rank five food samples in the order of least protein to most protein. *Obtain your teacher's permission before carrying out your investigation.*

Data Table			
Name of Dip	Percent Fat (% Daily Value)	Labeled Fat-Free?	Result of Test

The Cell in Its Environment

Reading Preview

Key Concepts
- How do most small molecules cross the cell membrane?
- Why is osmosis important to cells?
- What is the difference between passive transport and active transport?

Key Terms
- selectively permeable
- diffusion • osmosis
- passive transport
- active transport

Target Reading Skill
Building Vocabulary
A definition states the meaning of a word or phrase. After you read the section, reread the paragraphs that contain definitions of Key Terms. Use all the information you have learned to write a definition of each Key Term in your own words.

Lab zone · Discover **Activity**

How Do Molecules Move?
1. Stand with your classmates in locations that are evenly spaced throughout the classroom.
2. Your teacher will spray an air freshener into the room. When you first smell the air freshener, raise your hand.
3. Note how long it takes for other students to smell the scent.

Think It Over
Developing Hypotheses How was each student's distance from the teacher related to when he or she smelled the air freshener? Develop a hypothesis about why this pattern occurred.

As darkness fell, the knight urged his horse toward the castle. The weary knight longed for the safety of the castle, with its thick walls of stone and strong metal gates. The castle's gatekeeper opened the gates and slowly lowered the drawbridge. The horse clopped across the bridge, and the knight sighed with relief. Home at last!

Like ancient castles, cells have structures that protect their contents from the world outside. All cells are surrounded by a cell membrane that separates the cell from the outside environment. The cell membrane is **selectively permeable,** which means that some substances can pass through the membrane while others cannot.

Cells, like castles, must let things enter and leave. Cells must let in needed materials, such as oxygen and food molecules. In contrast, waste materials must move out of cells. Oxygen, food molecules, and waste products all must pass through the cell membrane.

Diffusion

Substances that can move into and out of a cell do so by one of three methods: diffusion, osmosis, or active transport. **Diffusion is the main method by which small molecules move across the cell membrane.** Diffusion (dih FYOO zhun) is the process by which molecules move from an area of higher concentration to an area of lower concentration. The concentration of a substance is the amount of the substance in a given volume. For example, suppose you dissolve 1 gram of sugar in 1 liter of water. The concentration of the sugar solution is 1 gram per liter.

If you did the Discover activity, you observed diffusion in action. The area where the air freshener was sprayed had many molecules of freshener. The molecules gradually moved from this area of higher concentration to the other parts of the classroom, where there were fewer molecules of freshener—and thus a lower concentration.

What Causes Diffusion? Molecules are always moving. As they move, the molecules bump into one another. The more molecules there are in an area, the more collisions there will be. Collisions cause molecules to push away from one another. Over time, the molecules of a substance will continue to spread out. Eventually, they will be spread evenly throughout the area.

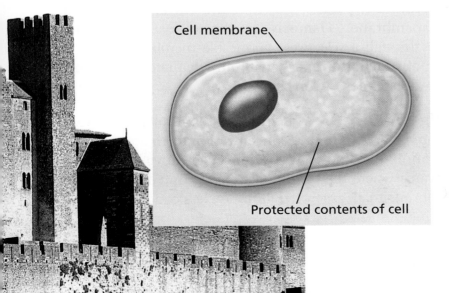

FIGURE 22
A Selective Barrier
The walls of a castle protected the inhabitants within, and the castle gatekeeper allowed only certain people to pass through. Similarly, the cell membrane protects the contents of the cell and helps control the materials that enter and leave.

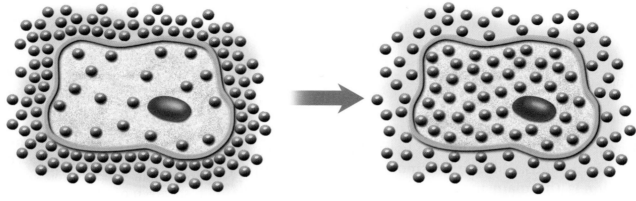

Before Diffusion
There is a higher concentration of oxygen molecules outside the cell than inside the cell.

After Diffusion
The concentration of oxygen molecules is the same outside and inside the cell.

FIGURE 23
Diffusion in Action
Molecules move by diffusion from an area of higher concentration to an area of lower concentration. Predicting *What would happen if the concentration of oxygen molecules outside the cell was lower than inside the cell?*

For: More on cellular transport
Visit: PHSchool.com
Web Code: ced-3014

Diffusion of Oxygen Have you ever used a microscope to observe one-celled organisms in pond water? These organisms obtain the oxygen they need to survive from the water around them. Luckily for them, there are many more molecules of oxygen in the water outside the cell than there are inside the cell. In other words, there is a higher concentration of oxygen molecules in the water than inside the cell. Remember that the cell membrane is permeable to oxygen molecules. The oxygen molecules diffuse from the area of higher concentration—the pond water—through the cell membrane to the area of lower concentration—the inside of the cell.

 **By what process do small molecules move into cells?**

Osmosis
Like oxygen, water passes easily into and out of cells through the cell membrane. **Osmosis** is the diffusion of water molecules through a selectively permeable membrane. **Because cells cannot function properly without adequate water, many cellular processes depend on osmosis.**

Osmosis and Diffusion Remember that molecules tend to move from an area of higher concentration to an area of lower concentration. In osmosis, water molecules move by diffusion from an area where they are highly concentrated through the cell membrane to an area where they are less concentrated.

Effects of Osmosis Osmosis can have important consequences for the cell. Look at Figure 24 to see the effect of osmosis on cells. In Figure 24A, a red blood cell is bathed in a solution in which the concentration of water is the same as it is inside the cell. This is the normal shape of a red blood cell.

Contrast this shape to the cell in Figure 24B. The red blood cell is floating in water that contains a lot of salt. The concentration of water molecules outside the cell is lower than the concentration of water molecules inside the cell. This difference in concentration occurs because the salt takes up space in the salt water. Therefore, there are fewer water molecules in the salt water outside the cell compared to the water inside the cell. As a result, water moves out of the cell by osmosis. When water moves out, cells shrink.

In Figure 24C, the red blood cell is floating in water that contains a very small amount of salt. The water inside the cell contains more salt than the solution outside the cell. Thus, the concentration of water outside the cell is greater than it is inside the cell. The water moves into the cell, causing it to swell.

 **Reading Checkpoint** How is osmosis related to diffusion?

Lab zone Try This Activity

Diffusion in Action
Here's how you can observe the effects of diffusion.

1. Fill a small, clear plastic cup with cold water. Place the cup on the table and allow it to sit until there is no movement in the water.
2. Use a plastic dropper to add one large drop of food coloring to the water.
3. Observe the water every minute. Note any changes that take place. Continue to observe until you can no longer see any changes.

Inferring What role did diffusion play in the changes you observed?

FIGURE 24
Effects of Osmosis on Cells
In osmosis, water diffuses through a selectively permeable membrane.

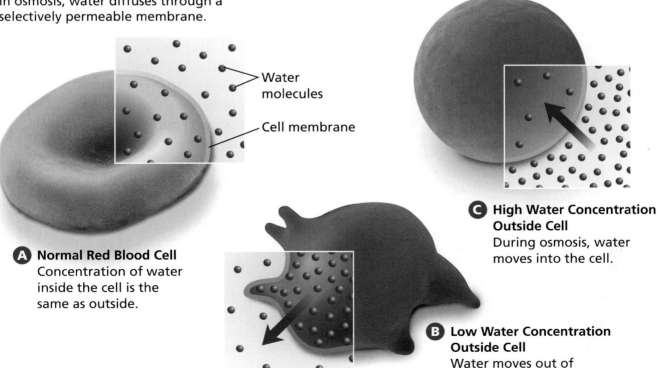

Water molecules

Cell membrane

A **Normal Red Blood Cell**
Concentration of water inside the cell is the same as outside.

B **Low Water Concentration Outside Cell**
Water moves out of the cell during osmosis.

C **High Water Concentration Outside Cell**
During osmosis, water moves into the cell.

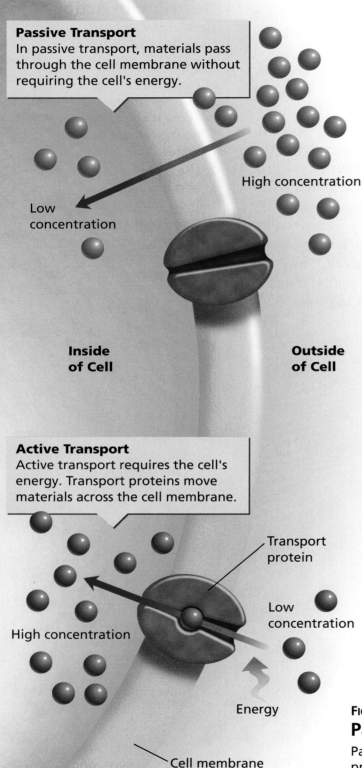

Passive Transport
In passive transport, materials pass through the cell membrane without requiring the cell's energy.

Low concentration

High concentration

Inside of Cell

Outside of Cell

Active Transport
Active transport requires the cell's energy. Transport proteins move materials across the cell membrane.

High concentration

Transport protein

Low concentration

Energy

Cell membrane

Active Transport

If you have ever ridden a bicycle down a long hill, you know that it doesn't take any of your energy to go fast. But you do have to use some of your energy to pedal back up the hill. For a cell, moving materials through the cell membrane by diffusion and osmosis is like cycling downhill. These processes do not require the cell to use its own energy. The movement of dissolved materials through a cell membrane without using cellular energy is called **passive transport.**

What if a cell needs to take in a substance that is present in a higher concentration inside the cell than outside? The cell would have to move the molecules in the opposite direction than they naturally move by diffusion. Cells can do this, but they have to use energy—just as you would use energy to pedal back up the hill. **Active transport** is the movement of materials through a cell membrane using cellular energy. **Active transport requires the cell to use its own energy, while passive transport does not.**

Transport Proteins Cells have several ways of moving materials by active transport. In one method, transport proteins in the cell membrane "pick up" molecules outside the cell and carry them in, using energy. Figure 25 illustrates this process. Transport proteins also carry molecules out of cells in a similar way. Some substances that are carried into and out of cells in this way include calcium, potassium, and sodium.

FIGURE 25
Passive and Active Transport
Passive and active transport are two processes by which materials pass through the cell membrane.
Interpreting Diagrams *What is the function of a transport protein?*

Transport by Engulfing Figure 26 shows another method of active transport. First, the cell membrane surrounds and engulfs, or encloses, a particle. Once the particle is engulfed, the cell membrane wraps around the particle and forms a vacuole within the cell. The cell must use energy in this process.

Why Cells Are Small As you know, most cells are so small that you cannot see them without a microscope. Have you ever wondered why cells are so small? One reason is related to how materials move into and out of cells.

As a cell's size increases, more of its cytoplasm is located farther from the cell membrane. Once a molecule enters a cell, it is carried to its destination by a stream of moving cytoplasm, somewhat like the way currents in the ocean move a raft. But in a very large cell, the streams of cytoplasm must travel farther to bring materials to all parts of the cell. It would take much longer for a molecule to reach the center of a very large cell than it would in a small cell. Likewise, it would take a long time for wastes to be removed. If a cell grew too large, it could not function well enough to survive.

FIGURE 26
Amoeba Engulfing Food
This single-celled amoeba is surrounding a smaller organism. The amoeba will engulf the organism and use it for food. Engulfing is a form of active transport.

 **Reading Checkpoint** **What prevents cells from growing very large?**

Section 4 Assessment

Target Reading Skill Building Vocabulary Use your definitions to help answer the questions below.

Reviewing Key Concepts

1. **a. Defining** What is diffusion?
   b. Relating Cause and Effect Use diffusion to explain what happens when you drop a sugar cube into a mug of hot tea.
2. **a. Defining** What is osmosis?
   b. Describing Describe how water molecules move through the cell membrane during osmosis.
   c. Applying Concepts A selectively permeable membrane separates solutions A and B. The concentration of water molecules in Solution B is higher than that in Solution A. Describe how the water molecules will move.
3. **a. Comparing and Contrasting** How is active transport different from passive transport?
   b. Reviewing What are transport proteins?
   c. Explaining Explain why transport proteins require energy to function in active transport.

Math Practice

A scientist dissolves 60 g of sugar in 3 L of water.

4. **Calculating a Concentration** Calculate the concentration of the solution in grams per liter.
5. **Ratios** Express the concentration as a ratio.

① Discovering Cells

Key Concepts

- Cells are the basic units of structure and function in living things.
- The invention of the microscope enabled people to discover and learn about cells.
- The cell theory states the following: All living things are composed of cells. Cells are the basic units of structure and function in living things. All cells are produced from other cells.
- The lenses in light microscopes magnify an object by bending the light that passes through them.
- Electron microscopes use a beam of electrons instead of light to produce a magnified image.

Key Terms

cell   microscope   cell theory

② Looking Inside Cells

Key Concepts

- A plant's cell wall protects and supports the cell.
- The cell membrane controls what substances come into and out of a cell.
- The nucleus directs the cell's activities.
- Mitochondria convert energy in food molecules to energy the cell can use.
- The endoplasmic reticulum carries materials throughout the cell.
- Ribosomes produce proteins.
- The Golgi bodies receive materials, package them, and distribute them.
- Chloroplasts capture energy from sunlight and use it to produce food for the cell.
- Vacuoles are the storage areas of cells.
- Lysosomes contain chemicals that break down certain materials in the cell.
- In many-celled organisms, cells are often organized into tissues, organs, and organ systems.
- A bacterial cell has a cell wall and cell membrane, but no nucleus. Its genetic material is found in the cytoplasm.

Key Terms

organelle	ribosome
cell wall	Golgi body
cell membrane	chloroplast
nucleus	vacuole
cytoplasm	lysosome
mitochondria	
endoplasmic reticulum	

③ Chemical Compounds in Cells

Key Concepts

- An element is any substance that cannot be broken down into simpler substances.
- When two or more elements combine chemically, they form a compound.
- Important groups of organic compounds found in living things are carbohydrates, proteins, lipids, and nucleic acids.
- Without water, most chemical reactions within cells could not take place.

Key Terms

element	enzyme
compound	lipid
carbohydrate	nucleic acid
protein	DNA
amino acid	RNA

④ The Cell in Its Environment

Key Concepts

- Diffusion is the main method by which small molecules move across the cell membrane.
- Osmosis is important to cells because cells cannot function properly without adequate water.
- Active transport requires the cell to use energy, while passive transport does not.

Key Terms

selectively permeable
diffusion
osmosis
passive transport
active transport

Review and Assessment

Go Online
PHSchool.com

For: Self-Assessment
Visit: PHSchool.com
Web Code: cea-3010

Organizing Information

Concept Mapping Copy the concept map. Then complete the map to show the types of organic compounds. (For more about Concept Mapping, see the Skills Handbook.)

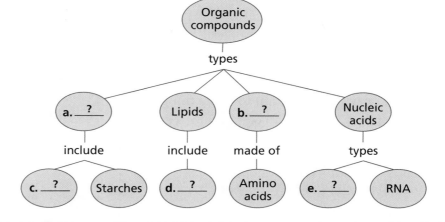

Reviewing Key Terms

Choose the letter of the best answer.

1. All living things are composed of
   a. blood.
   b. chloroplasts.
   c. vacuoles.
   d. cells.

2. In plant and animal cells, the control center of the cell is the
   a. chloroplast.
   b. cytoplasm.
   c. nucleus.
   d. Golgi body.

3. A storage compartment of the cell is the
   a. cell wall.
   b. lysosome.
   c. endoplasmic reticulum.
   d. vacuole.

4. Starch is an example of a
   a. nucleic acid.
   b. protein.
   c. lipid.
   d. carbohydrate.

5. The process by which water moves across a cell membrane is called
   a. osmosis.
   b. active transport.
   c. organelle.
   d. resolution.

If the statement is true, write _true_. If it is false, change the underlined word or words to make the statement true.

6. Cells were discovered using <u>electron</u> microscopes.

7. <u>Ribosomes</u> produce proteins.

8. The cells of <u>plants and animals</u> lack nuclei.

9. Both DNA and RNA are <u>proteins</u>.

10. The cell membrane is <u>selectively permeable</u>.

Writing in Science

Dialogue A dialogue is a conversation. Write a dialogue that might have taken place between Schleiden and Schwann. The scientists should discuss their observations and conclusions.

Cell Structure and Function
Video Preview
Video Field Trip
▶ Video Assessment

Review and Assessment

Checking Concepts

11. What role did the microscope play in the development of the cell theory?

12. Describe the function of the cell wall.

13. Explain the difference between elements and compounds.

14. How are enzymes important to living things?

15. What are the functions of DNA and RNA?

16. Why is water important in the cell?

17. What is diffusion? What function does diffusion have in the cell?

18. Explain the relationship between cell size and the movement of materials into and out of cells.

Thinking Critically

19. **Applying Concepts** Do the cells below come from a plant or an animal? Explain your answer.

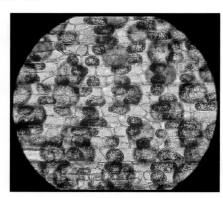

20. **Comparing and Contrasting** How are plant and animal cells similar? How are they different? To answer these questions, make a list of the different organelles in each cell. Explain how each organelle is vital to the life and function of a plant or animal.

21. **Predicting** Suppose a cell did not have a supply of amino acids and could not produce them. What effect might this have on the cell?

22. **Comparing and Contrasting** Explain how active transport is different from osmosis.

Math Practice

23. **Ratios** A solution consists of 24 g of table salt dissolved in 2 L of water. Express the concentration of salt in the form of a ratio.

Applying Skills

Use the diagrams to answer Questions 24–26.

A scientist watered the plant in Figure A with salt water. After 30 minutes, the plant looked as you see it in Figure B.

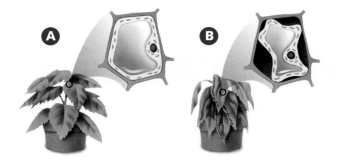

24. **Observing** How did the plant cells change after the plant was watered?

25. **Inferring** Describe a process that would lead to the changes in the plant cells.

26. **Developing Hypotheses** Suppose the scientist were to water the plant in B with fresh (unsalted) water. Develop a hypothesis about what would happen to the plant. Explain your hypothesis.

Lab zone Chapter **Project**

Performance Assessment Bring in your egg, graph, and any diagrams you made. As a class, discuss your results and conclusions. Then, as a group, try to answer these questions: What happened to the eggshell? What process took place at each stage of the experiment?

Standardized Test Prep

Choose the letter of the best answer.

1. A reasonable estimate for the size of a cell's nucleus is
   A 0.003 mm.
   B 3 mm.
   C 0.003 m.
   D 3 m.

2. A compound microscope has two lenses. One lens has a magnification of 15 and the other lens has a magnification of 40. What is the total magnification of the microscope?
   F 55
   G 150
   H 25
   J 600

3. A tissue in an animal produces and releases chemicals that are used by cells throughout the animal's body. Cells in that tissue probably have a larger than normal number of
   A lysosomes.
   B mitochondria.
   C Golgi bodies.
   D nuclei.

Use the diagram below and your knowledge of science to answer Questions 4 and 5.

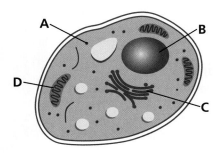

4. Which organelle contains instructions for directing the cell's functions?
   F A
   G B
   H C
   J D

5. In which organelle is food energy converted to energy that the cell can use?
   A A
   B B
   C C
   D D

Constructed Response

6. Describe the structure of proteins, and explain how proteins play an important role in the cell.

Chapter 2

Cell Processes and Energy

Sunlight on these maple leaves powers the process of photosynthesis. ▶

42 ◆ C

Lab zone™ Chapter Project

Shine On!

Every morning at sunrise, tiny living factories start a manufacturing process called photosynthesis. The power they use is sunlight. In this project, you will investigate how light affects one familiar group of photosynthesizers—plants.

Your Goal To determine how different lighting conditions affect the health and growth of plants

To complete the project, you will

- write up a plan to grow plants under different lighting conditions
- care for your plants daily, and keep careful records of their health and growth for three weeks
- graph your data, and draw conclusions about the effect of light on plant growth
- follow the safety guidelines in Appendix A

Plan It! Brainstorm with classmates to answer these questions: What different light conditions might you test? What plants will you use? How will you measure health and growth? How can you be sure your results are due to the light conditions? Write up your plan and submit it to your teacher.

Photosynthesis

Reading Preview

Key Concepts
- How does the sun supply living things with the energy they need?
- What happens during the process of photosynthesis?

Key Terms
- photosynthesis • autotroph
- heterotroph • pigment
- chlorophyll • stomata

Target Reading Skill

Sequencing A sequence is the order in which the steps in a process occur. As you read, create a flowchart that shows the steps in photosynthesis. Put each step in a separate box in the flowchart in the order in which it occurs.

Steps in Photosynthesis

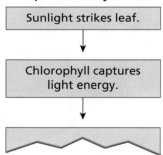

Sunlight strikes leaf.

Chlorophyll captures light energy.

Discover Activity

Where Does the Energy Come From?

1. Obtain a solar-powered calculator that does not use batteries. Place the calculator in direct light.
2. Cover the solar cells with your finger. Note how your action affects the number display.
3. Uncover the solar cells. What happens to the number display?
4. Now cover all but one of the solar cells. How does that affect the number display?

Think It Over

Inferring From your observations, what can you infer about the energy that powers the calculator?

On a plain in Africa, a herd of zebras peacefully eat the grass. But watch out—the zebras' grazing will soon be harshly interrupted. A group of lions is about to attack the herd. The lions will kill one of the zebras and eat it.

Both the zebras and the lions use the food they eat to obtain energy. Every living thing needs energy. All cells need energy to carry out their functions, such as making proteins and transporting substances into and out of the cell. The zebra's meat supplies the lion's cells with the energy they need, just as the grass provides the zebra's cells with energy. But plants and certain other organisms, such as algae and some bacteria, obtain their energy in a different way. These organisms use the energy in sunlight to make their own food.

Plants such as grass use energy from the sun to make their own food.

The zebra obtains energy by eating grass.

FIGURE 1
Energy From the Sun
The sun supplies energy for most living things, directly or indirectly. **Relating Cause and Effect** *How does sunlight provide food for the zebra?*

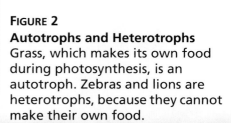

The lion obtains energy by feeding on the zebra.

Sources of Energy

The process by which a cell captures energy in sunlight and uses it to make food is called **photosynthesis** (foh toh SIN thuh sis). The term *photosynthesis* comes from the Greek words *photo*, which means "light," and *synthesis*, which means "putting together."

Nearly all living things obtain energy either directly or indirectly from the energy of sunlight captured during photosynthesis. Grass obtains energy directly from sunlight, because it makes its own food during photosynthesis. When the zebra eats the grass, it gets energy that has been stored in the grass. Similarly, the lion obtains energy stored in the zebra. The zebra and lion both obtain the sun's energy indirectly, from the energy that the grass obtained through photosynthesis.

Plants manufacture their own food through the process of photosynthesis. An organism that makes its own food is called an **autotroph** (AWT oh trahf). An organism that cannot make its own food, including animals such as the zebra and the lion, is called a **heterotroph** (HET ur oh trahf). Many heterotrophs obtain food by eating other organisms. Some heterotrophs, such as fungi, absorb their food from other organisms.

 **Reading Checkpoint** What are autotrophs?

FIGURE 2
Autotrophs and Heterotrophs
Grass, which makes its own food during photosynthesis, is an autotroph. Zebras and lions are heterotrophs, because they cannot make their own food.

The Two Stages of Photosynthesis

Photosynthesis is a complex process. **During photosynthesis, plants and some other organisms use energy from the sun to convert carbon dioxide and water into oxygen and sugars.** The process of photosynthesis is shown in Figure 3. You can think of photosynthesis as taking place in two stages: capturing the sun's energy and producing sugars. You're probably familiar with many two-stage processes. To make a cake, for example, the first stage is to combine the ingredients to make the batter. The second stage is to bake the batter. To get the desired result—the cake—both stages must occur in the correct order.

Stage 1: Capturing the Sun's Energy The first stage of photosynthesis involves capturing the energy in sunlight. In plants, this energy-capturing process occurs mostly in the leaves. Recall that chloroplasts are green organelles inside plant cells. The green color comes from **pigments,** colored chemical compounds that absorb light. The main photosynthetic pigment in chloroplasts is **chlorophyll.**

Chlorophyll functions in a manner similar to that of the solar "cells" in a solar-powered calculator. Solar cells capture the energy in light and use it to power the calculator. Similarly, chlorophyll captures light energy and uses it to power the second stage of photosynthesis.

FIGURE 3
Two Stages of Photosynthesis

Photosynthesis has two stages, as shown in the diagram.
Interpreting Diagrams *Which stage requires light?*

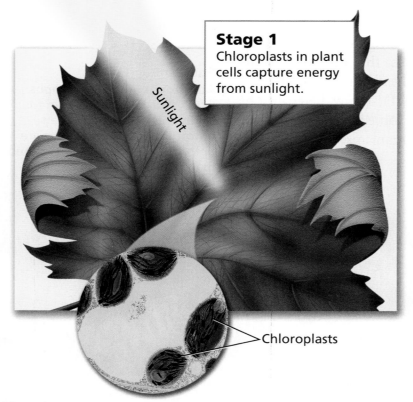

Stage 1
Chloroplasts in plant cells capture energy from sunlight.

Sunlight

Chloroplasts

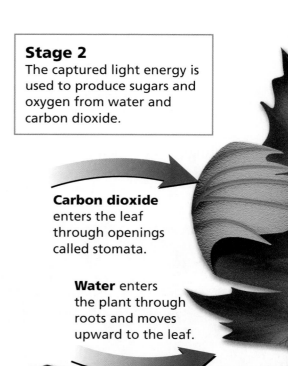

Stage 2
The captured light energy is used to produce sugars and oxygen from water and carbon dioxide.

Carbon dioxide enters the leaf through openings called stomata.

Water enters the plant through roots and moves upward to the leaf.

Stage 2: Using Energy to Make Food In the next stage of photosynthesis, the cell uses the captured energy to produce sugars. The cell needs two raw materials for this stage: water (H_2O) and carbon dioxide (CO_2). In plants, the roots absorb water from the soil. The water then moves up through the plant's stem to the leaves. Carbon dioxide is one of the gases in the air. Carbon dioxide enters the plant through small openings on the undersides of the leaves called **stomata** (STOH muh tuh) (singular *stoma*). Once in the leaves, the water and carbon dioxide move into the chloroplasts.

Inside the chloroplasts, the water and carbon dioxide undergo a complex series of chemical reactions. The reactions are powered by the energy captured in the first stage. These reactions produce chemicals as products. One product is a sugar that has six carbon atoms. Six-carbon sugars have the chemical formula $C_6H_{12}O_6$. Recall that sugars are a type of carbohydrate. Cells can use the energy in the sugar to carry out important cell functions.

The other product of photosynthesis is oxygen (O_2), which exits the leaf through the stomata. In fact, almost all the oxygen in Earth's atmosphere was produced by living things through the process of photosynthesis.

Reading Checkpoint What makes plants green?

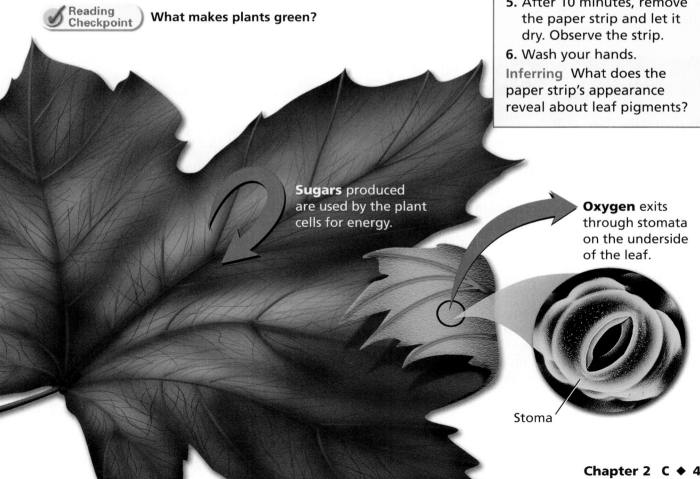

Sugars produced are used by the plant cells for energy.

Oxygen exits through stomata on the underside of the leaf.

Stoma

The Photosynthesis Equation The events of photosynthesis can be summed up by the following chemical equation:

$$6\,CO_2 \quad + \quad 6\,H_2O \xrightarrow{\text{light energy}} C_6H_{12}O_6 \;+\; 6\,O_2$$

carbon dioxide   water   a sugar   oxygen

Notice that the raw materials—six molecules of carbon dioxide and six molecules of water—are on the left side of the equation. The products—one molecule of a sugar and six molecules of oxygen—are on the right side of the equation. An arrow, which you can read as "yields," connects the raw materials to the products. Light energy, which is necessary for the chemical reaction to occur, is written above the arrow.

What happens to the sugar produced in photosynthesis? Plant cells use some of the sugar for food. The cells break down the sugar molecules to release the energy they contain. This energy can then be used to carry out the plant's functions. Some sugar molecules are converted into other compounds, such as cellulose. Other sugar molecules may be stored in the plant's cells for later use. When you eat food from plants, such as potatoes or carrots, you are eating the plant's stored energy.

FIGURE 4
Stored energy
When you eat a carrot, you obtain energy stored during photosynthesis.

> **Reading Checkpoint**   **In the photosynthesis equation, what does the arrow mean?**

Section 1 Assessment

Target Reading Skill Sequencing Use your flowchart about photosynthesis to help answer Question 2.

Reviewing Key Concepts

1. **a. Reviewing** Why do living things need energy?
   b. Explaining How do plants obtain energy?
   c. Applying Concepts An insect eats a leaf. Explain how the insect depends on the sun for energy.
2. **a. Reviewing** What chemical equation sums up the events of photosynthesis?
   b. Comparing and Contrasting What are the substances needed for photosynthesis? What substances are produced during photosynthesis?
   c. Making Generalizations Would you expect a plant to produce more oxygen on a cloudy day or a sunny day? Explain.

Writing in Science

Job Qualifications When people apply for jobs, they often must complete a job application form in which they describe their qualifications for a job. Suppose that you are a leaf, and that you are applying for a job in a photosynthesis factory. Write a paragraph in which you summarize your qualifications for the job of photosynthesis. Your paragraph should include the following words: *chloroplasts, chlorophyll, light, energy, water, carbon dioxide,* and *stomata.*

Reading Preview

Key Concepts
- What events occur during respiration?
- What is fermentation?

Key Terms
- respiration • fermentation

⊙ Target Reading Skill

Using Prior Knowledge Your prior knowledge is what you already know before you read about a topic. Before you read, write a definition of respiration in a graphic organizer like the one below. As you read, revise your definition based on what you learn.

What You Know
1. Definition of respiration:

What You Learned
1.

Lab zone · Discover **Activity**

What Is a Product of Respiration?

1. 🔧 Put on your goggles. Fill two test tubes half full of warm water. Add 5 mL of sugar to one of the test tubes. Put the tubes in a test-tube rack.
2. Add 0.5 mL of dried yeast (a single-celled organism) to each tube. Stir the contents of each tube with a straw. Place a stopper snugly in the top of each tube.
3. Observe any changes that occur in the two test tubes over the next 10 to 15 minutes.

Think It Over

Observing What changes occurred in each test tube? How can you account for any differences that you observed?

You and your friend have been hiking all morning. You look for a flat rock to sit on, so you can eat the lunch you packed. The steepest part of the trail is ahead. You'll need a lot of energy to get to the top of the mountain. That energy will come from food.

Before food can provide your body with energy, it must pass through your digestive system. There, the food is broken down into small molecules. These small molecules can then pass out of the digestive system and into your bloodstream. Next, the molecules travel through the bloodstream to the cells of your body. Inside the cells, the energy in the molecules is released. In this section, you'll learn how your body's cells obtain energy from the food you eat.

FIGURE 5
Energy
Vigorous exercise, such as hiking, requires a lot of energy.

FIGURE 6
Energy From Respiration
All organisms need energy to live. The leopard frog uses energy to leap great distances. Although the mushrooms don't move, they still need energy to grow and reproduce.

What Is Respiration?

After you eat a meal, your body converts some of the food into glucose, a type of sugar. **Respiration** is the process by which cells obtain energy from glucose. **During respiration, cells break down simple food molecules such as sugar and release the energy they contain.** Because living things need a continuous supply of energy, the cells of all living things carry out respiration continuously. Plant cells, as well as animal cells, respire.

Storing and Releasing Energy Energy stored in cells is something like money you put in a savings account in a bank. When you want to buy something, you withdraw some of the money. Cells store and use energy in a similar way. During photosynthesis, plants capture the energy from sunlight and "save" it in the form of carbohydrates, including sugars and starches. Similarly, when you eat a meal, you add to your body's energy savings account. When cells need energy, they "withdraw" it by breaking down the carbohydrates in the process of respiration.

Breathing and Respiration The term *respiration* has two meanings. You have probably used it to mean "breathing," that is, moving air in and out of your lungs. To avoid confusion, the respiration process that takes place inside cells is sometimes called cellular respiration. The two meanings of the term *respiration* do point out a connection, however. Breathing brings oxygen, which is usually necessary for cellular respiration, into your lungs.

 **Reading Checkpoint** What is respiration?

The Two Stages of Respiration Like photosynthesis, respiration is a two-stage process. The first stage takes place in the cytoplasm of the organism's cells. There, molecules of glucose are broken down into smaller molecules. Oxygen is not involved, and only a small amount of energy is released.

The second stage of respiration takes place in the mitochondria. There, the small molecules are broken down into even smaller molecules. These chemical reactions require oxygen, and they release a great deal of energy. This is why the mitochondria are sometimes called the "powerhouses" of the cell.

Trace the steps in the breakdown of glucose in Figure 7. Note that energy is released in both stages. Two other products of respiration are carbon dioxide and water. These products diffuse out of the cell. In most animals, the carbon dioxide and some water leave the body during exhalation, or breathing out. Thus, when you breathe in, you take in oxygen—a raw material for respiration. When you breathe out, you release carbon dioxide and water—products of respiration.

The Respiration Equation Although respiration occurs in a series of complex steps, the overall process can be summarized in the following equation:

$$C_6H_{12}O_6 + 6\,O_2 \longrightarrow 6\,CO_2 + 6\,H_2O + energy$$

sugar   oxygen   carbon dioxide   water

Notice that the raw materials for respiration are sugar and oxygen. Plants and other organisms that undergo photosynthesis make their own sugar. The glucose in the cells of animals and other organisms comes from the food they consume. The oxygen used in respiration comes from the air or water surrounding the organism.

FIGURE 7
Two Stages of Respiration
Respiration, like photosynthesis, takes place in two stages.
Interpreting Diagrams *In which stage of respiration is oxygen used?*

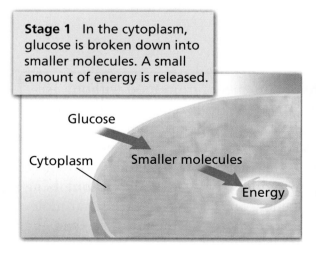

Stage 1 In the cytoplasm, glucose is broken down into smaller molecules. A small amount of energy is released.

Glucose

Cytoplasm   Smaller molecules

Energy

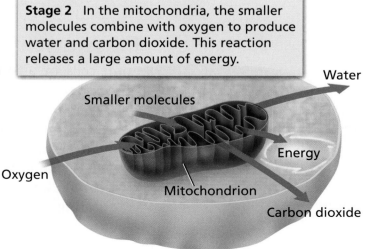

Stage 2 In the mitochondria, the smaller molecules combine with oxygen to produce water and carbon dioxide. This reaction releases a large amount of energy.

Water

Smaller molecules

Energy

Oxygen

Mitochondrion

Carbon dioxide

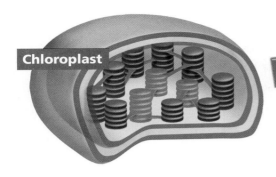

Chloroplast

Sugar and Oxygen

Photosynthesis
During photosynthesis, plants use carbon dioxide and release oxygen.

$$6\ CO_2 + 6\ H_2O \longrightarrow C_6H_{12}O_6 + 6\ O_2$$

Respiration
During respiration, organisms use oxygen and release carbon dioxide.

$$C_6H_{12}O_6 + 6\ O_2 \longrightarrow 6\ CO_2 + 6\ H_2O$$

Carbon Dioxide and Water

Mitochondrion

FIGURE 8
Photosynthesis and Respiration
You can think of photosynthesis and respiration as opposite processes.
Comparing and Contrasting
Which process uses oxygen? Which uses carbon dioxide?

Comparing Photosynthesis and Respiration Can you notice anything familiar about the equation for respiration? You are quite right if you said it is the opposite of the equation for photosynthesis. This is an important point. During photosynthesis, carbon dioxide and water are used to produce sugars and oxygen. During respiration, the sugar glucose and oxygen are used to produce carbon dioxide and water. Photosynthesis and respiration can be thought of as opposite processes.

Together, these two processes form a cycle that keeps the levels of oxygen and carbon dioxide fairly constant in Earth's atmosphere. As you can see in Figure 8, living things use both gases over and over again.

Reading Checkpoint   **Which process—photosynthesis or respiration—produces water?**

Fermentation

Some cells are able to obtain energy from food without using oxygen. For example, some single-celled organisms live where there is no oxygen, such as deep in the ocean or in the mud of lakes or swamps. These organisms obtain their energy through **fermentation,** an energy-releasing process that does not require oxygen. **Fermentation provides energy for cells without using oxygen.** The amount of energy released from each sugar molecule during fermentation, however, is much lower than the amount released during respiration.

Go Online
SciLINKS

For: Links on cellular respiration
Visit: www.SciLinks.org
Web Code: scn-0322

Alcoholic Fermentation One type of fermentation occurs when yeast and some other single-celled organisms break down sugars. This process is sometimes called alcoholic fermentation because alcohol is one of the products. The other products are carbon dioxide and a small amount of energy.

The products of alcoholic fermentation are important to bakers and brewers. The carbon dioxide produced by yeast creates air pockets in bread dough, causing it to rise. Carbon dioxide is also the source of bubbles in alcoholic drinks such as beer and sparkling wine.

Lactic Acid Fermentation Another type of fermentation takes place at times in your body. You've probably felt its effects. Think of a time when you ran as fast as you could for as long as you could. Your leg muscles were pushing hard against the ground, and you were breathing quickly.

No matter how hard you breathed, your muscle cells used up the oxygen faster than it could be replaced. Because your cells lacked oxygen, fermentation occurred. The fermentation supplied your cells with energy. One product of this type of fermentation is an acid known as lactic acid. When lactic acid builds up, you feel a painful sensation in your muscles. Your muscles feel weak and sore.

FIGURE 9
Lactic Acid Fermentation
When an athlete's muscles run out of oxygen, lactic acid fermentation supplies the cells with energy.

 **Reading Checkpoint** **Which kind of fermentation is important to bakers?**

Section 2 Assessment

Target Reading Skill

Using Prior Knowledge Review your graphic organizer about respiration. List two things that you learned about respiration.

Reviewing Key Concepts

1. a. Reviewing What happens during respiration?
 b. Reviewing What is the equation for respiration?
 c. Comparing and Contrasting Compare the equations for respiration and photosynthesis.
 d. Relating Cause and Effect Explain why cellular respiration adds carbon dioxide to the atmosphere, but photosynthesis does not.

2. a. Identifying What is the process in which cells obtain energy without using oxygen?
 b. Inferring How would athletes be affected if this process could not take place?
 c. Predicting Is this process more likely to occur during a short run or a long walk? Explain your answer.

Lab zone **At-Home Activity**

Make Bread With an adult family member, follow a recipe in a cookbook to make a loaf of bread using yeast. Explain to your family what causes the dough to rise. After you bake the bread, observe a slice and look for evidence that fermentation occurred.

Exhaling Carbon Dioxide

Problem

Is there a relationship between exercise and the amount of carbon dioxide you exhale?

Skills Focus

predicting, controlling variables

Materials

- 2 250-mL beakers
- bromthymol blue solution (0.1% solution), 30 mL
- 2 straws
- stopwatch or watch with second hand
- graduated cylinder, 25 mL
- paper towels

Procedure

PART 1 Testing for Carbon Dioxide

1. Label one beaker "Beaker 1" and the other beaker "Beaker 2." Beaker 1 will be the control in the experiment.

2. Bromthymol blue can be used to test for the presence of carbon dioxide. To see how this works, fill each beaker with 15 mL of bromthymol solution. **CAUTION:** *Bromthymol blue can stain skin and clothing. Avoid spilling or splashing it on yourself.*

3. Note and record the color of the solution in both beakers.

4. Place a straw in Beaker 2. Gently blow through the straw into the solution until the solution changes color. **CAUTION:** *Use the straw to breathe out only. Do not suck the solution back through the straw.* Your partner should begin timing when you first blow through the straw and stop as soon as the solution changes color. Record the time that has elapsed.

PART 2 Exercise and Carbon Dioxide

5. In Part 1 you timed the change of color without exercising first. Predict how long it would take the solution to change color if you conduct the test after you exercise. Design an experiment to test your prediction. Be sure to include a plan for recording your results and steps to review your results.

6. Write down the steps of your experiment and get your teacher's approval. Then, conduct your experiment. **CAUTION:** *Do not over-exert yourself. If you have a medical condition that limits your ability to exercise, do not take part in the exercise portion of this experiment.*

Analyze and Conclude

1. **Measuring** How long did it take for the solution to change color the first time you did the test (without exercising)?

2. **Drawing Conclusions** How did exercising affect the amount of time it took for the solution to change color?

3. **Predicting** What was your prediction in Step 5 based upon? Was your prediction accurate?

4. **Controlling Variables** In Part 2, what variables did you need to control? Explain how you controlled those variables.

5. **Communicating** Write a paragraph that relates the results of your experiment to the process of cellular respiration. Be sure to explain how increased cellular activity affects carbon dioxide output.

More to Explore

Some plants grow in water. If you added bromthymol blue to the water, do you think it would turn color? *(Hint:* What might happen to the carbon dioxide that the plants produce during respiration?)

Cell Division

Reading Preview

Key Concepts
- What events take place during the three stages of the cell cycle?
- How does the structure of DNA help account for the way in which DNA copies itself?

Key Terms
- cell cycle
- interphase
- replication
- mitosis
- chromosome
- cytokinesis

Target Reading Skill

Sequencing As you read, make a cycle diagram that shows the events in the cell cycle, including the phases of mitosis. Write each event in a separate circle.

The Cell Cycle

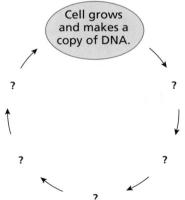

Cell grows and makes a copy of DNA.

? ?

? ?

?

Discover Activity

Lab zone

What Are the Yeast Cells Doing?

1. Use a plastic dropper to transfer some yeast cells from a yeast culture to a microscope slide. Your teacher has prepared the slide by drying methylene blue stain onto it. Add a coverslip and place the slide under a microscope.

2. Examine the cells on the slide. Use low power first, then high power. Look for what appears to be two cells attached to each other. One cell may be larger than the other. Draw what you see.

Think It Over

Developing Hypotheses What process do you think the "double cells" are undergoing? Develop a hypothesis that might explain what you see.

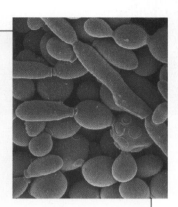

In the early autumn, many local fairs run pumpkin contests. Proud growers enter their largest pumpkins, hoping to win a prize. The pumpkin below has a mass greater than 600 kilograms! This giant pumpkin began as a small flower. How did the pumpkin grow so big?

A pumpkin grows in size by increasing both the size and the number of its cells. A single cell grows and then divides, forming two cells. Then two cells grow and divide, forming four, and so on. This process of cell growth and division does not occur only in pumpkins, though. In fact, many cells in your body are dividing as you read this page.

Prize-winning pumpkin ▲

Stage 1: Interphase

How do little pigs get to be big pigs? Their cells grow and divide, over and over. The regular sequence of growth and division that cells undergo is known as the **cell cycle.** During the cell cycle, a cell grows, prepares for division, and divides into two new cells, which are called "daughter cells." Each of the daughter cells then begins the cell cycle again. You can see details of the cell cycle in Figure 12. Notice that the cell cycle is divided into three main stages: interphase, mitosis, and cytokinesis.

The first stage of the cell cycle is called **interphase.** Interphase is the period before cell division. **During interphase, the cell grows, makes a copy of its DNA, and prepares to divide into two cells.**

Growing During the first part of interphase, the cell grows to its full size and produces structures it needs. For example, the cell makes new ribosomes and produces enzymes. Copies are made of both mitochondria and chloroplasts.

Copying DNA In the next part of interphase, the cell makes an exact copy of the DNA in its nucleus in a process called **replication.** Recall that DNA is found in the chromatin in the nucleus. DNA holds all the information that the cell needs to carry out its functions. Replication of DNA is very important, since each daughter cell must have a complete set of DNA to survive. At the end of DNA replication, the cell contains two identical sets of DNA. You will learn the details of DNA replication later in this section.

Preparing for Division Once the DNA has replicated, preparation for cell division begins. The cell produces structures that it will use to divide into two new cells. At the end of interphase, the cell is ready to divide.

 **Reading Checkpoint** What is replication?

Stage 2: Mitosis

Once interphase is complete, the second stage of the cell cycle begins. **Mitosis** (my TOH sis) is the stage during which the cell's nucleus divides into two new nuclei. **During mitosis, one copy of the DNA is distributed into each of the two daughter cells.**

Scientists divide mitosis into four parts, or phases: prophase, metaphase, anaphase, and telophase. During prophase, the threadlike chromatin in the nucleus condenses to form double-rod structures called **chromosomes.** Each chromosome has two rods because the cell's DNA has replicated, and each rod in a chromosome is an exact copy of the other. Each identical rod in a chromosome is called a chromatid. Notice in Figure 11 that the two chromatids are held together by a structure called a centromere.

As the cell progresses through metaphase, anaphase, and telophase, the chromatids separate from each other and move to opposite ends of the cell. Then two nuclei form around the chromatids at the two ends of the cell.

FIGURE 10
Bigger Pig, More Cells
The mother pig has more cells in her body than her small piglets.

FIGURE 11
Chromosomes
During mitosis, the chromatin condenses to form chromosomes. Each chromosome consists of two identical strands, or chromatids. *Applying Concepts During which phase of mitosis do the chromosomes form?*

Chromosomes ▼

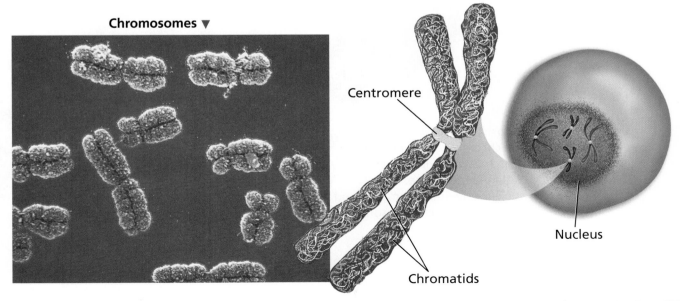

Centromere

Chromatids

Nucleus

FIGURE 12
The Cell Cycle

Cells undergo an orderly sequence of events as they grow and divide. The sequence shown here is a typical cell cycle in an animal cell. *Comparing and Contrasting Compare the location of the chromosomes during metaphase and anaphase.*

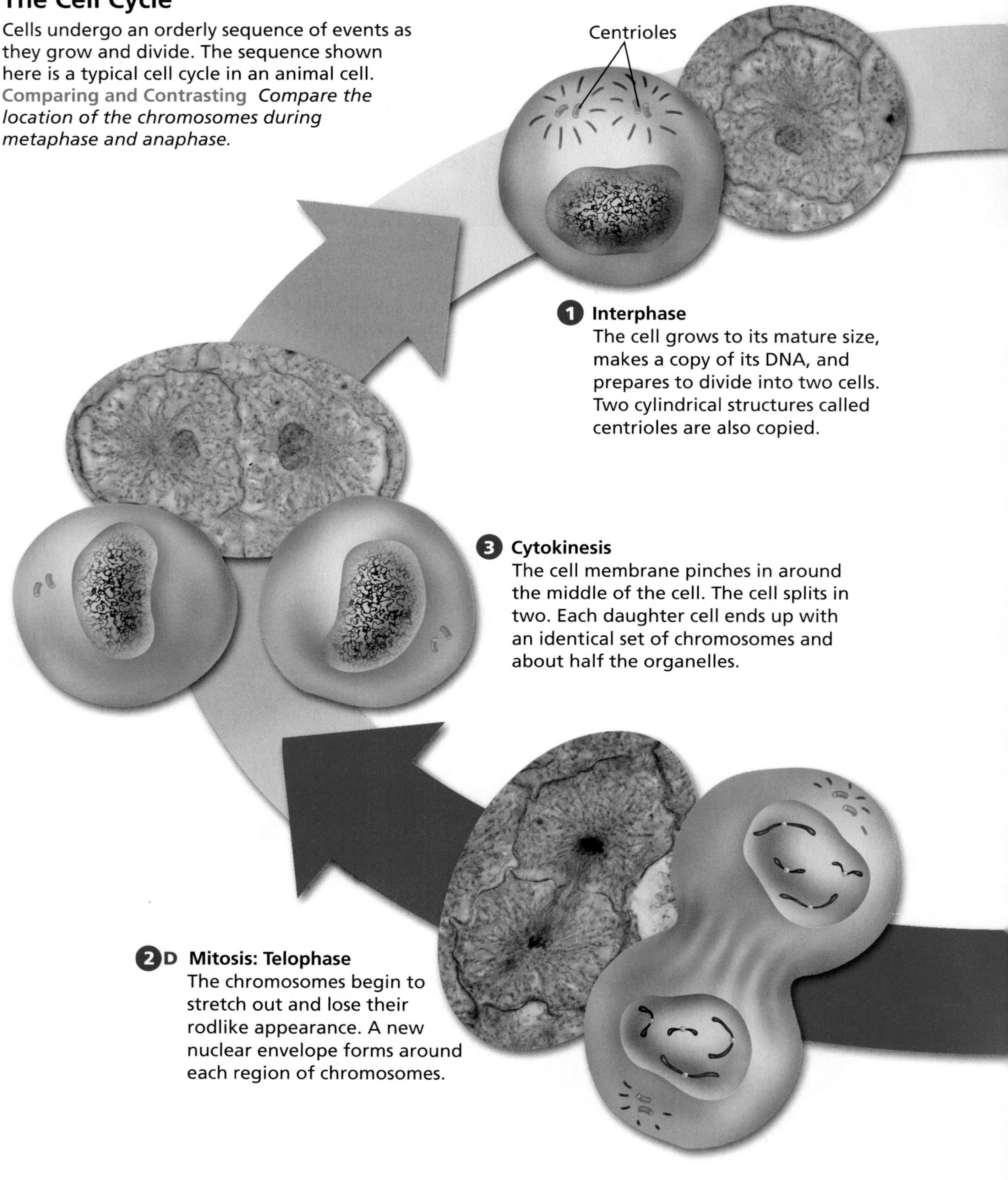

Centrioles

1 Interphase
The cell grows to its mature size, makes a copy of its DNA, and prepares to divide into two cells. Two cylindrical structures called centrioles are also copied.

3 Cytokinesis
The cell membrane pinches in around the middle of the cell. The cell splits in two. Each daughter cell ends up with an identical set of chromosomes and about half the organelles.

2 D Mitosis: Telophase
The chromosomes begin to stretch out and lose their rodlike appearance. A new nuclear envelope forms around each region of chromosomes.

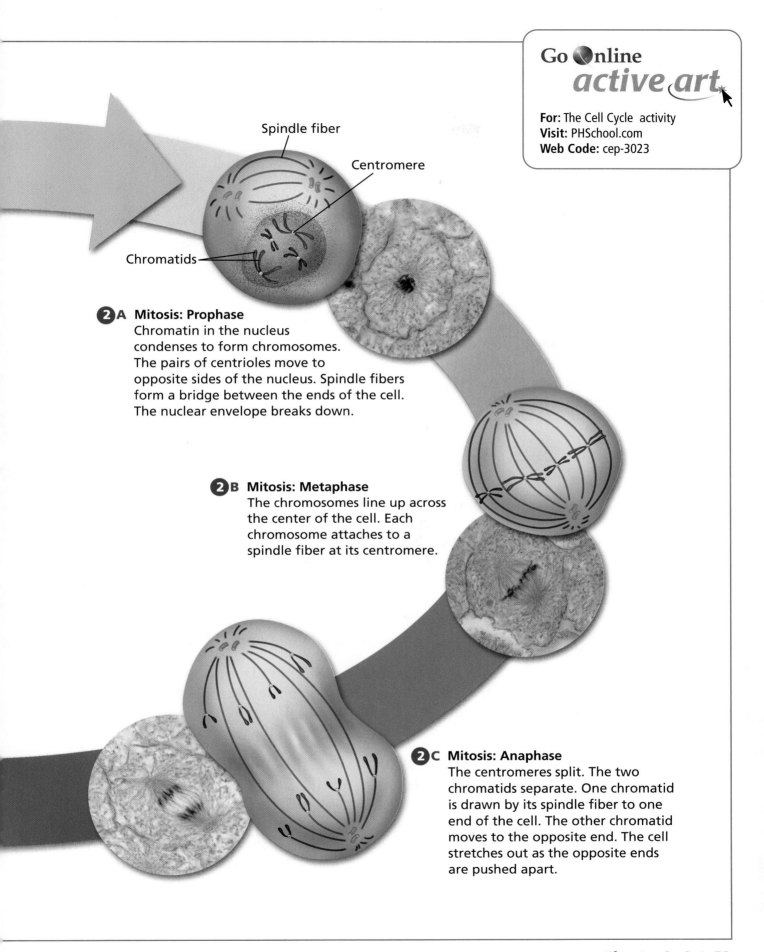

Go Online
active art

For: The Cell Cycle activity
Visit: PHSchool.com
Web Code: cep-3023

Spindle fiber

Centromere

Chromatids

2 A Mitosis: Prophase
Chromatin in the nucleus
condenses to form chromosomes.
The pairs of centrioles move to
opposite sides of the nucleus. Spindle fibers
form a bridge between the ends of the cell.
The nuclear envelope breaks down.

2 B Mitosis: Metaphase
The chromosomes line up across
the center of the cell. Each
chromosome attaches to a
spindle fiber at its centromere.

2 C Mitosis: Anaphase
The centromeres split. The two
chromatids separate. One chromatid
is drawn by its spindle fiber to one
end of the cell. The other chromatid
moves to the opposite end. The cell
stretches out as the opposite ends
are pushed apart.

Length of the Cell Cycle

How long does it take for a cell to go through one cell cycle? It all depends on the cell. A human liver cell, for example, completes one cell cycle in about 22 hours, as shown in the graph. Study the graph and then answer the following questions.

1. **Reading Graphs** What do the three curved arrows outside the circle represent?

2. **Reading Graphs** In what stage of the cell cycle is the wedge representing growth?

3. **Interpreting Data** In human liver cells, how long does it take DNA replication to occur?

4. **Drawing Conclusions** In human liver cells, what stage in the cell cycle takes the longest time?

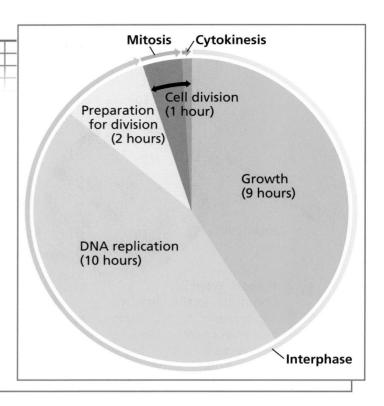

Mitosis Cytokinesis

Cell division (1 hour)

Preparation for division (2 hours)

Growth (9 hours)

DNA replication (10 hours)

Interphase

FIGURE 13
Cytokinesis in Plant Cells
During cytokinesis in plant cells, a cell plate forms between the two new nuclei.

Stage 3: Cytokinesis

The final stage of the cell cycle, which is called **cytokinesis** (sy toh kih NEE sis), completes the process of cell division. **During cytokinesis, the cytoplasm divides. The organelles are distributed into each of the two new cells.** Cytokinesis usually starts at about the same time as telophase. When cytokinesis is complete, two new cells, or daughter cells, have formed. Each daughter cell has the same number of chromosomes as the original parent cell. At the end of cytokinesis, each cell enters interphase, and the cycle begins again.

Cytokinesis in Animal Cells During cytokinesis in animal cells, the cell membrane squeezes together around the middle of the cell. The cytoplasm pinches into two cells. Each daughter cell gets about half of the organelles.

Cytokinesis in Plant Cells Cytokinesis is somewhat different in plant cells. A plant cell's rigid cell wall cannot squeeze together in the same way that a cell membrane can. Instead, a structure called a cell plate forms across the middle of the cell. The cell plate gradually develops into new cell membranes between the two daughter cells. New cell walls then form around the cell membranes.

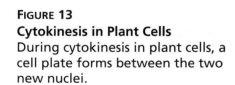 **Reading Checkpoint** **During what phase of mitosis does cytokinesis begin?**

Structure and Replication of DNA

DNA replication ensures that each daughter cell will have the genetic information it needs to carry out its activities. Before scientists could understand how DNA replicates, they had to know its structure. In 1952, Rosalind Franklin used an X-ray method to photograph DNA molecules. Her photographs helped James Watson and Francis Crick figure out the structure of DNA in 1953.

The Structure of DNA Notice in Figure 14 that a DNA molecule looks like a twisted ladder, or spiral staircase. The two sides of the DNA ladder are made up of molecules of a sugar called deoxyribose, alternating with molecules known as phosphates.

Each rung is made up of a pair of molecules called nitrogen bases. Nitrogen bases are molecules that contain the element nitrogen and other elements. DNA has four kinds of nitrogen bases: adenine (AD uh neen), thymine (THY meen), guanine (GWAH neen), and cytosine (SY tuh seen). The capital letters A, T, G, and C are used to represent the four bases.

The bases on one side of the ladder pair with the bases on the other side. Adenine (A) only pairs with thymine (T), while guanine (G) only pairs with cytosine (C). This pairing pattern is the key to understanding how DNA replication occurs.

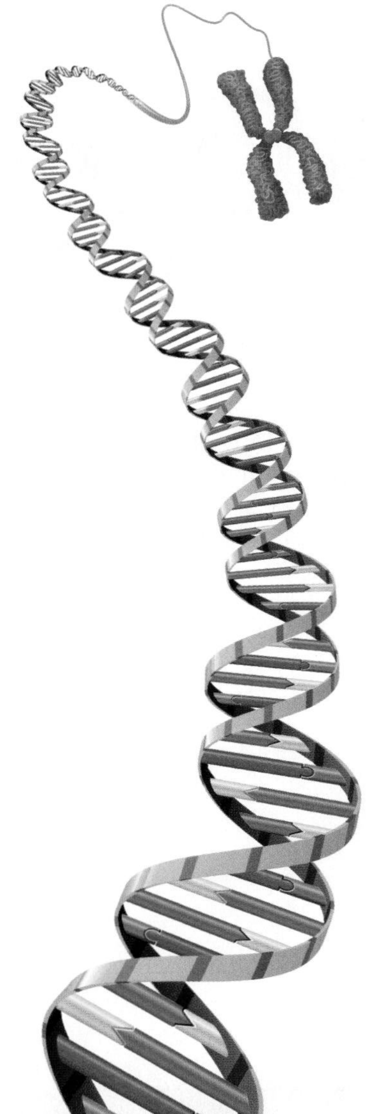

FIGURE 14
The Structure of DNA
The DNA molecule is shaped like a twisted ladder. Classifying *Which base always pairs with adenine?*

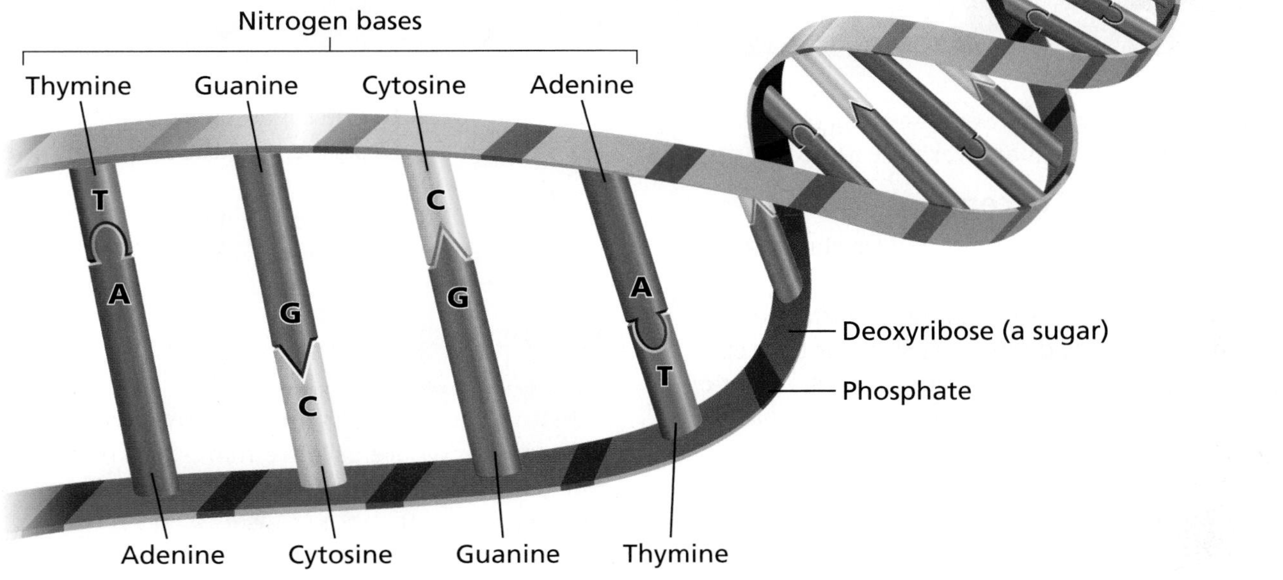

Nitrogen bases

Thymine Guanine Cytosine Adenine

T C

A G G A

G T

C

Deoxyribose (a sugar)

Phosphate

Adenine Cytosine Guanine Thymine

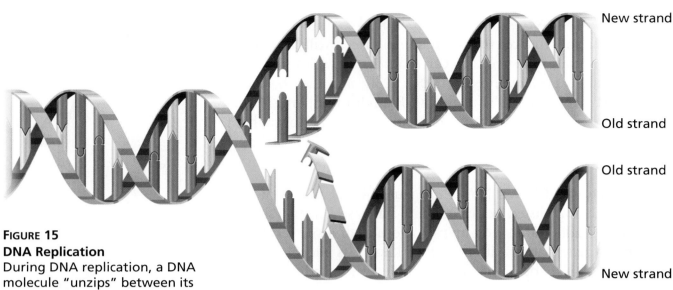

New strand

Old strand

Old strand

New strand

FIGURE 15

DNA Replication

During DNA replication, a DNA molecule "unzips" between its paired bases. New bases pair with the bases on each old strand. As a result, two identical DNA strands form.

The Replication Process DNA replication begins when the two sides of the DNA molecule unwind and separate, somewhat like a zipper unzipping. As you can see in Figure 15, the molecule separates between the paired nitrogen bases.

Next, nitrogen bases that are floating in the nucleus pair up with the bases on each half of the DNA molecule. **Because of the way in which the nitrogen bases pair with one another, the order of the bases in each new DNA molecule exactly matches the order in the original DNA molecule.** Adenine always pairs with thymine, while guanine always pairs with cytosine. Once the new bases are attached, two new DNA molecules are formed.

 **Reading Checkpoint** During DNA replication, which base pairs with guanine?

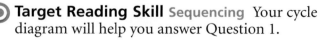 **Section 3 Assessment**

Target Reading Skill Sequencing Your cycle diagram will help you answer Question 1.

Reviewing Key Concepts

1. a. Reviewing What are the three stages of the cell cycle?

b. Summarizing Summarize what happens to chromosomes during the stage of the cell cycle in which the nucleus divides. Include the terms *prophase*, *metaphase*, *anaphase*, and *telophase*.

c. Interpreting Diagrams Look at Figure 12. What is the role of spindle fibers during cell division?

2. a. Listing List the nitrogen bases in DNA.

b. Describing Describe how the nitrogen bases pair in a DNA molecule.

c. Inferring One section of a strand of DNA has the base sequence AGATTC. What is the base sequence on the other strand?

Writing in Science

Writing Instructions Imagine that you work in a factory where cells are manufactured. Write instructions for newly forming cells on how to carry out cytokinesis. Provide instructions for both plant and animal cells.

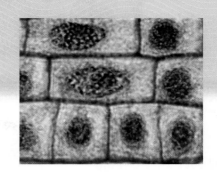

Multiplying by Dividing

Problem

How long do the stages of the cell cycle take?

Skills Focus

observing, calculating

Materials

- microscope
- colored pencils
- calculator (optional)
- prepared slides of onion root tip cells undergoing cell division

Procedure 🔧

1. Place the slide on the stage of a microscope. Use low power to locate a cell in interphase. Then switch to high power, and make a labeled drawing of the cell. **CAUTION:** *Slides and coverslips break easily. Do not allow the objective to touch the slide. If the slide breaks, notify your teacher. Do not touch broken glass.*

2. Repeat Step 1 to find cells in prophase, metaphase, anaphase, and telophase. Then copy the data table into your notebook.

3. Return to low power. Find an area of the slide with many cells undergoing cell division. Switch to the magnification that lets you see about 50 cells at once (for example, 100 ×).

4. Examine the cells row by row, and count the cells that are in interphase. Record that number in the data table under *First Sample*.

5. Examine the cells row by row four more times to count the cells in prophase, metaphase, anaphase, and telophase. Record the results.

6. Move to a new area on the slide. Repeat Steps 3–5 and record your counts in the column labeled *Second Sample*.

7. Fill in the column labeled *Total Number* by adding the numbers across each row in your data table.

8. Add the totals for the five stages to find the total number of cells counted.

Analyze and Conclude

1. **Observing** Which stage of the cell cycle did you observe most often?

2. **Calculating** The cell cycle for onion root tips takes about 720 minutes (12 hours). Use your data and the formula below to find the number of minutes each stage takes.

$$\text{Time for each stage} = \frac{\text{Number of cells at each stage}}{\text{Total number of cells counted}} \times 720 \text{ min}$$

3. **Communicating** Use the data to compare the amount of time spent in mitosis with the total time for the whole cell cycle. Write your answer in the form of a paragraph.

More to Explore

Examine prepared slides of animal cells undergoing cell division. Use drawings and descriptions to compare plant and animal mitosis.

Data Table			
Stage of Cell Cycle	First Sample	Second Sample	Total Number
Interphase			
Mitosis:			
Prophase			
Metaphase			
Anaphase			
Telophase			
Total number of cells counted			

Cancer

Reading Preview

Key Concepts
- How is cancer related to the cell cycle?
- What are some ways that cancer can be treated?

Key Terms
- cancer • mutation • tumor
- chemotherapy

 Target Reading Skill

Previewing Visuals When you preview, you look ahead at the material to be read. Preview Figure 17. Then write two questions that you have in a graphic organizer like the one below. As you read, answer your questions.

How Cancer Spreads

Q.	What is a tumor?
A.	
Q.	

The constellation Cancer ▶

Discover Activity

Lab zone

What Happens When There Are Too Many Cells?

1. Use tape to mark off a 1 m × 1 m square on the floor. The square represents an area inside the human body. Have two students stand in the square to represent cells.

2. Suppose each cell divides every 30 seconds, and then one cell dies. With a group of students, model this situation. After 30 seconds, two new students should enter the square and one student should leave the square.

3. Model another round of cell division by having three new students enter the square while one student leaves. Continue this process until no more students can fit in the square.

Think It Over

Predicting Use this activity to predict what would happen if some cells in a person's body divided faster than they should.

If you go outside on a clear night in spring, you may be able to see the constellation, or group of stars, called Cancer. The word *cancer* means "crab" in Latin, the language of the ancient Romans. According to an ancient Roman myth, the goddess Juno sent a giant crab to help kill the hero Hercules. Instead, Hercules crushed the crab with his foot. Juno then put the crab in the sky in the form of a constellation.

Today the word *cancer* still names the constellation, but it also names a disease. As the mythological crab threatened Hercules, the disease called cancer threatens human health. But doctors and scientists are making progress in treating and preventing cancer. As Hercules conquered the monster called Cancer, perhaps one day scientists will conquer the disease.

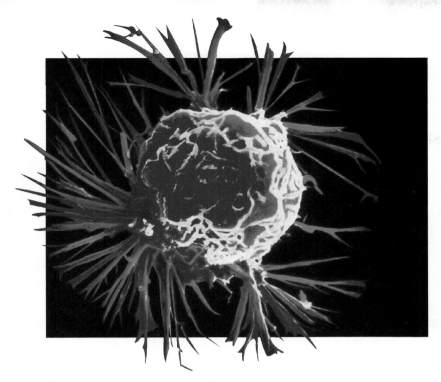

FIGURE 16
A Breast Cancer Cell
A cancer tumor begins as a single cell. A mutation in the cell's DNA disrupts the normal cell cycle.
Relating Cause and Effect *How does the cell behave as a result of the mutation?*

What Is Cancer?

Cancer is a disease in which cells grow and divide uncontrollably, damaging the parts of the body around them. Cancer is something like weeds in a garden. Weeds can overrun the garden plants, robbing them of the space, sunlight, and water they need. Similarly, cancer cells can overrun normal cells.

Cancer is actually not just one disease. In fact, there are more than 100 types of cancer. Cancer can occur in almost any part of the body. Cancers are often named by the place in the body where they begin. For example, lung cancer begins in the tissues of the lungs. In the United States today, lung cancer is the leading cause of cancer deaths among both men and women.

How Cancer Begins Scientists think that cancer begins when something damages a portion of the DNA in a chromosome. The damage causes a change in the DNA called a **mutation.** DNA contains all the instructions necessary for life. Damage to the DNA can cause cells to function abnormally.

Normally, the cells in one part of the body live in harmony with the cells around them. Cells that go through the cell cycle divide in a controlled way. **Cancer begins when mutations disrupt the normal cell cycle, causing cells to divide in an uncontrolled way.** Without the normal controls on the cell cycle, the cells grow too large and divide too often.

At first, one cell develops in an abnormal way. As the cell divides over and over, the repeated divisions produce more and more abnormal cells. In time, these cells form a tumor. A **tumor** is a mass of abnormal cells that develops when cancerous cells divide and grow uncontrollably.

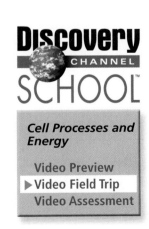

Discovery
CHANNEL
SCHOOL™

Cell Processes and Energy

Video Preview
▶Video Field Trip
Video Assessment

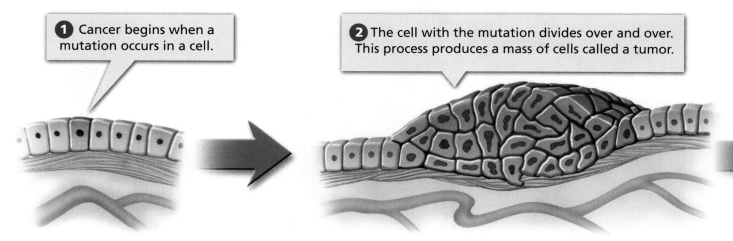

1 Cancer begins when a mutation occurs in a cell.

2 The cell with the mutation divides over and over. This process produces a mass of cells called a tumor.

FIGURE 17
How Cancer Spreads
A cancerous tumor is a mass of cells that divide uncontrollably.
Interpreting Diagrams *How can cancer spread from one part of the body to another?*

How Cancer Spreads Figure 17 shows how a tumor forms. Tumors often take years to grow to a noticeable size. During that time, the cells become more and more abnormal as they continue to divide. Some of the cancerous cells may break off the tumor and enter the bloodstream. In this way, the cancer can spread to other areas of the body.

 **Reading Checkpoint** **What is the first step that leads to the development of a tumor?**

Treating and Preventing Cancer

Scientists are making progress in the battle against cancer. Treatments offer hope for cancer patients. In addition, people can take steps that help prevent the disease.

Treating Cancer If a person is diagnosed with cancer, there are a variety of treatments. **There are three common ways to treat cancer: surgery, radiation, and drugs that destroy the cancer cells.**

When a cancer is detected before it has spread to other parts of the body, surgery is usually the best treatment. If doctors can completely remove the cancerous tumor, a person may be cured. If, however, the cancer has spread or if the tumor cannot be removed, doctors may use radiation. Radiation consists of beams of high-energy waves. Fast-growing cancer cells are more likely than normal cells to be destroyed by radiation.

Chemotherapy is another form of cancer treatment. **Chemotherapy** is the use of drugs to treat a disease. Cancer-treatment drugs are carried throughout the body by the bloodstream. These drugs kill cancer cells or slow their growth.

Scientists continue to look for new ways to treat cancer. If scientists can discover how the cell cycle is controlled, they may find ways to stop cancer cells from multiplying.

Go Online
SCLINKS **NSTA**

For: Links on cancer
Visit: www.SciLinks.org
Web Code: scn-0324

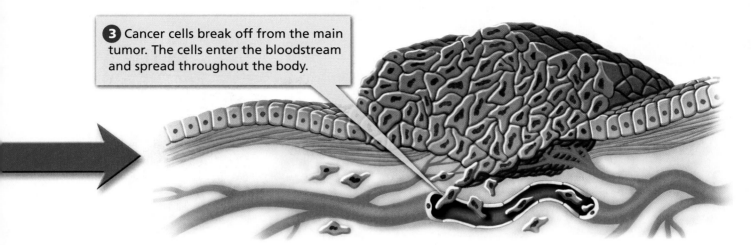

❸ Cancer cells break off from the main tumor. The cells enter the bloodstream and spread throughout the body.

Preventing Cancer People can reduce their chances of developing cancer by avoiding smoking, eating a healthful diet, and protecting their skin from bright sunlight. When people repeatedly inhale tobacco smoke, lung cancer and other forms of cancer may result. Unhealthful diets may lead to almost as many cancer deaths as does tobacco. A diet high in fatty foods, such as fatty meats and fried foods, is especially harmful. Eating a lot of fruits and vegetables may help lower the risk for some types of cancer.

Most skin cancers are caused by the ultraviolet light in sunlight. If people limit their exposure to bright sunlight, they can reduce their risk of getting skin cancer.

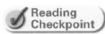 **Reading Checkpoint** **How can exposure to bright sunlight lead to cancer?**

Section 4 Assessment

Target Reading Skill Previewing Visuals Refer to your questions and answers about Figure 17 to help answer Question 1 below.

Reviewing Key Concepts

1. a. Defining What is cancer?
   b. Comparing and Contrasting How are cancer cells different from normal cells?
   c. Relating Cause and Effect What is the relationship between cancer and DNA?
2. a. Identifying Identify the three ways in which cancer is treated.
   b. Explaining Which method is almost always a part of the treatment for very small tumors that have not spread to other parts of the body? Explain why this method is chosen.

c. Inferring Why is a combination of methods typically used to treat cancer that has spread beyond the original tumor?

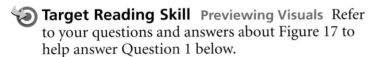 **Lab zone** **At-Home Activity**

A Cancer-Prevention Diet With your family, discuss what cancer is and how it spreads. Then explain that a diet that is low in fat can help prevent some forms of cancer. Work with members of your family to plan some low-fat meals. You might find new recipes for low-fat foods and prepare them together.

When Should New Medicines Be Made Available?

A woman is seriously ill with cancer. She has read about a new drug that shows promise in treating the type of cancer she has. The woman asks her doctor for the medicine. The doctor, however, tells her that she cannot have the drug. The new medicine is still being tested, and it has not yet been approved for use. When the cancer patient hears this news, she feels angry and helpless.

The Issues

Why Does Drug Approval Take So Long?

Before a new medicine becomes available, it must undergo extensive testing. The testing of new medicines is regulated by the Food and Drug Administration, or FDA, which is an agency of the United States government. The FDA tries to balance two important needs. First, sick people need to have the best treatments available, including promising new drugs. Second, patients need to be protected from drugs that do not work or are harmful.

It takes several years of testing for a new drug to be approved. The lengthy testing process is designed to ensure that the new medicine works, and that it is safe. Scientists begin by using chemical tests and computer programs to determine the drug's characteristics. Then the drug is tested on animals to see whether it is safe and effective. Next, the drug is extensively tested on human volunteers. If the results of the tests on human volunteers are good, the drug becomes available to patients who may benefit from it.

Testing for Safety and Effectiveness
To ensure that new medicines are safe and effective, they are tested on animals before being tested on humans.

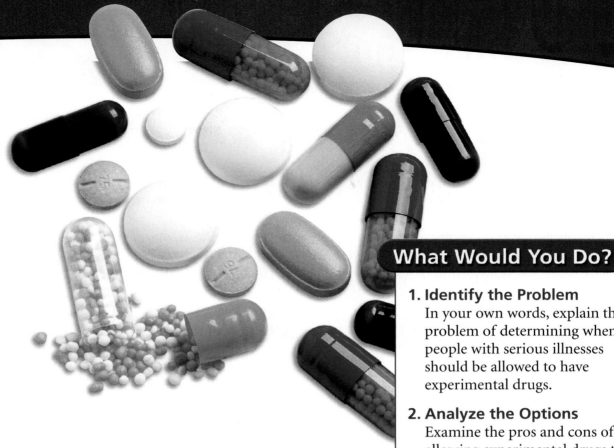

Should Drugs Be Available Sooner?

While a new drug is being tested, the only patients who can get the drug are the volunteers who take part in the tests. Other patients—even those who are very sick—do not usually have access to the drug. However, in rare cases, if a new medicine shows special promise in fighting a life-threatening disease, such as AIDS or cancer, the FDA may make it available sooner than usual.

Risks of Making Drugs Available Too Soon

Some people are critical of the FDA's efforts to make new drugs available more quickly. Early-approval drugs have not undergone the extensive testing required for most drugs. Therefore, the effectiveness of the drugs has not been fully demonstrated.

In addition, long-term use of the drugs may have harmful side effects. For example, long-term use of some drugs can increase the risk that people will develop harmful conditions or diseases, such as some types of cancer. Long-term side effects cannot usually be detected without years of testing.

What Would You Do?

1. Identify the Problem
In your own words, explain the problem of determining when people with serious illnesses should be allowed to have experimental drugs.

2. Analyze the Options
Examine the pros and cons of allowing experimental drugs to be released before the entire testing process is complete. List the possible benefits of releasing a drug early. Also identify the risks that patients take when they use medicines that have not been fully tested.

3. Find a Solution
Suppose a patient has heard about a promising new drug that has been approved without the full testing procedure. To take this drug, the patient must stop using a standard treatment that may be safer but less effective. Write a conversation between a doctor and the patient in which they discuss the pros and cons of the new drug.

For: More on new medicines
Visit: PHSchool.com
Web Code: ceh-3020

Study Guide

① Photosynthesis

Key Concepts

- Nearly all living things obtain energy either directly or indirectly from the energy of sunlight captured during photosynthesis.

- During photosynthesis, plants and some other organisms use energy from the sun to convert carbon dioxide and water into oxygen and sugars.

- The equation for photosynthesis is

$$6\,CO_2 + 6\,H_2O \longrightarrow C_6H_{12}O_6 + 6\,O_2.$$

Key Terms

photosynthesis
autotroph
heterotroph
pigment
chlorophyll
stomata

② Respiration

Key Concepts

- During respiration, cells break down simple food molecules such as sugar and release the energy they contain.

- The respiration equation is

$$C_6H_{12}O_6 + 6\,O_2 \longrightarrow$$
$$6\,CO_2 + 6\,H_2O + \text{energy}.$$

- Fermentation provides energy for cells without using oxygen.

Key Terms

respiration
fermentation

③ Cell Division

Key Concepts

- During interphase, the cell grows, makes a copy of its DNA, and prepares to divide into two cells.

- During mitosis, one copy of the DNA is distributed into each of the two daughter cells.

- During cytokinesis, the cytoplasm divides. The organelles are distributed into each of the two new cells.

- Because of the way in which the nitrogen bases pair with one another, the order of the bases in each new DNA molecule exactly matches the order in the original DNA molecule.

Key Terms

cell cycle
interphase
replication
mitosis
chromosome
cytokinesis

④ Cancer

Key Concepts

- Cancer begins when mutations disrupt the normal cell cycle, causing cells to divide in an uncontrolled way.

- There are three common ways to treat cancer: surgery, radiation, and drugs that destroy the cancer cells.

Key Terms

cancer   tumor
mutation   chemotherapy

Review and Assessment

Organizing Information

Comparing and Contrasting
Copy the compare/contrast table about photosynthesis and respiration. Complete the table to compare these processes. (For more information on compare/contrast tables, see the Skills Handbook.)

Comparing Photosynthesis and Respiration

Feature	Photosynthesis	Respiration
Raw materials	Water and carbon dioxide	a. ___?___
Products	b. ___?___	c. ___?___
Is energy released?	d. ___?___	Yes

Reviewing Key Terms

Choose the letter of the best answer.

1. The organelle in which photosynthesis takes place is the
   a. mitochondrion.
   b. chloroplast.
   c. chlorophyll.
   d. nucleus.

2. What process produces carbon dioxide?
   a. photosynthesis
   b. replication
   c. mutation
   d. respiration

3. The process in which a cell makes an exact copy of its DNA is called
   a. fermentation.
   b. respiration.
   c. replication.
   d. reproduction.

4. What happens during cytokinesis?
   a. A spindle forms.
   b. Chloroplasts release energy.
   c. The cytoplasm divides.
   d. Chromosomes divide.

5. A mass of cancer cells is called a
   a. tumor.
   b. chromosome.
   c. mutation.
   d. mitochondrion.

If the statement is true, write *true*. If it is false, change the underlined word or words to make the statement true.

6. An organism that makes its own food is <u>an autotroph</u> .

7. During <u>respiration</u>, most energy is released in the mitochondria.

8. An energy-releasing process that does not require oxygen is <u>replication</u>.

9. The stage of the cell cycle when DNA replication occurs is called <u>telophase</u>.

10. <u>Uncontrolled</u> cell division is a characteristic of cancer.

Writing in Science

Brochure Suppose you are a volunteer who works with cancer patients. Write a brochure that could be given to cancer patients and their families. The brochure should explain what cancer is and how it is treated.

DISCOVERY CHANNEL **SCHOOL**

Cell Processes and Energy
Video Preview
Video Field Trip
▶ Video Assessment

Review and Assessment

Checking Concepts

11. Briefly explain what happens to energy from the sun during photosynthesis.

12. What are the raw materials needed for photosynthesis? What are the products?

13. Why do organisms need to carry out the process of respiration?

14. Describe what happens during interphase.

15. How do the events in the cell cycle ensure that the genetic information in the daughter cells will be identical to that of the parent cell?

16. Describe how cancer usually begins to develop in the body.

17. Explain why it is important for people to wear protective clothing or use sunscreen when they are outdoors in bright sunlight.

Thinking Critically

18. **Predicting** Suppose a volcano threw so much ash into the air that it blocked most of the sunlight that usually strikes Earth. How might this affect the ability of animals to obtain the energy they need to live?

19. **Comparing and Contrasting** Explain the relationship between the processes of breathing and cellular respiration.

20. **Relating Cause and Effect** Do plant cells need to carry out respiration? Explain.

21. **Inferring** The diagram below shows part of one strand of a DNA molecule. What would the bases on the other strand be?

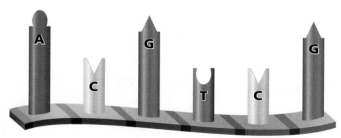

22. **Making Judgments** What information could you give someone to persuade him or her not to start smoking?

Applying Skills

Use the table below to answer Questions 23–26.

Percentages of Nitrogen Bases in the DNA of Various Organisms

Nitrogen Base	Human	Wheat	E. coli Bacterium
Adenine	30%	27%	24%
Guanine	20%	23%	26%
Thymine	30%	27%	24%
Cytosine	20%	23%	26%

23. **Graphing** For each organism, draw a bar graph to show the percentages of each nitrogen base in its DNA.

24. **Interpreting Data** What is the relationship between the amounts of adenine and thymine in the DNA of each organism? What is the relationship between the amounts of guanine and cytosine?

25. **Inferring** Based on your answer to Question 24, what can you infer about the structure of DNA in these three organisms?

26. **Applying Concepts** Suppose cytosine made up 28% of the nitrogen bases in an organism. What percentage of the organism's nitrogen bases should be thymine? Explain.

Lab zone Chapter Project

Performance Assessment Bring in your plants, recorded observations, and graphs to share with the class. Be prepared to describe your experimental plan and explain your results. How well did you follow your experimental plan? What did you learn about photosynthesis and light from the experiment you performed?

Standardized Test Prep

Choose the letter of the best answer.

1. A researcher places part of a plant in a beaker of water. She observes that the plant leaves release bubbles of gas when she shines a light on the beaker. The leaves do not release gas when the beaker is placed in the dark. Based on her observations, which of the following is the most logical inference?
   A The plant is undergoing cellular respiration.
   B The plant is breathing.
   C Light is breaking down molecules of air.
   D The plant is undergoing photosynthesis.

2. A scientist performed an experiment to determine the effect of temperature on the length of the cell cycle. On the basis of the data in the table below, how long would you expect the cell cycle to be at 5°C ?
   F less than 13.3 hours
   G more than 54.6 hours
   H between 29.8 and 54.6 hours
   J about 20 hours

Effect of Temperature on Length of Onion Cell Cycle	
Temperature (°C)	**Length of Cell Cycle (hours)**
10	54.6
15	29.8
20	18.8
25	13.3

3. Which of the following statements is true?
   A Plants cannot respire because they have no mitochondria.
   B Photosynthesis produces energy.
   C Animals cannot photosynthesize.
   D Only plants photosynthesize and only animals respire.

4. Which of the following nitrogen base pairs can be found in DNA?
   F A-G
   G T-C
   H G-T
   J A-T

Constructed Response

5. Explain the relationship between cell division and cancer. How do scientists believe cancer starts? What causes a tumor to form?

Chapter Preview

interactive Textbook

These spaniel puppies and their mother resemble each other in many ways. ▶

Lab zone™ Chapter **Project**

All in the Family

Did you ever wonder why some offspring resemble their parents while others do not? In this chapter, you'll learn how offspring come to have traits similar to those of their parents. You'll create a family of "paper pets" to explore how traits pass from parents to offspring.

Your Goal To create a "paper pet" that will be crossed with a class-mate's pet, and to determine what traits the offspring will have

To complete this project success-fully, you must

● create your own unique paper pet with five different traits

● cross your pet with another pet to produce six offspring

● determine what traits the offspring will have, and explain how they came to have those traits

● follow the safety guidelines in Appendix A

Plan It! Cut out your pet from either blue or yellow construction paper. Choose other traits for your pet from this list: square eyes or round eyes; oval nose or triangular nose; pointed teeth or square teeth. Then create your pet using materials of your choice.

Mendel's Work

Reading Preview

Key Concepts
- What were the results of Mendel's experiments, or crosses?
- What controls the inheritance of traits in organisms?

Key Terms
- heredity • trait • genetics
- fertilization • purebred • gene
- alleles • dominant allele
- recessive allele • hybrid

Target Reading Skill

Outlining As you read, make an outline about Mendel's work. Use the red headings for the main ideas and the blue headings for the supporting ideas.

Mendel's Work
I. Mendel's experiments
A. Crossing pea plants
B.
C.

Lab zone Discover Activity

What Does the Father Look Like?

1. Observe the colors of the kitten in the photo. Record the kitten's coat colors and pattern. Include as many details as you can.
2. Observe the mother cat in the photo. Record her coat color and pattern.

Think It Over

Inferring Based on your observations, describe what you think the kitten's father might look like. Identify the evidence on which you based your inference.

In the mid nineteenth century, a priest named Gregor Mendel tended a garden in a central European monastery. Mendel's experiments in that peaceful garden would one day revolutionize the study of heredity. **Heredity** is the passing of physical characteristics from parents to offspring.

Mendel wondered why different pea plants had different characteristics. Some pea plants grew tall, while others were short. Some plants produced green seeds, while others had yellow seeds. Each different form of a characteristic, such as stem height or seed color, is called a **trait.** Mendel observed that the pea plants' traits were often similar to those of their parents. Sometimes, however, the plants had different traits from those of their parents.

Mendel experimented with thousands of pea plants to understand the process of heredity. Today, Mendel's discoveries form the foundation of **genetics,** the scientific study of heredity.

◄ Gregor Mendel

Mendel's Experiments

Figure 1 shows a pea plant's flower. The flower's petals surround the pistil and the stamens. The pistil produces female sex cells, or eggs. The stamens produce pollen, which contains the male sex cells, or sperm. A new organism begins to form when egg and sperm join in the process called **fertilization.** Before fertilization can happen in pea plants, pollen must reach the pistil of a pea flower. This process is called pollination.

Pea plants are usually self-pollinating. In self-pollination, pollen from a flower lands on the pistil of the same flower. Mendel developed a method by which he cross-pollinated, or "crossed," pea plants. To cross two plants, he removed pollen from a flower on one plant. He then brushed the pollen onto a flower on a second plant.

Crossing Pea Plants Suppose you wanted to study the inheritance of traits in pea plants. What could you do? Mendel decided to cross plants with contrasting traits—for example, tall plants and short plants. He started his experiments with purebred plants. A **purebred** organism is the offspring of many generations that have the same trait. For example, purebred short pea plants always come from short parent plants.

FIGURE 1
Crossing Pea Plants
Gregor Mendel crossed pea plants that had different traits. The illustrations show how he did this. **Interpreting Diagrams** *How did Mendel prevent self-pollination?*

1 To prevent self-pollination, Mendel removed the pollen-producing structures from a pink flower.

2 He used a brush to remove pollen from a white flower on another plant. He brushed this pollen onto the pink flower.

3 The egg cells in the pink flower were then fertilized by sperm from the white flower. After a time, peas formed in the pod.

The F$_1$ Offspring In one experiment, Mendel crossed pure-bred tall plants with purebred short plants. Scientists today call these parent plants the parental generation, or P generation. The offspring from this cross are the first filial (FIL ee ul) generation, or the F$_1$ generation. The word *filial* comes from *filia* and *filius*, the Latin words for "daughter" and "son."

In Figure 2, notice that all the offspring in the F$_1$ generation were tall. Even though one of the parent plants was short, none of the offspring were short. The shortness trait seemed to disappear!

The F$_2$ Offspring When the plants in the F$_1$ generation were full-grown, Mendel allowed them to self-pollinate. Surprisingly, the plants in the F$_2$ (second filial) generation were a mix of tall and short plants. The shortness trait had reappeared, even though none of the F$_1$ parent plants were short. Mendel counted the tall and short plants. About three fourths of the plants were tall, while one fourth were short.

Experiments With Other Traits Mendel also crossed pea plants with other contrasting traits. Compare the two forms of each trait in Figure 3. **In all of Mendel's crosses, only one form of the trait appeared in the F$_1$ generation. However, in the F$_2$ generation, the "lost" form of the trait always reappeared in about one fourth of the plants.**

 What did Mendel observe about the F$_2$ plants?

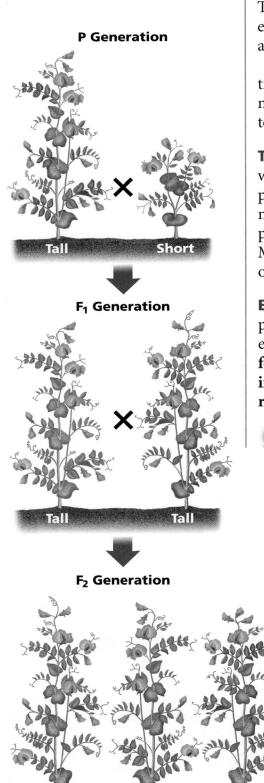

P Generation

F$_1$ Generation

F$_2$ Generation

FIGURE 2
Results of a Cross
When Mendel crossed purebred tall-stemmed plants with purebred short-stemmed plants, the first-generation offspring all had tall stems. Then he allowed the first-generation plants to self-pollinate. About 75 percent of the offspring had tall stems, and about 25 percent had short stems.

Genetics of Pea Plants							
Traits	Seed Shape	Seed Color	Seed Coat Color	Pod Shape	Pod Color	Flower Position	Stem Height
Controlled by Dominant Allele	Round	Yellow	Gray	Smooth	Green	Side	Tall
Controlled by Recessive Allele	Wrinkled	Green	White	Pinched	Yellow	End	Short

Dominant and Recessive Alleles

Mendel reached several conclusions on the basis of his experimental results. He reasoned that individual factors, or sets of genetic "information," must control the inheritance of traits in peas. The factors that control each trait exist in pairs. The female parent contributes one factor, while the male parent contributes the other factor. Finally, one factor in a pair can mask, or hide, the other factor. The tallness factor, for example, masked the shortness factor.

Genes and Alleles Today, scientists use the word **gene** for the factors that control a trait. **Alleles** (uh LEELZ) are the different forms of a gene. The gene that controls stem height in peas, for example, has one allele for tall stems and one allele for short stems. Each pea plant inherits two alleles from its parents—one allele from the egg and the other from the sperm. A pea plant may inherit two alleles for tall stems, two alleles for short stems, or one of each.

An organism's traits are controlled by the alleles it inherits from its parents. Some alleles are dominant, while other alleles are recessive. A **dominant allele** is one whose trait always shows up in the organism when the allele is present. A **recessive allele,** on the other hand, is hidden whenever the dominant allele is present. A trait controlled by a recessive allele will only show up if the organism does not have the dominant allele. Figure 3 shows dominant and recessive alleles in Mendel's crosses.

FIGURE 3
Mendel studied several traits in pea plants.
Interpreting Diagrams *Is yellow seed color controlled by a dominant allele or a recessive allele?*

Lab zone Skills Activity

Predicting

In fruit flies, long wings are dominant over short wings. A scientist crossed a purebred long-winged male fruit fly with a purebred short-winged female. Predict the wing length of the F_1 offspring. If the scientist crossed a hybrid male F_1 fruit fly with a hybrid F_1 female, what would their offspring probably be like?

In pea plants, the allele for tall stems is dominant over the allele for short stems. Pea plants with one allele for tall stems and one allele for short stems will be tall. The allele for tall stems masks the allele for short stems. Only pea plants that inherit two recessive alleles for short stems will be short.

Alleles in Mendel's Crosses In Mendel's cross for stem height, the purebred tall plants in the P generation had two alleles for tall stems. The purebred short plants had two alleles for short stems. The F_1 plants each inherited an allele for tall stems from the tall parent and an allele for short stems from the short parent. Therefore, each F_1 plant had one allele for tall stems and one for short stems. The F_1 plants are called hybrids. A **hybrid** (HY brid) organism has two different alleles for a trait. All the F_1 plants are tall because the dominant allele for tall stems masks the recessive allele for short stems.

When Mendel crossed the F_1 plants, some of the offspring in the F_2 generation inherited two dominant alleles for tall stems. These plants were tall. Other F_2 plants inherited one dominant allele for tall stems and one recessive allele for short stems. These plants were also tall. The rest of the F_2 plants inherited two recessive alleles for short stems. These plants were short.

Symbols for Alleles Geneticists use letters to represent alleles. A dominant allele is represented by a capital letter. For example, the allele for tall stems is represented by *T*. A recessive allele is represented by the lowercase version of the letter. So, the allele for short stems would be represented by *t*. When a plant inherits two dominant alleles for tall stems, its alleles are written as *TT*. When a plant inherits two recessive alleles for short stems, its alleles are written as *tt*. When a plant inherits one allele for tall stems and one allele for short stems, its alleles are written as *Tt*.

FIGURE 4
Black Fur, White Fur
In rabbits, the allele for black fur is dominant over the allele for white fur. **Inferring** *What combination of alleles must the white rabbit have?*

Significance of Mendel's Contribution Mendel's discovery of genes and alleles eventually changed scientists' ideas about heredity. Before Mendel, most people thought that the traits of an individual organism were simply a blend of their parents' characteristics. According to this idea, if a tall plant and a short plant were crossed, the offspring would all have medium height.

However, when Mendel crossed purebred tall and purebred short pea plants, the offspring were all tall. Mendel's experiments demonstrated that parents' traits do not simply blend in the offspring. Instead, traits are determined by individual, separate alleles inherited from each parent. Some of these alleles, such as the allele for short height in pea plants, are recessive. If a trait is determined by a recessive allele, the trait can seem to disappear in the offspring.

Unfortunately, the importance of Mendel's discovery was not recognized during his lifetime. Then, in 1900, three different scientists rediscovered Mendel's work. These scientists quickly recognized the importance of Mendel's ideas. Because of his work, Mendel is often called the Father of Genetics.

FIGURE 5
The Mendel Medal
Every year, to honor the memory of Gregor Mendel, an outstanding scientist is awarded the Mendel Medal.

 **Reading Checkpoint** If an allele is represented by a capital letter, what does this indicate?

Section 1 Assessment

Target Reading Skill Outlining Use the information in your outline about Mendel's work to help you answer the questions below.

Reviewing Key Concepts

1. a. Identifying In Mendel's cross for stem height, what contrasting traits did the pea plants in the P generation exhibit?

   b. Explaining What trait or traits did the plants in the F_1 generation exhibit? When you think of the traits of the parent plants, why is this result surprising?

   c. Comparing and Contrasting Contrast the offspring in the F_1 generation to the offspring in the F_2 generation. What did the differences in the F_1 and F_2 offspring show Mendel?

2. a. Defining What is a dominant allele? What is a recessive allele?

   b. Relating Cause and Effect Explain how dominant and recessive alleles for the trait of stem height determine whether a pea plant will be tall or short.

   c. Applying Concepts Can a short pea plant ever be a hybrid for the trait of stem height? Why or why not? As part of your explanation, write the letters that represent the alleles for stem height of a short pea plant.

Lab zone **At-Home Activity**

Gardens and Heredity Some gardeners save the seeds produced by flowers and plant them in the spring. If there are gardeners in your family, ask them how closely the plants that grow from these seeds resemble the parent plants. Are the offspring's traits ever different from those of the parents?

Take a Class Survey

Problem

Are traits controlled by dominant alleles more common than traits controlled by recessive alleles?

Skills Focus

developing hypotheses, interpreting data

Materials

• mirror (optional)

Procedure

PART 1 Dominant and Recessive Alleles

1. Write a hypothesis reflecting your ideas about the problem. Then copy the data table.

2. For each of the traits listed in the data table, work with a partner to determine which trait you have. Circle that trait in your data table.

3. Count the number of students in your class who have each trait. Record that number in your data table. Also record the total number of students.

PART 2 Are Your Traits Unique?

4. Look at the circle of traits on the opposite page. All the traits in your data table appear in the circle. Place the eraser end of your pencil on the trait in the small central circle that applies to you—either free ear lobes or attached ear lobes.

5. Look at the two traits touching the space your eraser is on. Move your eraser onto the next description that applies to you. Continue using your eraser to trace your traits until you reach a number on the outside rim of the circle. Share that number with your classmates.

Analyze and Conclude

1. **Observing** The traits listed under Trait 1 in the data table are controlled by dominant alleles. The traits listed under Trait 2 are controlled by recessive alleles. Which traits controlled by dominant alleles were shown by a majority of students? Which traits controlled by recessive alleles were shown by a majority of students?

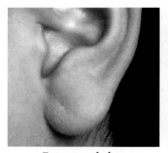

Free ear lobe

Widow's peak

Cleft chin

Dimple

Attached ear lobe

No widow's peak

No cleft chin

No dimple

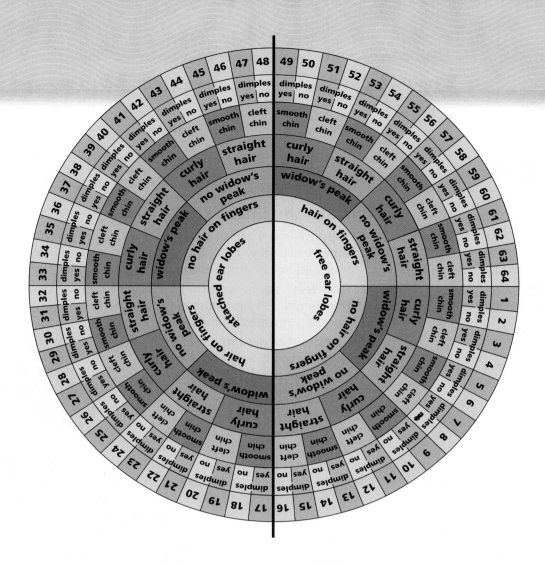

2. **Interpreting Data** How many students ended up on the same number on the circle of traits? How many students were the only ones to have their number? What do the results suggest about each person's combination of traits?

3. **Developing Hypotheses** Do your data support the hypothesis you proposed in Step 1? Write an answer with examples.

Design an Experiment

Do people who are related to each other show more genetic similarity than unrelated people? Write a hypothesis. Then design an experiment to test your hypothesis. *Obtain your teacher's permission before carrying out your investigation.*

Data Table				
Total Number of Students_____				
	Trait 1	Number	Trait 2	Number
A	Free ear lobes		Attached ear lobes	
B	Hair on fingers		No hair on fingers	
C	Widow's peak		No widow's peak	
D	Curly hair		Straight hair	
E	Cleft chin		Smooth chin	
F	Smile dimples		No smile dimples	

Probability and Heredity

Reading Preview

Key Concepts
- What is probability and how does it help explain the results of genetic crosses?
- What is meant by genotype and phenotype?
- What is codominance?

Key Terms
- probability
- Punnett square
- phenotype
- genotype
- homozygous
- heterozygous
- codominance

Target Reading Skill

Building Vocabulary After you read the section, reread the paragraphs that contain definitions of Key Terms. Use all the information you have learned to write a definition of each Key Term in your own words.

Go Online
SciLINKS NSTA

For: Links on probability and genetics
Visit: www.SciLinks.org
Web Code: scn-0332

Discover Activity

What's the Chance?
1. Suppose you were to toss a coin 20 times. Predict how many times the coin would land with heads up and how many times it would land with tails up.
2. Now test your prediction by tossing a coin 20 times. Record the number of times the coin lands with heads up and the number of times it lands with tails up.
3. Combine the data from the entire class. Record the total number of tosses, the number of heads, and the number of tails.

Think It Over
Predicting How did your results in Step 2 compare to your prediction? How can you account for any differences between your results and the class results?

On a brisk fall afternoon, the stands are packed with cheering football fans. Today is the big game between Riverton's North and South high schools, and it's almost time for the kickoff. Suddenly, the crowd becomes silent, as the referee is about to toss a coin. The outcome of the coin toss will decide which team kicks the ball and which receives it. The captain of the visiting North High team says "heads." If the coin lands with heads up, North High wins the toss and the right to decide whether to kick or receive the ball.

What is the chance that North High will win the coin toss? To answer this question, you need to understand the principles of probability.

Principles of Probability

If you did the Discover activity, you used the principles of **probability** to predict the results of a particular event. In this case, the event was the toss of a coin. **Probability is a number that describes how likely it is that an event will occur.**

Mathematics of Probability Each time you toss a coin, there are two possible ways that the coin can land—heads up or tails up. Each of these two events is equally likely to occur. In mathematical terms, you can say that the probability that a tossed coin will land with heads up is 1 in 2. There is also a 1 in 2 probability that the coin will land with tails up. A 1 in 2 probability can also be expressed as the fraction $\frac{1}{2}$ or as a percent—50 percent.

The laws of probability predict what is likely to occur, not necessarily what will occur. If you tossed a coin 20 times, you might expect it to land with heads up 10 times and with tails up 10 times. However, you might not get these results. You might get 11 heads and 9 tails, or 8 heads and 12 tails. The more tosses you make, the closer your actual results will be to the results predicted by probability.

 **Reading Checkpoint** **What is probability?**

Independence of Events When you toss a coin more than once, the results of one toss do not affect the results of the next toss. Each event occurs independently. For example, suppose you toss a coin five times and it lands with heads up each time. What is the probability that it will land with heads up on the next toss? Because the coin landed heads up on the previous five tosses, you might think that it would be likely to land heads up on the next toss. However, this is not the case. The probability of the coin landing heads up on the next toss is still 1 in 2, or 50 percent. The results of the first five tosses do not affect the result of the sixth toss.

FIGURE 6
A Coin Toss
The result of a coin toss can be explained by probability.

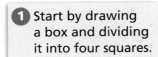

① Start by drawing a box and dividing it into four squares.

② Write the male parent's alleles along the top of the square and the female parent's alleles along the left side.

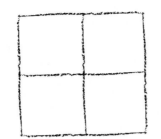

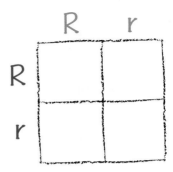

FIGURE 7

How to Make a Punnett Square

The diagrams show how to make a Punnett square. In this cross, both parents are heterozygous for the trait of seed shape. *R* represents the dominant round allele, and *r* represents the recessive wrinkled allele.

Lab zone Try This **Activity**

Coin Crosses

Here's how you can use coins to model Mendel's cross between two *Tt* pea plants.

1. Place a small piece of masking tape on each side of two coins.

2. Write a *T* (for tall) on one side of each coin and a *t* (for short) on the other.

3. Toss both coins together 20 times. Record the letter combinations that you obtain from each toss.

Interpreting Data How many of the offspring would be tall plants? (*Hint:* What different letter combinations would result in a tall plant?) How many would be short? Convert your results to percentages. Then compare your results to Mendel's.

Probability and Genetics

How is probability related to genetics? To answer this question, think back to Mendel's experiments with peas. Remember that Mendel carefully counted the offspring from every cross that he carried out. When Mendel crossed two plants that were hybrid for stem height (Tt), three fourths of the F_1 plants had tall stems. One fourth of the plants had short stems.

Each time Mendel repeated the cross, he obtained similar results. Mendel realized that the mathematical principles of probability applied to his work. He could say that the probability of such a cross producing a tall plant was 3 in 4. The probability of producing a short plant was 1 in 4. Mendel was the first scientist to recognize that the principles of probability can be used to predict the results of genetic crosses.

Punnett Squares A tool that can help you understand how the laws of probability apply to genetics is called a Punnett square. A **Punnett square** is a chart that shows all the possible combinations of alleles that can result from a genetic cross. Geneticists use Punnett squares to show all the possible outcomes of a genetic cross, and to determine the probability of a particular outcome.

Figure 7 shows how to construct a Punnett square. In this case, the Punnett square shows a cross between two hybrid pea plants with round seeds (Rr). The allele for round seeds (R) is dominant over the allele for wrinkled seeds (r). Each parent can pass either of its alleles, R or r, to its offspring. The boxes in the Punnett square represent the possible combinations of alleles that the offspring can inherit.

 Reading Checkpoint **What is a Punnett square?**

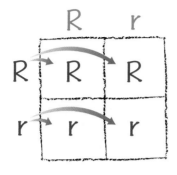

3 Copy the female parent's alleles into the boxes to their right.

	R	r
R	R	R
r	r	r

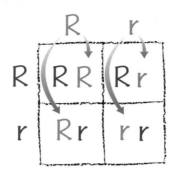

4 Copy the male parent's alleles into the boxes beneath them.

	R	r
R	R	R r
r	R r	r r

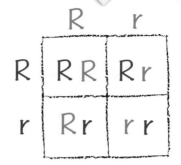

5 The completed Punnett square shows all the possible allele combinations in the offspring.

	R	r
R	RR	Rr
r	Rr	rr

Using a Punnett Square You can use a Punnett square to calculate the probability that offspring with a certain combination of alleles will result. **In a genetic cross, the allele that each parent will pass on to its offspring is based on probability.** The completed Punnett square in Figure 7 shows four possible combinations of alleles. The probability that an offspring will be *RR* is 1 in 4, or 25 percent. The probability that an offspring will be *rr* is also 1 in 4, or 25 percent. Notice, however, that the *Rr* allele combination appears in two boxes in the Punnett square. This is because there are two possible ways in which this combination can occur. So the probability that an offspring will be *Rr* is 2 in 4, or 50 percent.

When Mendel crossed hybrid plants with round seeds, he discovered that about three fourths of the plants (75 percent) had round seeds. The remaining one fourth of the plants (25 percent) produced wrinkled seeds. Plants with the *RR* allele combination would produce round seeds. So too would those plants with the *Rr* allele combination. Remember that the dominant allele masks the recessive allele. Only those plants with the *rr* allele combination would have wrinkled seeds.

Predicting Probabilities You can use a Punnett square to predict probabilities. For example, Figure 8 shows a cross between a purebred black guinea pig and a purebred white guinea pig. The allele for black fur is dominant over the allele for white fur. Notice that only one allele combination is possible in the offspring—*Bb*. All of the offspring will inherit the dominant allele for black fur. Because of this, all of the offspring will have black fur. There is a 100 percent probability that the offspring will have black fur.

FIGURE 8
Guinea Pig Punnett Square
This Punnett square shows a cross between a black guinea pig (*BB*) and a white guinea pig (*bb*).
Calculating What is the probability that an offspring will have white fur?

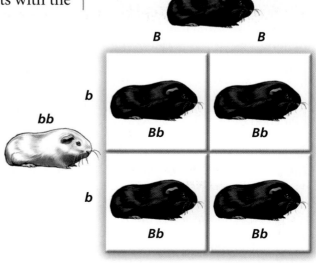

Math ▶ Analyzing Data

What Are the Genotypes?

Mendel allowed several F$_1$ pea plants with yellow seeds to self-pollinate. The graph shows the approximate numbers of the F$_2$ offspring with yellow seeds and with green seeds.

1. **Reading Graphs** How many F$_2$ offspring had yellow seeds? How many had green seeds?

2. **Calculating** Use the information in the graph to calculate the total number of offspring that resulted from this cross. Then calculate the percentage of the offspring with yellow peas, and the percentage with green peas.

3. **Inferring** Use the answers to Question 2 to infer the probable genotypes of the parent plants.

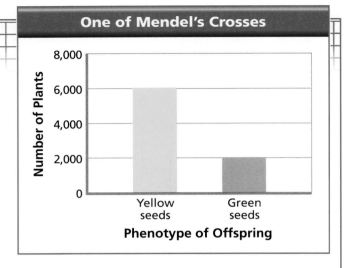

One of Mendel's Crosses

(*Hint:* Construct Punnett squares with the possible genotypes of the parents.)

Phenotypes and Genotypes

Two useful terms that geneticists use are **phenotype** (FEE noh typ) and **genotype** (JEN uh typ). **An organism's phenotype is its physical appearance, or visible traits. An organism's genotype is its genetic makeup, or allele combinations.**

To understand the difference between phenotype and genotype, look at Figure 9. The allele for smooth pea pods (*S*) is dominant over the allele for pinched pea pods (*s*). All of the plants with at least one dominant allele have the same phenotype—they all produce smooth pods. However, the plants can have two different genotypes—*SS* or *Ss*. If you were to look at the plants with smooth pods, you would not be able to tell the difference between those with the *SS* genotype and those with the *Ss* genotype. The plants with pinched pods, on the other hand, would all have the same phenotype—pinched pods—as well as the same genotype—*ss*.

Geneticists use two additional terms to describe an organism's genotype. An organism that has two identical alleles for a trait is said to be **homozygous** (hoh moh ZY gus) for that trait. A smooth-pod plant that has the alleles *SS* and a pinched-pod plant with the alleles *ss* are both homozygous. An organism that has two different alleles for a trait is **heterozygous** (het ur oh ZY gus) for that trait. A smooth-pod plant with the alleles *Ss* is heterozygous. Mendel used the term *hybrid* to describe heterozygous pea plants.

Phenotypes and Genotypes

Phenotype	Genotype
Smooth pods	*SS*
Smooth pods	*Ss*
Pinched pods	*ss*

FIGURE 9
The phenotype of an organism is its physical appearance. Its genotype is its genetic makeup.
Interpreting Tables How many genotypes are there for the smooth-pod phenotype?

 **Reading Checkpoint** If a pea plant's genotype is *Ss*, what is its phenotype?

Codominance

For all of the traits that Mendel studied, one allele was dominant while the other was recessive. This is not always the case. For some alleles, an inheritance pattern called **codominance** exists. **In codominance, the alleles are neither dominant nor recessive. As a result, both alleles are expressed in the offspring.**

Look at Figure 10. Mendel's principle of dominant and recessive alleles does not explain why the heterozygous chickens have both black and white feathers. The alleles for feather color are codominant—neither dominant nor recessive. As you can see, neither allele is masked in the heterozygous chickens. Notice also that the codominant alleles are written as capital letters with superscripts—F^B for black feathers and F^W for white feathers. As the Punnett square shows, heterozygous chickens have the $F^B F^W$ allele combination.

 **Reading Checkpoint** How are the symbols for codominant alleles written?

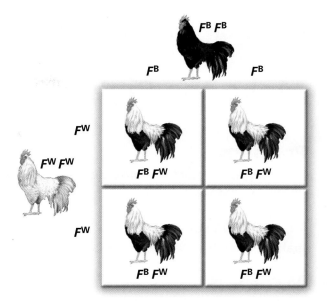

FIGURE 10
Codominance
The offspring of the cross in this Punnett square will have both black and white feathers.
Classifying *Will the offspring be heterozygous or homozygous? Explain your answer.*

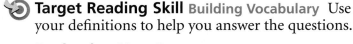

Section 2 Assessment

Target Reading Skill Building Vocabulary Use your definitions to help you answer the questions.

Reviewing Key Concepts

1. **a. Reviewing** What is probability?
   b. Explaining If you know the parents' alleles for a trait, how can you use a Punnett square to predict the probable genotypes of the offspring?
   c. Predicting A pea plant with round seeds has the genotype *Rr*. You cross this plant with a wrinkled-seed plant, genotype *rr*. What is the probability that the offspring will have wrinkled seeds? (Use a Punnett square to help with the prediction.)

2. **a. Defining** Define *genotype* and *phenotype*.
   b. Relating Cause and Effect Explain how two organisms can have the same phenotype but different genotypes. Give an example.
   c. Applying Concepts A pea plant has a tall stem. What are its possible genotypes?

3. **a. Explaining** What is codominance? Give an example of codominant alleles and explain why they are codominant.
   b. Applying Concepts What is the phenotype of a chicken with the genotype $F^B F^W$?

Math ▶ Practice

4. **Ratios** A scientist crossed a tall pea plant with a short pea plant. Of the offspring, 13 were tall and 12 were short. Write the ratio of each phenotype to the total number of offspring. Express the ratios as fractions.

5. **Percentage** Use the fractions to calculate the percentage of the offspring that were tall and the percentage that were short.

Make the Right Call!

Problem

How can you predict the possible results of genetic crosses?

Skills Focus

making models, interpreting data

Materials

- 2 small paper bags   • marking pen
- 3 blue marbles   • 3 white marbles

Procedure

1. Label one bag "Bag 1, Female Parent." Label the other bag "Bag 2, Male Parent." Then read over Part 1, Part 2, and Part 3 of this lab. Write a prediction about the kinds of off-spring you expect from each cross.

PART 1   Crossing Two Homozygous Parents

2. Copy the data table and label it *Data Table 1*. Then place two blue marbles in Bag 1. This pair of marbles represents the female parent's alleles. Use the letter *B* to represent the dominant allele for blue color.

3. Place two white marbles in Bag 2. Use the letter *b* to represent the recessive allele for white color.

4. For Trial 1, remove one marble from Bag 1 without looking in the bag. Record the result in your data table. Return the marble to the bag. Again, without looking in the bag, remove one marble from Bag 2. Record the result in your data table. Return the marble to the bag.

5. In the column labeled Offspring's Alleles, write *BB* if you removed two blue marbles, *bb* if you removed two white marbles, or *Bb* if you removed one blue marble and one white marble.

6. Repeat Steps 4 and 5 nine more times.

PART 2   Crossing Homozygous and Heterozygous Parents

7. Place two blue marbles in Bag 1. Place one white marble and one blue marble in Bag 2. Copy the data table again, and label it *Data Table 2*.

8. Repeat Steps 4 and 5 ten times.

Data Table			
Number _____			
Trial	Allele From Bag 1 (Female Parent)	Allele From Bag 2 (Male Parent)	Offspring's Alleles
1			
2			
3			
4			
5			
6			

PART 3 Crossing Two Heterozygous Parents

9. Place one blue marble and one white marble in Bag 1. Place one blue marble and one white marble in Bag 2. Copy the data table again and label it *Data Table 3*.

10. Repeat Steps 4 and 5 ten times.

Analyze and Conclude

1. **Making Models** Make a Punnett square for each of the crosses you modeled in Part 1, Part 2, and Part 3.

2. **Interpreting Data** According to your results in Part 1, how many different kinds of offspring are possible when the homozygous parents (*BB* and *bb*) are crossed? Do the results you obtained using the marble model agree with the results shown by a Punnett square?

3. **Predicting** According to your results in Part 2, what percentage of offspring are likely to be homozygous when a homozygous parent (*BB*) and a heterozygous parent (*Bb*) are crossed? What percentage of offspring are likely to be heterozygous? Does the model agree with the results shown by a Punnett square?

4. **Making Models** According to your results in Part 3, what different kinds of offspring are possible when two heterozygous parents (*Bb* × *Bb*) are crossed? What percentage of each type of offspring are likely to be produced? Does the model agree with the results of a Punnett square?

5. **Inferring** For Part 3, if you did 100 trials instead of 10 trials, would your results be closer to the results shown in a Punnett square? Explain.

6. **Communicating** In a paragraph, explain how the marble model compares with a Punnett square. How are the two methods alike? How are they different?

More to Explore

In peas, the allele for yellow seeds (*Y*) is dominant over the allele for green seeds (*y*). What possible crosses do you think could produce a heterozygous plant with yellow seeds (*Yy*)? Use the marble model and Punnett squares to test your predictions.

The Cell and Inheritance

Reading Preview

Key Concepts
- What role do chromosomes play in inheritance?
- What events occur during meiosis?
- What is the relationship between chromosomes and genes?

Key Term
- meiosis

Target Reading Skill
Identifying Supporting Evidence As you read, identify the evidence that supports the hypothesis that chromosomes are important in inheritance. Write the evidence in a graphic organizer.

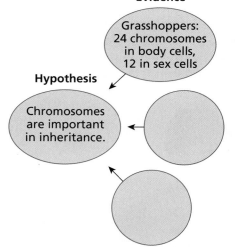

Evidence

Grasshoppers: 24 chromosomes in body cells, 12 in sex cells

Hypothesis

Chromosomes are important in inheritance.

Discover Activity

Which Chromosome Is Which?
Mendel did not know about chromosomes or their role in genetics. Today we know that genes are located on chromosomes.

1. Label two craft sticks with the letter *A*. The craft sticks represent a pair of chromosomes in the female parent. Turn the sticks face down on a piece of paper.
2. Label two more craft sticks with the letter *a*. These represent a pair of chromosomes in the male parent. Turn the sticks face down on another piece of paper.
3. Turn over one craft stick "chromosome" from each piece of paper. Move both sticks to a third piece of paper. These represent a pair of chromosomes in the offspring. Note the allele combination that the offspring received.

Think It Over
Making Models Use this model to explain how chromosomes are involved in the inheritance of alleles.

Mendel's work showed that genes exist. But scientists in the early twentieth century did not know what structures in cells contained genes. The search for the answer to this puzzle is something like a mystery story. The story could be called "The Clue in the Grasshopper's Cells."

In 1903, Walter Sutton, an American geneticist, was studying the cells of grasshoppers. He wanted to understand how sex cells (sperm and egg) form. Sutton focused on the movement of chromosomes during the formation of sex cells. He hypothesized that chromosomes were the key to understanding how offspring have traits similar to those of their parents.

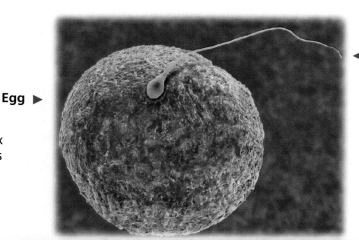

◀ **Sperm**

Egg ▶

FIGURE 11
Sex Cells
The large egg is a female sex cell, and the smaller sperm is a male sex cell.

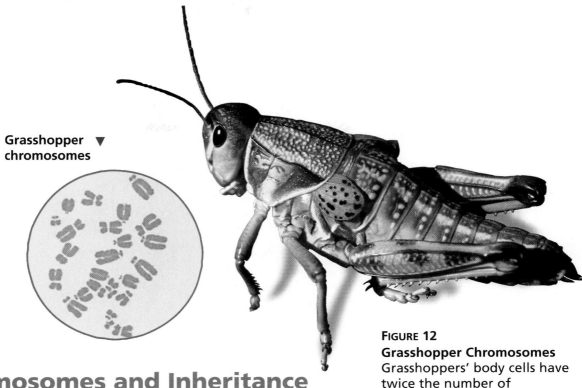

Grasshopper ▼
chromosomes

FIGURE 12
Grasshopper Chromosomes
Grasshoppers' body cells have twice the number of chromosomes as their sex cells.
Applying Concepts *What is the function of chromosomes?*

Chromosomes and Inheritance

Sutton needed evidence to support his hypothesis that chromosomes were important in the inheritance of traits. He found that evidence in grasshoppers' cells. The body cells of a grasshopper have 24 chromosomes. To his surprise, Sutton found that the grasshopper's sex cells have only 12 chromosomes. In other words, a grasshopper's sex cells have exactly half the number of chromosomes found in its body cells.

Chromosome Pairs Sutton observed what happened when a sperm cell and an egg cell joined during fertilization. The fertilized egg that formed had 24 chromosomes. As a result, the grasshopper offspring had exactly the same number of chromosomes in its cells as did each of its parents. The 24 chromosomes existed in 12 pairs. One chromosome in each pair came from the male parent, while the other chromosome came from the female parent.

Genes on Chromosomes Recall that alleles are different forms of a gene. Because of Mendel's work, Sutton knew that alleles exist in pairs in an organism. One allele in a pair comes from the organism's female parent and the other allele comes from the male parent. Sutton realized that paired alleles were carried on paired chromosomes. Sutton's idea came to be known as the chromosome theory of inheritance. **According to the chromosome theory of inheritance, genes are carried from parents to their offspring on chromosomes.**

 **Reading Checkpoint** What is the relationship between alleles and chromosomes?

FIGURE 13
Meiosis

During meiosis, a cell produces sex cells with half the number of chromosomes. **Interpreting Diagrams** *What happens before meiosis?*

1 Before Meiosis
Before meiosis begins, every chromosome in the parent cell is copied. Centromeres hold the two chromatids together.

2 Meiosis I
A The chromosome pairs line up in the center of the cell.

B The pairs separate and move to opposite ends of the cell.

C Two cells form, each with half the number of chromosomes. Each chromosome still has two chromatids.

Meiosis

How do sex cells end up with half the number of chromosomes as body cells? To answer this question, you need to understand the events that occur during meiosis. **Meiosis** (my OH sis) is the process by which the number of chromosomes is reduced by half to form sex cells—sperm and eggs.

What Happens During Meiosis You can trace the events of meiosis in Figure 13. In this example, each parent cell has four chromosomes arranged in two pairs. **During meiosis, the chromosome pairs separate and are distributed to two different cells. The resulting sex cells have only half as many chromosomes as the other cells in the organism.** The sex cells end up with only two chromosomes each—half the number found in the parent cell. Each sex cell has one chromosome from each original pair.

When sex cells combine to form an organism, each sex cell contributes half the normal number of chromosomes. Thus, the offspring gets the normal number of chromosomes—half from each parent.

Go Online
SciLINKS NSTA

For: Links on meiosis
Visit: www.SciLinks.org
Web Code: scn-0333

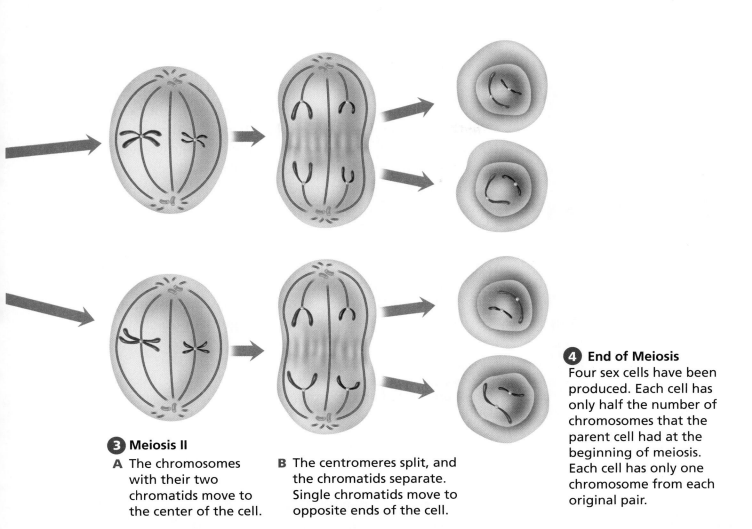

3 Meiosis II

A The chromosomes with their two chromatids move to the center of the cell.

B The centromeres split, and the chromatids separate. Single chromatids move to opposite ends of the cell.

4 End of Meiosis
Four sex cells have been produced. Each cell has only half the number of chromosomes that the parent cell had at the beginning of meiosis. Each cell has only one chromosome from each original pair.

Meiosis and Punnett Squares A Punnett square is actually a way to show the events that occur at meiosis. When the chromosome pairs separate and go into two different sex cells, so do the alleles carried on each chromosome. One allele from each pair goes to each sex cell.

In Figure 14, you can see how the Punnett square accounts for the separation of alleles during meiosis. As shown across the top of the Punnett square, half of the sperm cells from the male parent will receive the chromosome with the *T* allele. The other half of the sperm cells will receive the chromosome with the *t* allele. In this example, the same is true for the egg cells from the female parent, as shown down the left side of the Punnett square. Depending on which sperm cell combines with which egg cell, one of the allele combinations shown in the boxes will result.

FIGURE 14
Meiosis Punnett Square
Both parents are heterozygous for the trait of stem height. The Punnett square shows the possible allele combinations after fertilization.

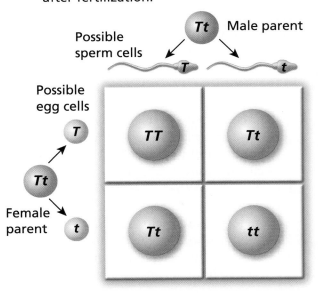

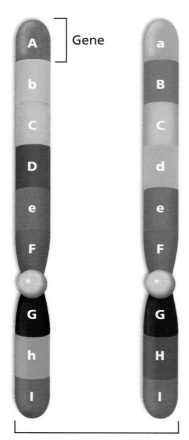

Gene

Chromosome pair

A Lineup of Genes

The body cells of humans contain 23 chromosome pairs, or 46 chromosomes. **Chromosomes are made up of many genes joined together like beads on a string.** Although you have only 23 pairs of chromosomes, your body cells each contain about 35,000 genes. Each gene controls a trait.

In Figure 15, one chromosome in the pair came from the female parent. The other chromosome came from the male parent. Notice that each chromosome in the pair has the same genes. The genes are lined up in the same order on both chromosomes. However, the alleles for some of the genes might be different. For example, the organism has the *A* allele on one chromosome and the *a* allele on the other. As you can see, this organism is heterozygous for some traits and homozygous for others.

FIGURE 15
Genes on Chromosomes
Genes are located on chromosomes. The chromosomes in a pair may have different alleles for some genes and the same alleles for others.
Classifying *For which genes is this organism homozygous? For which genes is it heterozygous?*

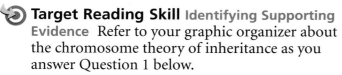

Section 3 Assessment

Target Reading Skill Identifying Supporting Evidence Refer to your graphic organizer about the chromosome theory of inheritance as you answer Question 1 below.

Reviewing Key Concepts

1. a. Comparing and Contrasting According to Sutton's observations, how does the number of chromosomes in a grasshopper's body cells compare to the number in its sex cells?
   b. Describing Describe what happens to the number of chromosomes when two grasshopper sex cells join in fertilization.
   c. Explaining How do Sutton's observations about chromosome number support the chromosome theory of inheritance?
2. a. Defining What is meiosis?
   b. Interpreting Diagrams Briefly describe meiosis I and meiosis II. Refer to Figure 13.
   c. Sequencing Use the events of meiosis to explain why a sex cell normally does not receive both chromosomes from a pair.

3. a. Describing How are genes arranged on a chromosome?
   b. Comparing and Contrasting How does the order of genes in one member of a chromosome pair compare to the order of genes on the other chromosome?

Writing in Science

Newspaper Interview You are a newspaper reporter in the early 1900s. You want to interview Walter Sutton about his work with chromosomes. Write three questions you would like to ask Sutton. Then, for each question, write answers that Sutton might have given.

The DNA Connection

Reading Preview

Key Concepts
- What forms the genetic code?
- How does a cell produce proteins?
- How can mutations affect an organism?

Key Terms
- messenger RNA
- transfer RNA

Target Reading Skill

Sequencing A sequence is the order in which the steps in a process occur. As you read, make a flowchart that shows protein synthesis. Put the steps of the process in separate boxes in the flowchart in the order in which they occur.

Protein Synthesis

DNA provides code to form messenger RNA.

↓

Messenger RNA attaches to ribosome.

↓

⌄⌄⌄

Discover **Activity**

Can You Crack the Code?

1. Use the Morse code in the chart to decode the question in the message below. The letters are separated by slash marks.

   • – – / • • • • / • / • – • / • / • – / • – • /
   • / – – • / • / – • / • / • • • / • – • • / – – – /
   – • – • / • – / – / • / – • • /

2. Write your answer to the question in Morse code.

3. Exchange your coded answer with a partner. Then decode your partner's answer.

Think It Over
Forming Operational Definitions Based on your results from this activity, write a definition of the word *code*. Then compare your definition to one in a dictionary.

A • –	N – •
B – • • •	O – – –
C – • – •	P • – – •
D – • •	Q – – • –
E •	R • – •
F • • – •	S • • •
G – – •	T –
H • • • •	U • • –
I • •	V • • • –
J • – – –	W • – –
K – • –	X – • • –
L • – • •	Y – • – –
M – –	Z – – • •

The young, white, ring-tailed lemur in the photograph below was born in a forest in southern Madagascar. White lemurs are extremely rare. Why was this lemur born with such an uncommon phenotype? To answer this question, you need to know how the genes on a chromosome control an organism's traits.

A white lemur and its mother ▶

The Genetic Code

The main function of genes is to control the production of proteins in an organism's cells. Proteins help to determine the size, shape, color, and many other traits of an organism.

Genes and DNA Recall that chromosomes are composed mostly of DNA. In Figure 16, you can see the relationship between chromosomes and DNA. Notice that a DNA molecule is made up of four different nitrogen bases—adenine (A), thymine (T), guanine (G), and cytosine (C). These bases form the rungs of the DNA "ladder."

A gene is a section of a DNA molecule that contains the information to code for one specific protein. A gene is made up of a series of bases in a row. The bases in a gene are arranged in a specific order—for example, ATGACGTAC. A single gene on a chromosome may contain anywhere from several hundred to a million or more of these bases. Each gene is located at a specific place on a chromosome.

Order of the Bases A gene contains the code that determines the structure of a protein. **The order of the nitrogen bases along a gene forms a genetic code that specifies what type of protein will be produced.** Remember that proteins are long-chain molecules made of individual amino acids. In the genetic code, a group of three DNA bases codes for one specific amino acid. For example, the base sequence CGT (cytosine-guanine-thymine) always codes for the amino acid alanine. The order of the three-base code units determines the order in which amino acids are put together to form a protein.

FIGURE 16
The DNA Code
Chromosomes are made of DNA. Each chromosome contains thousands of genes. The sequence of bases in a gene forms a code that tells the cell what protein to produce. Interpreting Diagrams *Where in the cell are chromosomes located?*

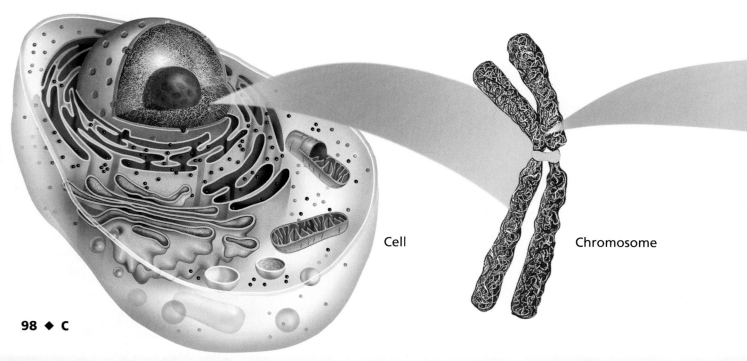

Cell

Chromosome

How Cells Make Proteins

The production of proteins is called protein synthesis. **During protein synthesis, the cell uses information from a gene on a chromosome to produce a specific protein.** Protein synthesis takes place on the ribosomes in the cytoplasm of a cell. As you know, the cytoplasm is outside the nucleus. The chromosomes, however, are found inside the nucleus. How, then, does the information needed to produce proteins get out of the nucleus and into the cytoplasm?

The Role of RNA Before protein synthesis can take place, a "messenger" must first carry the genetic code from the DNA inside the nucleus into the cytoplasm. This genetic messenger is called ribonucleic acid, or RNA.

Although RNA is similar to DNA, the two molecules differ in some important ways. Unlike DNA, which has two strands, RNA has only one strand. RNA also contains a different sugar molecule from the sugar found in DNA. Another difference between DNA and RNA is in their nitrogen bases. Like DNA, RNA contains adenine, guanine, and cytosine. However, instead of thymine, RNA contains uracil (YOOR uh sil).

Types of RNA There are several types of RNA involved in protein synthesis. **Messenger RNA** copies the coded message from the DNA in the nucleus, and carries the message to the ribosome in the cytoplasm. Another type of RNA, called **transfer RNA,** carries amino acids to the ribosome and adds them to the growing protein.

 **Reading Checkpoint** **How is RNA different from DNA?**

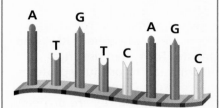
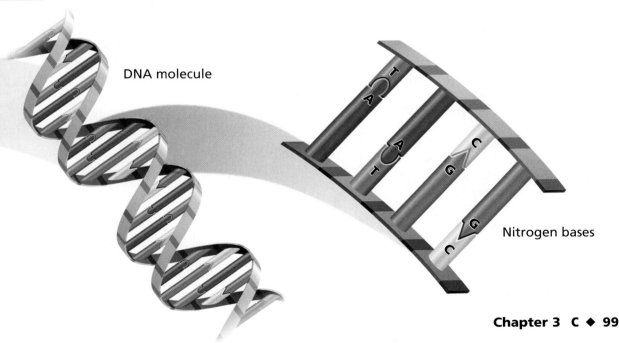

DNA molecule

Nitrogen bases

Translating the Code The process of protein synthesis is shown in Figure 17. Look at the illustration as you read the following steps.

❶ The first step is for a DNA molecule to "unzip" between its base pairs. Then one of the strands of DNA directs the production of a strand of messenger RNA. To form the RNA strand, RNA bases pair up with the DNA bases. The process is similar to the process in which DNA replicates. Cytosine always pairs with guanine. However, uracil—not thymine— pairs with adenine.

❷ The messenger RNA then leaves the nucleus and enters the cytoplasm. In the cytoplasm, messenger RNA attaches to a ribosome. On the ribosome, the messenger RNA provides the code for the protein molecule that will form. During protein synthesis, the ribosome moves along the messenger RNA strand.

FIGURE 17
Protein Synthesis

To make proteins, messenger RNA copies information from DNA in the nucleus. Messenger RNA and transfer RNA then use this information to produce proteins.
Interpreting Diagrams *In which organelle of the cell are proteins manufactured?*

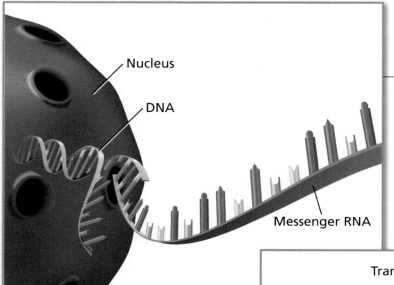

Nucleus

DNA

Messenger RNA

❷ **Messenger RNA Attaches to a Ribosome** ▼
When the messenger RNA enters the cytoplasm, it attaches to a ribosome, where production of the protein chain begins. The ribosome moves along the messenger RNA strand.

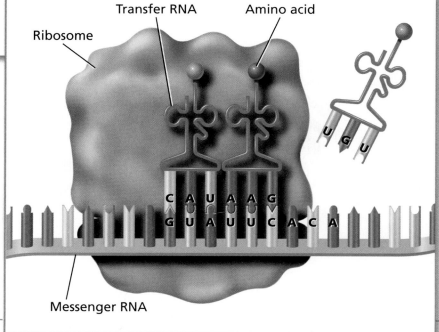

Transfer RNA   Amino acid

Ribosome

C A U A A G
G U A U U C A C A

U G U

Messenger RNA

❶ **Messenger RNA Production** ▲
In the nucleus, a DNA molecule serves as a "pattern" for making messenger RNA. The DNA molecule "unzips" between base pairs. RNA bases match up along one of the DNA strands. The genetic information in the DNA is transferred to the messenger RNA strand.

❸ Molecules of transfer RNA attach to the messenger RNA. The bases on the transfer RNA "read" the message by pairing up three-letter codes to bases on the messenger RNA. For example, you can see that a molecule of transfer RNA with the bases AAG pairs with the bases UUC on the messenger RNA. The molecules of transfer RNA carry specific amino acids. The amino acids link in a chain. The order of the amino acids in the chain is determined by the order of the three-letter codes on the messenger RNA.

❹ The protein molecule grows longer as each transfer RNA molecule puts the amino acid it is carrying along the growing protein chain. Once an amino acid is added to the protein chain, the transfer RNA is released into the cytoplasm and can pick up another amino acid. Each transfer RNA molecule always picks up the same kind of amino acid.

 **Reading Checkpoint** **What is the function of transfer RNA?**

Go Online
active art

For: Protein Synthesis activity
Visit: PHSchool.com
Web Code: cep-3034

❸ Transfer RNA Attaches to Messenger RNA ▼
Transfer RNA molecules carry specific amino acids to the ribosome. There they "read" the message in messenger RNA by matching up with three-letter codes of bases. The protein chain grows as each amino acid is attached.

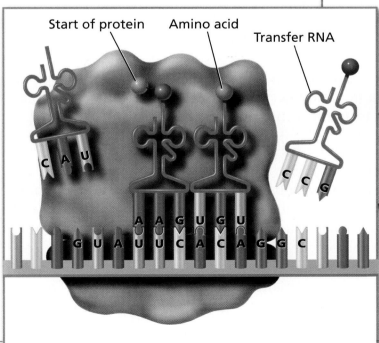

Start of protein   Amino acid   Transfer RNA

❹ Protein Production Continues ▲
The protein chain continues to grow until the ribosome reaches a three-letter code that acts as a stop sign. The ribosome then releases the completed protein.

Growing protein

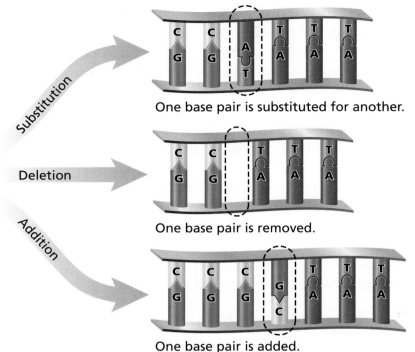

One base pair is substituted for another.

Deletion

One base pair is removed.

Addition

One base pair is added.

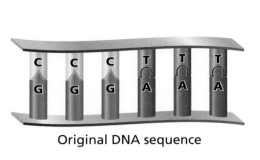

Original DNA sequence

FIGURE 18
Mutations in Genes
The illustration shows three types of mutations that can occur in genes.
Comparing and Contrasting *How are these mutations different from the mutations that occur when chromosomes do not separate during meiosis?*

Mutations

Suppose that a mistake occurred in one gene of a chromosome. Instead of the base A, for example, the DNA molecule might have the base G. Such a mistake is one type of mutation that can occur in a cell's hereditary material. Recall that a mutation is any change in a gene or chromosome. **Mutations can cause a cell to produce an incorrect protein during protein synthesis. As a result, the organism's trait, or phenotype, may be different from what it normally would have been.** In fact, the term *mutation* comes from a Latin word that means "change."

If a mutation occurs in a body cell, such as a skin cell, the mutation will not be passed on to the organism's offspring. If, however, a mutation occurs in a sex cell, the mutation can be passed on to an offspring and affect the offspring's phenotype.

Types of Mutations Some mutations are the result of small changes in an organism's hereditary material. For example, a single base may be substituted for another, or one or more bases may be removed from a section of DNA. This type of mutation can occur during the DNA replication process. Other mutations may occur when chromosomes don't separate correctly during meiosis. When this type of mutation occurs, a cell can end up with too many or too few chromosomes. The cell could also end up with extra segments of chromosomes.

Effects of Mutations Because mutations can introduce changes in an organism, they can be a source of genetic variety. Some mutations are harmful to an organism. A few mutations, however, are helpful, and others are neither harmful nor helpful. A mutation is harmful to an organism if it reduces the organism's chance for survival and reproduction.

Whether a mutation is harmful or not depends partly on the organism's environment. The mutation that led to the production of a white lemur would probably be harmful to an organism in the wild. The lemur's white color would make it more visible, and thus easier for predators to find. However, a white lemur in a zoo has the same chance for survival as a brown lemur. In a zoo, the mutation neither helps nor harms the lemur.

Helpful mutations, on the other hand, improve an organism's chances for survival and reproduction. Antibiotic resistance in bacteria is an example. Antibiotics are chemicals that kill bacteria. Gene mutations have enabled some kinds of bacteria to become resistant to certain antibiotics—that is, the antibiotics do not kill the bacteria that have the mutations. The mutations have improved the bacteria's ability to survive and reproduce.

 **Reading Checkpoint** **What are two types of mutations?**

FIGURE 19
Six-Toed Cat
Because of a mutation in one of its ancestors, this cat has six toes on each front paw.

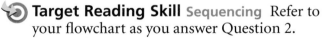

Section 4 Assessment

Target Reading Skill Sequencing Refer to your flowchart as you answer Question 2.

Reviewing Key Concepts

1. a. **Explaining** What is the relationship between a gene, a DNA molecule, and a protein?
   b. **Relating Cause and Effect** How does a DNA molecule determine the structure of a specific protein?
   c. **Inferring** The DNA base sequence GGG codes for the amino acid proline. Could this same base sequence code for a different amino acid? Why or why not?
2. a. **Listing** List the sequence of events that happens during protein synthesis.
   b. **Describing** What is messenger RNA? Describe how it performs its function.

   c. **Inferring** Does transfer RNA perform its function in the nucleus or cytoplasm? Explain your answer.
3. a. **Reviewing** How does a mutation in a gene affect the order of DNA bases?
   b. **Relating Cause and Effect** How can a mutation in a gene cause a change in an organism's phenotype?

Writing in Science

Compare/Contrast Paragraph Write a paragraph comparing and contrasting gene mutations and chromosome mutations. In your paragraph, explain what the two types of mutations are, and how they are similar and different.

① Mendel's Work

Key Concepts

- In all of Mendel's crosses, only one form of the trait appeared in the F_1 generation. However, in the F_2 generation, the "lost" form of the trait always reappeared in about one fourth of the plants.

- An organism's traits are controlled by the alleles it inherits from its parents. Some alleles are dominant, while other alleles are recessive.

Key Terms

heredity	gene
trait	alleles
genetics	dominant allele
fertilization	recessive allele
purebred	hybrid

② Probability and Heredity

Key Concepts

- Probability is the likelihood that a particular event will occur.

- In a genetic cross, the allele that each parent will pass on to its offspring is based on probability.

- An organism's phenotype is its physical appearance, or visible traits. An organism's genotype is its genetic makeup, or allele combinations.

- In codominance, the alleles are neither dominant nor recessive. As a result, both alleles are expressed in the offspring.

Key Terms

probability
Punnett square
phenotype
genotype
homozygous
heterozygous
codominance

③ The Cell and Inheritance

Key Concepts

- According to the chromosome theory of inheritance, genes are carried from parents to their offspring on chromosomes.

- During meiosis, the chromosome pairs separate and are distributed to two different cells. The resulting sex cells have only half as many chromosomes as the other cells in the organism.

- Chromosomes are made up of many genes joined together like beads on a string.

Key Term

meiosis

④ The DNA Connection

Key Concepts

- The order of the nitrogen bases along a gene forms a genetic code that specifies what type of protein will be produced.

- During protein synthesis, the cell uses information from a gene on a chromosome to produce a specific protein.

- Mutations can cause a cell to produce an incorrect protein during protein synthesis. As a result, the organism's trait, or phenotype, may be different from what it normally would have been.

Key Terms

messenger RNA
transfer RNA

Review and Assessment

Go Online
PHSchool.com

For: Self-Assessment
Visit: PHSchool.com
Web Code: cea-3030

Organizing Information

Concept Mapping Copy the concept map onto a separate sheet of paper. Then complete the concept map. (For more on Concept Mapping, see the Skills Handbook.)

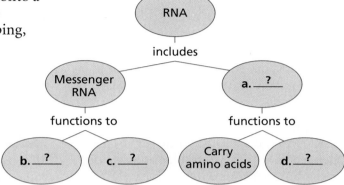

Reviewing Key Terms

Choose the letter of the best answer.

1. The different forms of a gene are called
   a. alleles.
   b. chromosomes.
   c. phenotypes.
   d. genotypes.

2. The likelihood that a particular event will occur is called
   a. chance.
   b. Punnett square.
   c. probability.
   d. recessive.

3. An organism with two identical alleles for a trait is
   a. heterozygous.
   b. homozygous.
   c. recessive.
   d. dominant.

4. If the body cells of an organism have 10 chromosomes, then the sex cells produced during meiosis would have
   a. 5 chromosomes.
   b. 10 chromosomes.
   c. 15 chromosomes.
   d. 20 chromosomes.

5. During protein synthesis, messenger RNA
   a. links one amino acid to another.
   b. releases the completed protein chain.
   c. provides a code from DNA in the nucleus.
   d. carries amino acids to the ribosome.

If the statement is true, write _true_. If it is false, change the underlined word or words to make the statement true.

6. The scientific study of heredity is called <u>genetics</u>.

7. An organism's physical appearance is its <u>genotype</u>.

8. In <u>codominance</u>, neither of the alleles is dominant or recessive.

9. Each transfer RNA molecule picks up one kind of <u>protein</u>.

10. Mutations in <u>body cells</u> are passed to offspring.

Writing in Science

Science Article You are a science reporter for a newspaper. Write an article about gene mutations. Explain what a mutation is and what determines whether it is helpful or harmful.

Genetics: The Science of Heredity
Video Preview
Video Field Trip
▶ Video Assessment

Review and Assessment

Checking Concepts

11. Describe what happened when Mendel crossed purebred tall pea plants with purebred short pea plants.

12. You toss a coin five times and it lands heads up each time. What is the probability that it will land heads up on the sixth toss? Explain your answer.

13. In guinea pigs, the allele for black fur (*B*) is dominant over the allele for white fur (*b*). In a cross between a heterozygous black guinea pig (*Bb*) and a homozygous white guinea pig (*bb*), what is the probability that an offspring will have white fur? Use a Punnett square to answer the question.

14. Describe the role of transfer RNA in protein synthesis.

15. How can mutations affect protein synthesis?

Thinking Critically

16. **Applying Concepts** In rabbits, the allele for a spotted coat is dominant over the allele for a solid-colored coat. A spotted rabbit was crossed with a solid-colored rabbit. The offspring all had spotted coats. What are the probable genotypes of the parents? Explain.

17. **Interpreting Diagrams** The diagram below shows a chromosome pair. For which genes is the organism heterozygous?

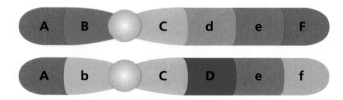

18. **Predicting** A new mutation in mice causes the coat to be twice as thick as normal. In what environments would this mutation be helpful? Why?

19. **Applying Concepts** If the body cells have 12 chromosomes, how many will the sex cells have?

20. **Relating Cause and Effect** Why are mutations that occur in an organism's body cells not passed on to its offspring?

Math Practice

21. **Percentage** A garden has 80 pea plants. Of the plants, 20 have short stems and 60 have tall stems. What percentage of the plants have short stems? What percentage have tall stems?

Applying Skills

Use the information in the table to answer Questions 22–24.

In peas, the allele for green pods (G) is dominant over the allele for yellow pods (g). The table shows the phenotypes of offspring produced from a cross of two plants with green pods.

Phenotype	Number of Offspring
Green pods	27
Yellow pods	9

22. **Calculating Percent** Calculate what percent of the offspring produce green pods. Calculate what percent have yellow pods.

23. **Inferring** What is the genotype of the offspring with yellow pods? What are the possible genotypes of the offspring with green pods?

24. **Drawing Conclusions** What are the genotypes of the parents? How do you know?

Lab zone Chapter **Project**

Performance Assessment Finalize your display of your pet's family. Be prepared to discuss the inheritance patterns in your pet's family. Examine your classmates' exhibits. See which offspring look most like, and least like, their parents. Can you find any offspring that "break the laws" of inheritance?

Standardized Test Prep

Choose the letter of the best answer.

1. Which of the following is the first step in the formation of sex cells in an organism that has eight chromosomes?

  A The two chromatids of each chromosome separate.

  B Chromosome pairs line up next to each other in the center of the cell.

  C The DNA in the eight chromosomes is copied.

  D The chromatids move apart, producing cells with four chromosomes each.

The Punnett square below shows a cross between two pea plants, each with round seeds. Use the Punnett square to answer Questions 2–4.

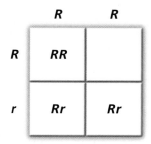

2. The missing genotype in the empty square is correctly written as

  F Rr.

  G rR.

  H rr.

  J RR.

3. Which statement is true about the cross shown in the Punnett square?

  A Both parents are heterozygous for the trait.

  B Both parents are homozygous for the trait.

  C One parent is heterozygous and the other is homozygous for the trait.

  D The trait is controlled by codominant alleles.

4. What percentage of the offspring of this cross will produce round seeds?

  F 0%

  G 25%

  H 50%

  J 100%

5. A section of DNA has the base sequence GCTTAA. The corresponding messenger RNA base sequence will be

  A GCTTAA.

  B CGAAUU.

  C CGAATT.

  D UUTTCG.

Constructed Response

6. Compare the processes and outcomes of mitosis and meiosis.

Chapter Preview

interactive Textbook

The members of this family resemble one another because they share some alleles. ▶

Lab zone™ Chapter **Project**

Teach Others About a Trait

People inherit alleles for traits from their parents. Some traits, such as keen eyesight, are beneficial. Other traits, such as colorblindness, can present challenges. In this project you will design a display to help teach younger children about a genetically inherited trait. You and your group will need to research the inheritance pattern of your selected trait.

Your Goal To design and build an educational tool or display that can be used to educate young children

The display you create should

- illustrate how the trait is inherited and whom it can affect
- explain whether the trait is dominant, recessive, or codominant
- contain an interactive question and answer section that includes a way of predicting the probability that a person will inherit the trait
- stand by itself and be easy to set up

Plan It! Begin by choosing a trait and researching its inheritance pattern. Then determine how the display will look and the materials you need. Determine what is the best method to make the display interactive. Plan to test your display on a younger audience to assess their understanding and then revise your design.

Human Inheritance

Reading Preview

Key Concepts
- What are some patterns of inheritance in humans?
- What are the functions of the sex chromosomes?
- What is the relationship between genes and the environment?

Key Terms
- multiple alleles
- sex chromosomes
- sex-linked gene
- carrier

Target Reading Skill
Identifying Main Ideas As you read the Patterns of Human Inheritance section, write the main idea—the biggest or most important idea—in a graphic organizer like the one below. Then write three supporting details that further explain the main idea.

Main Idea

Human traits are controlled by single genes with two alleles, single genes with . . .

Detail	Detail	Detail

Lab zone   Discover **Activity**

How Tall Is Tall?

1. Choose a partner. Measure each other's height to the nearest 5 centimeters. Record your measurements on the chalkboard.

2. Create a bar graph showing the number of students at each height. Plot the heights on the horizontal axis and the number of students on the vertical axis.

Think It Over

Inferring Do you think height in humans is controlled by a single gene, as it is in peas? Explain your answer.

The arrival of a baby is a happy event. Eagerly, the parents and grandparents gather around to admire the newborn baby. "Don't you think she looks like her father?" "Yes, but she has her mother's eyes."

When a baby is born, the parents, their families, and their friends try to determine whom the baby resembles. Chances are good that the baby will look a little bit like both parents. That is because both parents pass alleles for traits on to their offspring.

FIGURE 1
Family Resemblance
Because children inherit alleles for traits from their mother and father, children often look like their parents.

Patterns of Human Inheritance

Take a few seconds to look at the other students in your classroom. Some people have curly hair; others have straight hair. Some people are tall, some are short, and many others are in between. You'll probably see eyes of many different colors, ranging from pale blue to dark brown. The different traits you see are determined by a variety of inheritance patterns. **Some human traits are controlled by single genes with two alleles, and others by single genes with multiple alleles. Still other traits are controlled by many genes that act together.**

Single Genes With Two Alleles A number of human traits are controlled by a single gene with one dominant allele and one recessive allele. These human traits have two distinctly different phenotypes, or physical appearances.

For example, a widow's peak is a hairline that comes to a point in the middle of the forehead. The allele for a widow's peak is dominant over the allele for a straight hairline. The Punnett square in Figure 2 illustrates a cross between two parents who are heterozygous for a widow's peak. Trace the possible combinations of alleles that a child may inherit. Notice that each child has a 3 in 4, or 75 percent, probability of having a widow's peak. There is only a 1 in 4, or 25 percent, probability that a child will have a straight hairline. When Mendel crossed peas that were heterozygous for a trait, he obtained similar percentages in the offspring.

FIGURE 2
Widow's Peak Punnett Square
This Punnett square shows a cross between two parents with widow's peaks.
Interpreting Diagrams *What are the possible genotypes of the offspring? What percentage of the offspring will have each genotype?*

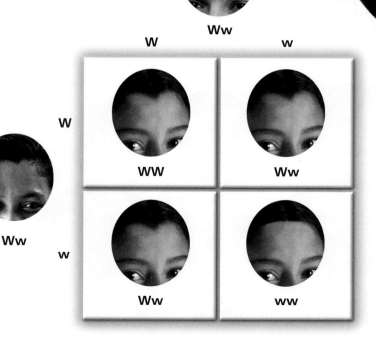

FIGURE 3
Inheritance of Blood Type
Blood type is determined by a single gene with three alleles. This chart shows which combinations of alleles result in each blood type.

Alleles of Blood Types	
Blood Type	**Combination of Alleles**
A	$I^A I^A$ or $I^A i$
B	$I^B I^B$ or $I^B i$
AB	$I^A I^B$
O	ii

FIGURE 4
Many Phenotypes
Skin color in humans is determined by three or more genes. Different combinations of alleles for each of the genes result in a wide range of possible skin colors.

Single Genes With Multiple Alleles Some human traits are controlled by a single gene that has more than two alleles. Such a gene is said to have **multiple alleles**—three or more forms of a gene that code for a single trait. Even though a gene may have multiple alleles, a person can carry only two of those alleles. This is because chromosomes exist in pairs. Each chromosome in a pair carries only one allele for each gene.

Human blood type is controlled by a gene with multiple alleles. There are four main blood types—A, B, AB, and O. Three alleles control the inheritance of blood types. The allele for blood type A and the allele for blood type B are codominant. The allele for blood type A is written as I^A. The allele for blood type B is written I^B. The allele for blood type O—written i—is recessive. Recall that when two codominant alleles are inherited, neither allele is masked. A person who inherits an I^A allele from one parent and an I^B allele from the other parent will have type AB blood. Figure 3 shows the allele combinations that result in each blood type. Notice that only people who inherit two i alleles have type O blood.

Traits Controlled by Many Genes If you completed the Discover activity, you saw that height in humans has more than two distinct phenotypes. In fact, there is an enormous variety of phenotypes for height. Some human traits show a large number of phenotypes because the traits are controlled by many genes. The genes act together as a group to produce a single trait. At least four genes control height in humans, so there are many possible combinations of genes and alleles. Skin color is another human trait that is controlled by many genes.

 Reading Checkpoint **Why do some traits exhibit a large number of phenotypes?**

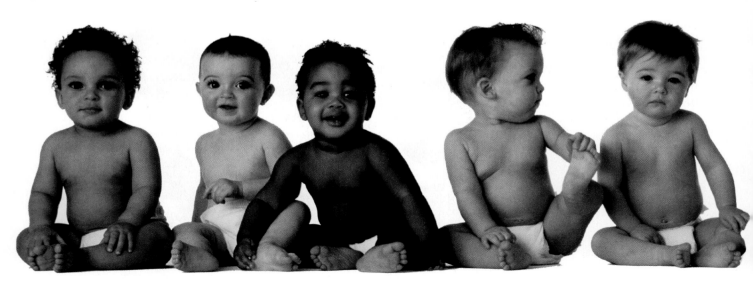

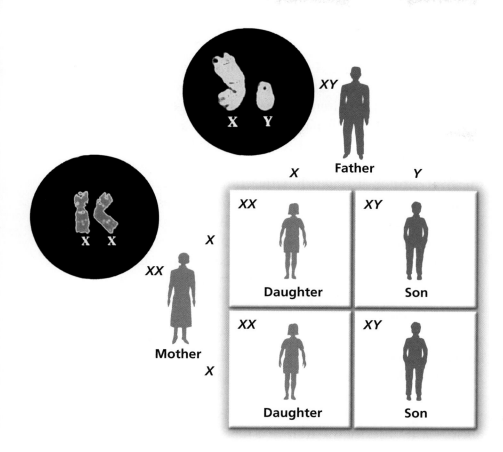

FIGURE 5
Male or Female?
As this Punnett square shows, there is a 50 percent probability that a child will be a girl and a 50 percent probability that a child will be a boy.
Interpreting Diagrams *What sex will the child be if a sperm with a Y chromosome fertilizes an egg?*

The Sex Chromosomes

The **sex chromosomes** are one of the 23 pairs of chromosomes in each body cell. **The sex chromosomes carry genes that determine whether a person is male or female. They also carry genes that determine other traits.**

Girl or Boy? The sex chromosomes are the only chromosome pair that do not always match. If you are a girl, your two sex chromosomes match. The two chromosomes are called X chromosomes. If you are a boy, your sex chromosomes do not match. One of them is an X chromosome, and the other is a Y chromosome. The Y chromosome is much smaller than the X chromosome.

Sex Chromosomes and Fertilization What happens to the sex chromosomes when egg and sperm cells form? Since both of a female's sex chromosomes are X chromosomes, all eggs carry one X chromosome. Males, however, have two different sex chromosomes. Therefore, half of a male's sperm cells carry an X chromosome, while half carry a Y chromosome.

When a sperm cell with an X chromosome fertilizes an egg, the egg has two X chromosomes. The fertilized egg will develop into a girl. When a sperm with a Y chromosome fertilizes an egg, the egg has one X chromosome and one Y chromosome. The fertilized egg will develop into a boy.

Lab zone Try This **Activity**

The Eyes Have It
One inherited trait is eye dominance—the tendency to use one eye more than the other. Here's how you can test yourself for this trait.

1. Hold your hand out in front of you at arm's length. Point your finger at an object across the room.
2. Close your right eye. With only your left eye open, observe how far your finger appears to move.
3. Repeat Step 2 with the right eye open. With which eye did your finger seem to remain closer to the object? That eye is dominant.

Designing Experiments
Is eye dominance related to hand dominance—whether a person is right-handed or left-handed? Design an experiment to find out. *Obtain your teacher's permission before carrying out your experiment.*

Sex-Linked Genes The genes for some human traits are carried on the sex chromosomes. Genes on the X and Y chromosomes are often called **sex-linked genes** because their alleles are passed from parent to child on a sex chromosome. Traits controlled by sex-linked genes are called sex-linked traits. One sex-linked trait is red-green colorblindness. A person with this trait cannot distinguish between red and green.

Recall that females have two X chromosomes, whereas males have one X chromosome and one Y chromosome. Unlike most chromosome pairs, the X and Y chromosomes have different genes. Most of the genes on the X chromosome are not on the Y chromosome. Therefore, an allele on an X chromosome may have no corresponding allele on a Y chromosome.

Like other genes, sex-linked genes can have dominant and recessive alleles. In females, a dominant allele on one X chromosome will mask a recessive allele on the other X chromosome. But in males, there is usually no matching allele on the Y chromosome to mask the allele on the X chromosome. As a result, any allele on the X chromosome—even a recessive allele—will produce the trait in a male who inherits it. Because males have only one X chromosome, males are more likely than females to have a sex-linked trait that is controlled by a recessive allele.

FIGURE 6
Colorblindness
The lower photo shows how a red barn and green fields look to a person with red-green colorblindness.

Normal vision

Red-green colorblind vision

Inheritance of Colorblindness Colorblindness is a trait controlled by a recessive allele on the X chromosome. Many more males than females have red-green colorblindness. You can understand why this is the case by examining the Punnett square in Figure 7. Both parents in this example have normal color vision. Notice, however, that the mother is a carrier of colorblindness. A **carrier** is a person who has one recessive allele for a trait and one dominant allele. A carrier of a trait controlled by a recessive allele does not have the trait. However, the carrier can pass the recessive allele on to his or her offspring. In the case of sex-linked traits, only females can be carriers.

As you can see in Figure 7, there is a 25 percent probability that this couple will have a colorblind child. Notice that none of the couple's daughters will be colorblind. On the other hand, the sons have a 50 percent probability of being colorblind. For a female to be colorblind, she must inherit two recessive alleles for colorblindness, one from each parent. A male needs to inherit only one recessive allele. This is because there is no gene for color vision on the Y chromosome. Thus, there is no allele that could mask the recessive allele on the X chromosome.

Go Online
SciLINKS

For: Links on genetics
Visit: www.SciLinks.org
Web Code: scn-0341

Reading Checkpoint What is the sex of a person who is a carrier for colorblindness?

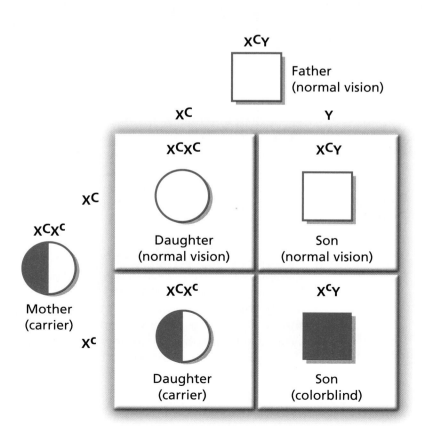

FIGURE 7
Colorblindness Punnett Square
Red-green colorblindness is a sex-linked trait. A girl who receives only one recessive allele (written X^c) for red-green colorblindness will not have the trait. However, a boy who receives one recessive allele will be colorblind.
Applying Concepts *What allele combination would a daughter need to inherit to be colorblind?*

The Effect of Environment

In humans and other organisms, the effects of genes are often influenced by the environment—an organism's surroundings. **Many of a person's characteristics are determined by an interaction between genes and the environment.**

You have learned that several genes work together to help determine human height. However, people's heights are also influenced by their environments. People's diets can affect their height. A diet lacking in protein, certain minerals, or certain vitamins can prevent a person from growing as tall as might be possible.

Environmental factors can also affect human skills, such as playing a musical instrument. For example, physical traits such as muscle coordination and a good sense of hearing will help a musician play well. But the musician also needs instruction on how to play the instrument. Musical instruction is an environmental factor.

 **Reading Checkpoint** How can environmental factors affect a person's height?

FIGURE 8
Heredity and Environment
When a person plays a violin, genetically determined traits such as muscle coordination interact with environmental factors such as time spent in practice.

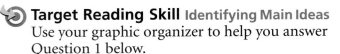

Section 1 Assessment

Target Reading Skill Identifying Main Ideas Use your graphic organizer to help you answer Question 1 below.

Reviewing Key Concepts

1. a. Identifying Identify three patterns of inheritance in humans. Give an example of a trait that follows each pattern.

   b. Summarizing How many human blood types are there? Summarize how blood type is inherited.

   c. Drawing Conclusions Aaron has blood type O. Can either of his parents have blood type AB? Explain your answer.

2. a. Reviewing What are the functions of the sex chromosomes?

   b. Comparing and Contrasting Contrast the sex chromosomes found in human females and human males.

   c. Relating Cause and Effect Explain how red-green colorblindness is inherited. Why is the condition more common in males than in females?

3. a. Reviewing Are a person's characteristics determined only by genes? Explain.

   b. Applying Concepts Explain what factors might work together to enable a great soccer player to kick a ball a long distance.

Writing in Science

Heredity and Environment Think of an ability you admire, such as painting, dancing, snowboarding, or playing games skillfully. Write a paragraph explaining how genes and the environment might work together to enable a person to develop this ability.

Human Genetic Disorders

Reading Preview

Key Concepts
- What are two major causes of genetic disorders in humans?
- How do geneticists trace the inheritance of traits?
- How are genetic disorders diagnosed and treated?

Key Terms
- genetic disorder • pedigree
- karyotype

Target Reading Skill
Comparing and Contrasting As you read, compare and contrast the types of genetic disorders by completing a table like the one below.

Disorder	Description	Cause
Cystic fibrosis	Abnormally thick mucus	Loss of three DNA bases

Discover **Activity**

How Many Chromosomes?
The photo at right shows the chromosomes from a cell of a person with Down syndrome, a genetic disorder. The chromosomes have been sorted into pairs.

1. Count the number of chromosomes in the photo.
2. How does the number of chromosomes compare to the usual number of chromosomes in human cells?

Think It Over
Inferring How do you think a cell could have ended up with this number of chromosomes? (*Hint:* Think about the events that occur during meiosis.)

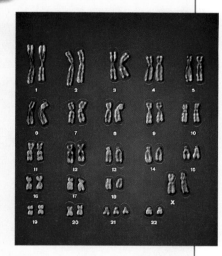

The air inside the stadium was hot and still. The crowd cheered loudly as the runners approached the starting blocks. At the crack of the starter's gun, the runners leaped into motion and sprinted down the track. Seconds later, the race was over. The runners, bursting with pride, hugged each other and their coaches. These athletes were running in the Special Olympics, a competition for people with disabilities. Many of the athletes who compete in the Special Olympics have disabilities that result from genetic disorders.

◀ **Runners in the Special Olympics**

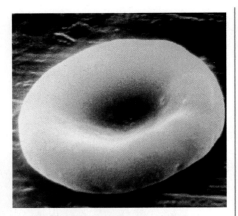

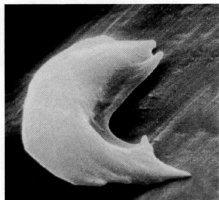

FIGURE 9
Sickle-Cell Disease
Normally, red blood cells are shaped like round disks (top). In a person with sickle-cell disease, red blood cells can become sickle-shaped (bottom).

Causes of Genetic Disorders

A **genetic disorder** is an abnormal condition that a person inherits through genes or chromosomes. **Some genetic disorders are caused by mutations in the DNA of genes. Other disorders are caused by changes in the overall structure or number of chromosomes.** In this section, you will learn about some common genetic disorders.

Cystic Fibrosis Cystic fibrosis is a genetic disorder in which the body produces abnormally thick mucus in the lungs and intestines. The thick mucus fills the lungs, making it hard for the affected person to breathe. Cystic fibrosis is caused by a recessive allele on one chromosome. The recessive allele is the result of a mutation in which three bases are removed from a DNA molecule.

Sickle-Cell Disease Sickle-cell disease affects hemoglobin, a protein in red blood cells that carries oxygen. When oxygen concentrations are low, the red blood cells of people with the disease have an unusual sickle shape. Sickle-shaped red blood cells clog blood vessels and cannot carry as much oxygen as normal cells. The allele for the sickle-cell trait is codominant with the normal allele. A person with two sickle-cell alleles will have the disease. A person with one sickle-cell allele will produce both normal hemoglobin and abnormal hemoglobin. This person usually will not have symptoms of the disease.

Hemophilia Hemophilia is a genetic disorder in which a person's blood clots very slowly or not at all. People with the disorder do not produce one of the proteins needed for normal blood clotting. The danger of internal bleeding from small bumps and bruises is very high. Hemophilia is caused by a recessive allele on the X chromosome. Because hemophilia is a sex-linked disorder, it occurs more frequently in males than in females.

Down Syndrome In Down syndrome, a person's cells have an extra copy of chromosome 21. In other words, instead of a pair of chromosomes, a person with Down syndrome has three of that chromosome. Down syndrome most often occurs when chromosomes fail to separate properly during meiosis. People with Down syndrome have some degree of mental retardation. Heart defects are also common, but can be treated.

 **Reading Checkpoint** **How is the DNA in the sickle-cell allele different from the normal allele?**

Pedigrees

Imagine that you are a geneticist who is interested in tracing the occurrence of a genetic disorder through several generations of a family. What would you do? **One important tool that geneticists use to trace the inheritance of traits in humans is a pedigree.** A **pedigree** is a chart or "family tree" that tracks which members of a family have a particular trait.

The trait in a pedigree can be an ordinary trait, such as a widow's peak, or a genetic disorder, such as cystic fibrosis. Figure 10 shows a pedigree for albinism, a condition in which a person's skin, hair, and eyes lack normal coloring.

FIGURE 10
A Pedigree
The father in the photograph has albinism. The pedigree shows the inheritance of the allele for albinism in three generations of a family. **Interpreting Diagrams** *Where is an albino male shown in the pedigree?*

Go Online
active art

For: Pedigree activity
Visit: PHSchool.com
Web Code: cep-3042

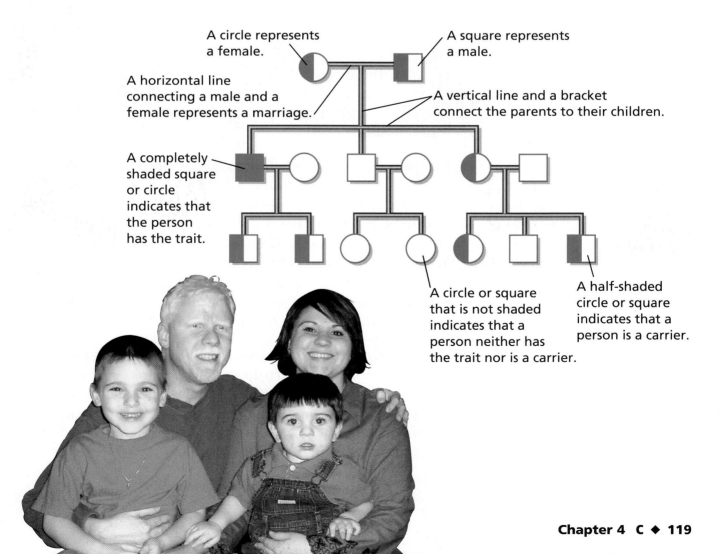

A circle represents a female.

A square represents a male.

A horizontal line connecting a male and a female represents a marriage.

A vertical line and a bracket connect the parents to their children.

A completely shaded square or circle indicates that the person has the trait.

A circle or square that is not shaded indicates that a person neither has the trait nor is a carrier.

A half-shaded circle or square indicates that a person is a carrier.

FIGURE 11
Living With Hemophilia

With proper care, people with hemophilia can manage their disorder. **Interpreting Diagrams** *In the pedigree, how many people have hemophilia?*

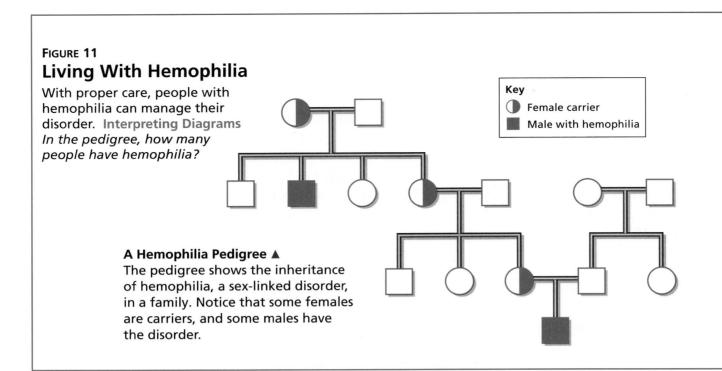

Key
◐ Female carrier
■ Male with hemophilia

A Hemophilia Pedigree ▲
The pedigree shows the inheritance of hemophilia, a sex-linked disorder, in a family. Notice that some females are carriers, and some males have the disorder.

Managing Genetic Disorders

Years ago, doctors had only Punnett squares and pedigrees to help them predict whether a child might have a genetic disorder. **Today, doctors use tools such as karyotypes to help diagnose genetic disorders. People with genetic disorders are helped through medical care, education, job training, and other methods.**

Karyotypes To detect chromosomal disorders such as Down syndrome, a doctor examines the chromosomes from a person's cells. The doctor uses a karyotype to examine the chromosomes. A **karyotype** (KA ree uh typ) is a picture of all the chromosomes in a cell. The chromosomes in a karyotype are arranged in pairs. A karyotype can reveal whether a person has the correct number of chromosomes in his or her cells. If you did the Discover activity, you saw a karyotype from a girl with Down syndrome.

Genetic Counseling A couple that has a family history of a genetic disorder may turn to a genetic counselor for advice. Genetic counselors help couples understand their chances of having a child with a particular genetic disorder. Genetic counselors use tools such as karyotypes, pedigree charts, and Punnett squares to help them in their work.

 **Reading Checkpoint** **What do genetic counselors do?**

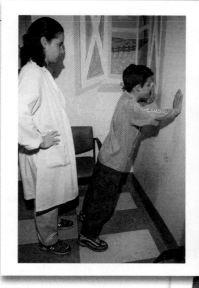

Physical Therapy ▶
Trained medical workers help hemophilia patients cope with their disorder. Here, a boy receives physical therapy.

Sports ▶
A boy with hemophilia learns how to play golf. The disorder does not stop people from living active lives.

Dealing With Genetic Disorders People with genetic disorders face serious challenges, but help is available. Medical treatments help people with some disorders. For example, physical therapy helps remove mucus from the lungs of people with cystic fibrosis. People with sickle-cell disease take folic acid, a vitamin, to help their bodies manufacture red blood cells. Because of education and job training, adults with Down syndrome can find work in hotels, banks, restaurants, and other places of employment. Fortunately, most genetic disorders do not prevent people from living active, productive lives.

Section 2 Assessment

Target Reading Skill

Comparing and Contrasting Use the information in your table to help you answer Question 1 below.

Reviewing Key Concepts

1. a. Identifying Identify the two major causes of genetic disorders in humans.
   b. Explaining Which of those two major causes is responsible for Down syndrome?
   c. Describing How are the cells of a person with Down syndrome different from those of a person without the disorder?

2. a. Defining What is a pedigree?
   b. Inferring Why are pedigrees helpful in understanding genetic disorders?

   c. Applying Concepts Sam has hemophilia. Sam's brother, mother, and father do not have hemophilia. Draw a pedigree showing who has the disorder and who is a carrier.

3. a. Reviewing What is a karyotype?
   b. Inferring Would a karyotype reveal the presence of sickle-cell disease? Why or why not?

Writing in Science

Creating a Web Site Create an imaginary Web site to inform the public about genetic disorders. Write a description of one disorder for the Web site.

Family Puzzle

Problem

A husband and wife want to understand the probability that their children might inherit cystic fibrosis. How can you use the information in the box labeled Case Study to predict the probability?

Skills Focus

interpreting data, predicting

Materials

• 12 index cards • scissors • marker

Procedure

1. Read the Case Study. In your notebook, draw a pedigree that shows all the family members. Use circles to represent the females, and squares to represent the males. Shade in the circles or squares representing the individuals who have cystic fibrosis.

2. You know that cystic fibrosis is controlled by a recessive allele. To help you figure out Joshua and Bella's family pattern, create a set of cards to represent the alleles. Cut each of six index cards into four smaller cards. On 12 of the small cards, write *N* to represent the dominant normal allele. On the other 12 small cards, write *n* for the recessive allele.

Case Study: Joshua and Bella

• Joshua and Bella have a son named Ian. Ian has been diagnosed with cystic fibrosis.

• Joshua and Bella are both healthy.

• Bella's parents are both healthy.

• Joshua's parents are both healthy.

• Joshua's sister, Sara, has cystic fibrosis.

3. Begin by using the cards to represent Ian's alleles. Since he has cystic fibrosis, what alleles must he have? Write in this genotype next to the pedigree symbol for Ian.

4. Joshua's sister, Sara, also has cystic fibrosis. What alleles does she have? Write in this genotype next to the pedigree symbol that represents Sara.

5. Now use the cards to figure out what genotypes Joshua and Bella must have. Write their genotypes next to their symbols in the pedigree.

6. Work with the cards to figure out the genotypes of all other family members. Fill in each person's genotype next to his or her symbol in the pedigree. If more than one genotype is possible, write in both genotypes.

Analyze and Conclude

1. **Interpreting Data** What were the possible genotypes of Joshua's parents? What were the genotypes of Bella's parents?

2. **Predicting** Joshua also has a brother. What is the probability that he has cystic fibrosis? Explain.

3. **Communicating** Imagine that you are a genetic counselor. A couple asks why you need information about many generations of their families to draw conclusions about a hereditary condition. Write an explanation you can give to them.

More to Explore

Review the pedigree that you just studied. What data suggest that the traits are not sex-linked? Explain.

Advances in Genetics

Reading Preview

Key Concepts
- What are three ways of producing organisms with desired traits?
- What is the goal of the Human Genome Project?

Key Terms
- selective breeding
- inbreeding • hybridization
- clone • genetic engineering
- gene therapy • genome

Target Reading Skill

Asking Questions Before you read, preview the red headings. In a graphic organizer like the one below, ask a question for each heading. As you read, write answers to your questions.

Advances in Genetics

Question	Answer
What is selective breeding?	Selective breeding is . . .

Discover Activity

Lab zone

What Do Fingerprints Reveal?

1. Label a sheet of paper with your name. Then roll one of your fingers from side to side on an ink pad. Make a fingerprint by carefully rolling your inked finger on the paper.
2. Divide into groups. Each group should choose one member to use the same finger to make a second fingerprint on a sheet of paper. Leave the paper unlabeled.
3. Exchange your group's fingerprints with those from another group. Compare each labeled fingerprint with the fingerprint on the unlabeled paper. Decide whose fingerprint it is.
4. Wash your hands after completing this activity.

Think It Over

Observing Why are fingerprints used to identify people?

Would you like to have your picture taken with a 9,000-year-old family member? Adrian Targett, a history teacher in the village of Cheddar in England, has actually done that. All that's left of his ancient relative, known as "Cheddar Man," is a skeleton. The skeleton was discovered in a cave near the village. DNA analysis indicates that Targett and Cheddar Man are relatives.

Like your fingerprints, your DNA is different from everyone else's. Because of advances in genetics, DNA evidence can show many things, such as family relationships.

FIGURE 12
Distant Relatives
Adrian Targett visits his distant relative, Cheddar Man. Unfortunately, Cheddar Man cannot respond to questions about life 9,000 years ago.

FIGURE 13
Inbreeding
Turkeys such as the one with white feathers were developed by inbreeding. Breeders started with wild turkeys.

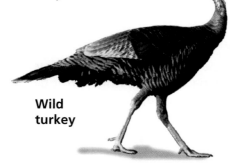

Wild turkey

Domestic turkey

Selective Breeding

Genetic techniques have enabled people to produce organisms with desirable traits. **Selective breeding, cloning, and genetic engineering are three methods for developing organisms with desirable traits.**

The process of selecting organisms with desired traits to be parents of the next generation is called **selective breeding**. Thousands of years ago, in what is now Mexico, the food that we call corn was developed in this way. Every year, farmers saved seeds from the healthiest plants that produced the best food. In the spring, they planted those seeds. By repeating this process over and over, farmers developed plants that produced better corn. People have used selective breeding with many different plants and animals. Two selective breeding techniques are inbreeding and hybridization.

Inbreeding The technique of **inbreeding** involves crossing two individuals that have similar characteristics. For example, suppose a male and a female turkey are both plump and grow quickly. Their offspring will probably also have those desirable qualities. Inbred organisms have alleles that are very similar to those of their parents.

Inbred organisms are genetically very similar. Therefore, inbreeding increases the probability that organisms may inherit alleles that lead to genetic disorders. For example, inherited hip problems are common in many breeds of dogs.

Hybridization In **hybridization** (hy brid ih ZAY shun), breeders cross two genetically different individuals. The hybrid organism that results is bred to have the best traits from both parents. For example, a farmer might cross corn that produces many kernels with corn that is resistant to disease. The result might be a hybrid corn plant with both of the desired traits.

✓ **Reading Checkpoint** **What is the goal of hybridization?**

FIGURE 14
Hybridization
McIntosh and Red Delicious apples were crossed to produce Empire apples.
Applying Concepts *What desirable traits might breeders have been trying to produce?*

McIntosh   **Red Delicious**   **Empire**

Changing Rice Production

The graph shows how worldwide rice production changed between 1965 and 2000. New, hybrid varieties of rice plants are one factor that has affected the amount of rice produced.

Worldwide Rice Production

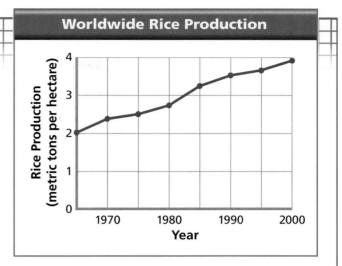

1. **Reading Graphs** According to the graph, how did rice production change between 1965 and 2000?

2. **Reading Graphs** How many metric tons of rice per hectare were produced in 1965? How many were produced in 2000?

3. **Calculating** Calculate the approximate difference between rice production in 1965 and 2000.

4. **Developing Hypotheses** What factors besides new varieties of plants might help account for the difference in rice production between 1965 and 2000?

Cloning

For some organisms, a technique called cloning can be used to produce offspring with desired traits. A **clone** is an organism that has exactly the same genes as the organism from which it was produced. It isn't hard to clone some kinds of plants, such as an African violet. Just cut a stem from one plant, and put the stem in soil. Water it, and soon you will have a whole new plant. The new plant is genetically identical to the plant from which the stem was cut.

Researchers have also cloned animals such as sheep and pigs. The methods for cloning these animals are complex. They involve taking the nucleus of an animal's body cell and using that nucleus to produce a new animal.

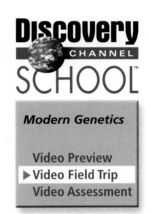
Modern Genetics

Video Preview
▶ Video Field Trip
Video Assessment

Reading Checkpoint How can a clone of a plant be produced?

FIGURE 15
Cloned Goats
These goats were produced by cloning.

Genetic Engineering

Geneticists have developed another powerful technique for producing organisms with desired traits. In this process, called **genetic engineering**, genes from one organism are transferred into the DNA of another organism. Genetic engineering can produce medicines and improve food crops.

Genetic Engineering in Bacteria One type of genetically engineered bacteria produces a protein called insulin. Injections of insulin are needed by many people with diabetes. Recall that bacteria have a single DNA molecule in the cytoplasm. Some bacterial cells also contain small circular pieces of DNA called plasmids. In Figure 16, you can see how scientists insert the DNA for a human gene into the plasmid of a bacterium.

FIGURE 16
Genetic Engineering

Scientists use genetic engineering to create bacterial cells that produce important human proteins such as insulin.
Interpreting Diagrams *How does a human insulin gene become part of a plasmid?*

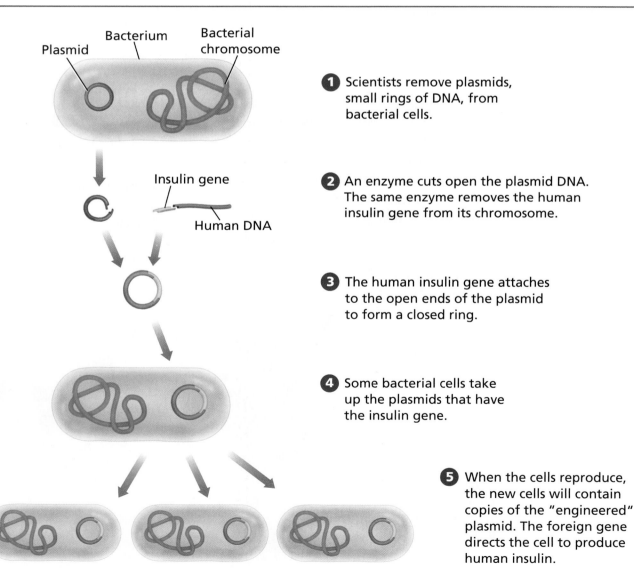

1 Scientists remove plasmids, small rings of DNA, from bacterial cells.

Insulin gene

Human DNA

2 An enzyme cuts open the plasmid DNA. The same enzyme removes the human insulin gene from its chromosome.

3 The human insulin gene attaches to the open ends of the plasmid to form a closed ring.

4 Some bacterial cells take up the plasmids that have the insulin gene.

5 When the cells reproduce, the new cells will contain copies of the "engineered" plasmid. The foreign gene directs the cell to produce human insulin.

Plasmid
Bacterium
Bacterial chromosome

Normal
zebra danio ▲

Genetically ▶
engineered
zebra danios

Once the gene is inserted into the plasmid, the bacterial cell and all its offspring will contain this human gene. As a result, the bacteria produce the protein that the human gene codes for—in this case, insulin. Because bacteria reproduce quickly, large amounts of insulin can be produced in a short time.

Genetic Engineering in Other Organisms Scientists can also use genetic engineering techniques to insert genes into animals. For example, human genes can be inserted into the cells of cows. The cows then produce the human protein for which the gene codes in their milk. Scientists have used this technique to produce the blood clotting protein needed by people with hemophilia.

Genes have also been inserted into the cells of plants, such as tomatoes and rice. Some of the genes enable the plants to survive in cold temperatures or in poor soil. Other genetically engineered crops can resist insect pests.

Gene Therapy Someday it may be possible to use genetic engineering to correct some genetic disorders in humans. This process, called **gene therapy**, will involve inserting copies of a gene directly into a person's cells. For example, doctors may be able to treat hemophilia by replacing the defective allele on the X chromosome. The person's blood would then clot normally.

Concerns About Genetic Engineering Some people are concerned about the long-term effects of genetic engineering. For example, some people think that genetically engineered crops may not be entirely safe. People fear that these crops may harm the environment or cause health problems in humans. To address such concerns, scientists are trying to learn more about the effects of genetic engineering.

✓ Reading Checkpoint How do genetic engineering techniques enable scientists to produce clotting proteins?

FIGURE 17
Genetically Engineered Fish
The bright red zebra danios are the result of genetic engineering.

For: Links on genetic engineering
Visit: www.SciLinks.org
Web Code: scn-0343

Lab zone Skills **Activity**

Communicating
Suppose you work for a drug company that uses genetically engineered bacteria to produce insulin. Write an advertisement for the drug that includes a simplified explanation of how the drug is produced.

Learning About Human Genetics

Recent advances have enabled scientists to learn a great deal about human genetics. The Human Genome Project and DNA fingerprinting are two applications of this new knowledge.

The Human Genome Project Imagine trying to crack a code that is 6 billion letters long. That's exactly what scientists working on the Human Genome Project have been doing. A **genome** is all the DNA in one cell of an organism. **The main goal of the Human Genome Project has been to identify the DNA sequence of every gene in the human genome.** The Human Genome Project has completed a "first draft" of the human genome. The scientists have learned that the DNA of humans has at least 30,000 genes. The average gene has about 3,000 bases. Scientists will some day know the DNA sequence of every human gene.

DNA Fingerprinting DNA technology used in the Human Genome Project can also identify people and show whether people are related. DNA from a person's cells is broken down into small pieces, or fragments. Selected fragments are used to produce a pattern called a DNA fingerprint. Except for identical twins, no two people have exactly the same DNA fingerprint. You will learn more about DNA fingerprinting in Technology and Society.

FIGURE 18
The Human Genome Project
Scientists on the Human Genome Project continue to study human DNA.

 **Reading Checkpoint** **About how many genes are in the human genome?**

Section 3 Assessment

Target Reading Skill Asking Questions Work with a partner to check your answers in your graphic organizer.

Reviewing Key Concepts

1. a. Listing List three methods that scientists can use to develop organisms with desirable traits.
b. Describing Briefly describe each method.
c. Applying Concepts Lupita has a houseplant. Which method would be the best way of producing a similar plant for a friend? Explain your answer.
2. a. Defining What is a genome?
b. Explaining What is the Human Genome Project?

c. Relating Cause and Effect How might knowledge gained from the Human Genome Project be used in gene therapy?

Lab zone At-Home Activity

Food and Selective Breeding Go to a grocery store with a parent or other family member. Discuss how fruits and vegetables have been produced by selective breeding. Choose a fruit or vegetable, and identify the traits that make it valuable.

Guilty or Innocent?

Problem

A crime scene may contain hair, skin, or blood from a criminal. These materials all contain DNA that can be used to make a DNA fingerprint. A DNA fingerprint, which consists of a series of bands, is something like a bar code. How can a DNA fingerprint identify individuals?

Skills Focus

drawing conclusions, inferring

Materials

- 4–6 bar codes
- hand lens

Procedure

1. Look at the photograph of DNA band patterns shown at right. Each person's DNA produces a unique pattern of these bands.

2. Now look at the Universal Product Code, also called a bar code, shown below the DNA bands. A bar code can be used as a model of a DNA band pattern. Compare the bar code with the DNA bands to see what they have in common. Record your observations.

3. Suppose that a burglary has taken place, and you're the detective leading the investigation. Your teacher will give you a bar code that represents DNA from blood found at the crime scene. You arrange to have DNA samples taken from several suspects. Write a sentence describing what you will look for as you try to match each suspect's DNA to the DNA sample from the crime scene.

4. You will now be given bar codes representing DNA samples taken from the suspects. Compare those bar codes with the bar code that represents DNA from the crime scene.

5. Use your comparisons to determine whether any of the suspects was present at the crime scene.

Analyze and Conclude

1. **Drawing Conclusions** Based on your findings, were any of the suspects present at the crime scene? Support your conclusion with specific evidence.

2. **Inferring** Why do people's DNA patterns differ so greatly?

3. **Drawing Conclusions** How would your conclusions be affected if you learned that the suspect whose DNA matched the evidence had an identical twin?

4. **Communicating** Suppose you are a defense lawyer. DNA evidence indicates that the bloodstain at the scene of a crime belongs to your client. Do you think this DNA evidence should be enough to convict your client? Write a speech you might give to the jury in defense of your client.

More to Explore

Do you think the DNA fingerprints of a parent and a child would show any similarities? Explain your thinking.

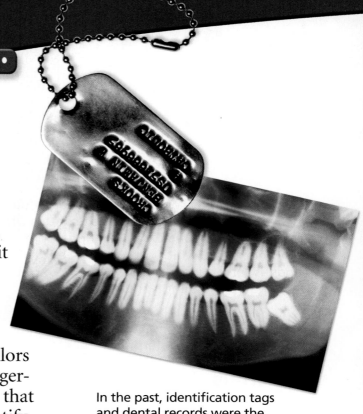

DNA Fingerprinting

What do you have that no one else has? Unless you are an identical twin, your DNA is unique. Because one person's DNA is like no one else's, it can be used to produce genetic "fingerprints." These fingerprints can tie a person to the scene of a crime. They can prevent the wrong person from going to jail. They can also be used to identify skeletal remains. Today, soldiers and sailors give blood and saliva samples so their DNA fingerprints can be saved. Like the identification tags that soldiers wear, DNA records can be used to identify the bodies of unknown soldiers or civilians.

In the past, identification tags and dental records were the main methods for identifying skeletal remains.

T T C G A A T T C G A A T T C T G A A T T C T A G A A T T C G A A

T T C G   A A T T C G   A A T T C T G   A A T T C T A G   A A T T C G A A

4 bases   6 bases   7 bases   8 bases   8 bases

This enzyme cuts the DNA every time it encounters the DNA sequence GAATTC.

1 After a sample of DNA is extracted from the body, an enzyme cuts the DNA strand into several smaller pieces.

2 The cut-up DNA fragments are loaded into a gel that uses electric current to separate fragments. Larger fragments of DNA move through the gel more slowly than the smaller fragments.

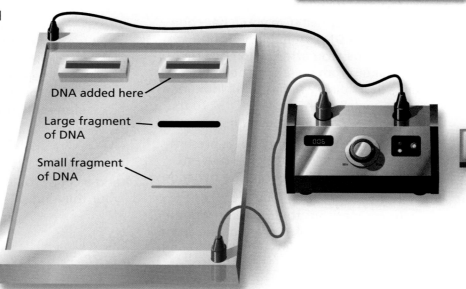

DNA added here

Large fragment of DNA

Small fragment of DNA

Analyzing DNA

In one method of DNA analysis, DNA from saliva, blood, bones, teeth, or other fluids or tissues is taken from cells. Special enzymes are added to cut the DNA into small pieces. Selected pieces are put into a machine that runs an electric current through the DNA and sorts the pieces by size. The DNA then gets stained and photographed. When developed, a unique banded pattern, similar to a product bar code, is revealed. The pattern can be compared to other samples of DNA to determine a match.

Limitations of DNA Fingerprinting

Like all technology, DNA fingerprinting has its limitations. DNA is very fragile and the films produced can be difficult to read if the DNA samples are old. In rare instances, DNA from the people testing the samples can become mixed in with the test samples and produce inaccurate results. DNA testing is also time consuming and expensive.

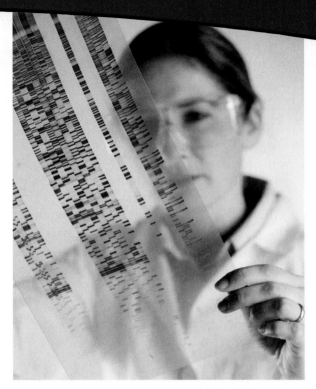

▲ **Scientist reading a DNA fingerprint**

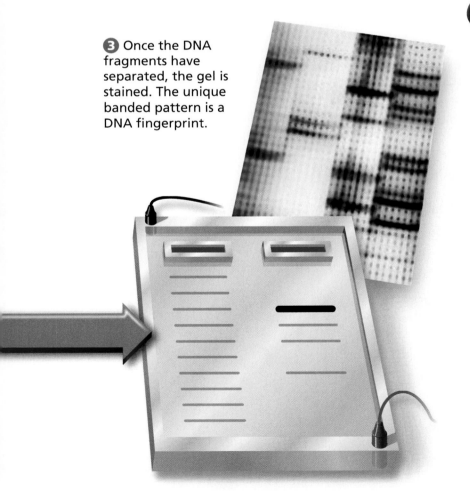

❸ Once the DNA fragments have separated, the gel is stained. The unique banded pattern is a DNA fingerprint.

Weigh the Impact

1. Identify the Need
Make a list of at least five situations in which DNA fingerprinting could be useful.

2. Research
Research the situations you listed in Question 1 to find out if DNA analysis is or can be used in each.

3. Write
Choose one application of DNA analysis and write one or two paragraphs to explain when the application can be used.

Go Online
PHSchool.com

For: More on DNA fingerprinting
Visit: PHSchool.com
Web Code: ceh-3040

1 Human Inheritance

Key Concepts

- Some human traits are controlled by single genes with two alleles, and others by single genes with multiple alleles. Still other traits are controlled by many genes that act together.

- The sex chromosomes carry genes that determine whether a person is male or female. They also carry genes that determine other traits.

- Many of a person's characteristics are determined by an interaction between genes and the environment.

Key Terms

multiple alleles
sex chromosomes
sex-linked gene
carrier

3 Advances in Genetics

Key Concepts

- Selective breeding, cloning, and genetic engineering are three methods for developing organisms with desirable traits.

- The main goal of the Human Genome Project has been to identify the DNA sequence of every gene in the human genome.

Key Terms

selective breeding
inbreeding
hybridization
clone
genetic engineering
gene therapy
genome

2 Human Genetic Disorders

Key Concepts

- Some genetic disorders are caused by mutations in the DNA of genes. Other disorders are caused by changes in the overall structure or number of chromosomes.

- One important tool that geneticists use to trace the inheritance of traits in humans is a pedigree.

- Today doctors use tools such as karyotypes to help detect genetic disorders. People with genetic disorders are helped through medical care, education, job training, and other methods.

Key Terms

genetic disorder
pedigree
karyotype

Review and Assessment

Go Online
PHSchool.com

For: Self-Assessment
Visit: PHSchool.com
Web Code: cea-3040

Organizing Information

Concept Mapping Copy the concept map about human traits onto a separate sheet of paper. Then complete it and add a title. (For more on Concept Mapping, see the Skills Handbook.)

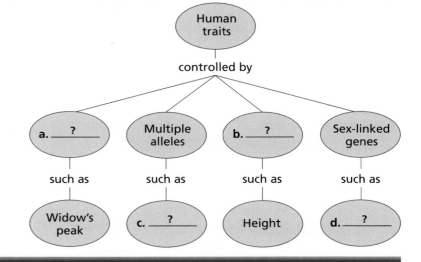

Human traits
controlled by

a. ___?___   Multiple alleles   b. ___?___   Sex-linked genes

such as   such as   such as   such as

Widow's peak   c. ___?___   Height   d. ___?___

Reviewing Key Terms

Choose the letter of the best answer.

1. A human trait that is controlled by a single gene with multiple alleles is
   a. dimples.   **b.** blood type.
   c. height.   **d.** skin color.

2. A sex-linked disorder is
   a. cystic fibrosis.
   b. sickle-cell disease.
   c. hemophilia.
   d. Down syndrome.

3. Which of the following would most likely be used to diagnose Down syndrome?
   a. a karyotype
   b. a pedigree
   c. a blood-clotting test
   d. a Punnett square

4. Inserting a human gene into a bacterial plasmid is an example of
   a. inbreeding.
   b. selective breeding.
   c. DNA fingerprinting.
   d. genetic engineering.

5. An organism that has the same genes as the organism from which it was produced is called a
   a. clone.   **b.** hybrid.
   c. genome.   **d.** pedigree.

If the statement is true, write *true*. If it is false, change the underlined word or words to make the statement true.

6. A widow's peak is a human trait that is controlled by <u>a single gene</u>.

7. A <u>male</u> inherits two X chromosomes.

8. A <u>karyotype</u> tracks which members of a family have a trait.

9. <u>Hybridization</u> is the crossing of two genetically similar organisms.

10. A <u>genome</u> is all the DNA in one cell of an organism.

Writing in Science

Fact Sheet You are a scientist in a cloning lab. Write a fact sheet that explains what the process of cloning involves. Describe at least one example.

DISCOVERY CHANNEL **SCHOOL**

Modern Genetics

Video Preview
Video Field Trip
▶ Video Assessment

Review and Assessment

Checking Concepts

11. Explain why there are a wide variety of phenotypes for skin color in humans.

12. Traits controlled by recessive alleles on the X chromosome are more common in males than in females. Explain why.

13. What is sickle-cell disease? How is this disorder inherited?

14. What is a pedigree? How do geneticists use pedigrees?

15. Describe two ways in which people with genetic disorders can be helped.

16. Explain how a horse breeder might use selective breeding to produce horses that have golden coats.

17. Describe how gene therapy might be used in the future to treat a person with hemophilia.

18. What is the Human Genome Project?

Thinking Critically

19. **Problem Solving** A woman with normal color vision has a colorblind daughter. What are the genotypes and phenotypes of both parents?

20. **Calculating** If a mother is a carrier of hemophilia and the father does not have hemophilia, what is the probability that their son will have the trait? Explain your answer.

21. **Interpreting Diagrams** The allele for cystic fibrosis is recessive. Identify which members of the family in the pedigree have cystic fibrosis and which are carriers.

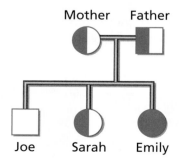

Applying Skills

Use the Punnett square to answer Questions 22–24.

The Punnett square below shows how muscular dystrophy, a sex-linked recessive disorder, is inherited.

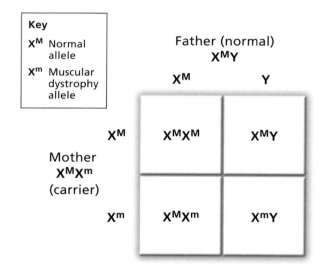

22. **Interpreting Data** What is the probability that a daughter of these parents will have muscular dystrophy? Explain your answer.

23. **Interpreting Data** What is the probability that a son of these parents will have muscular dystrophy? Explain your answer.

24. **Inferring** Is it possible for a woman to have muscular dystrophy? Why or why not?

Lab zone Chapter **Project**

Performance Assessment Present your display board to your class. Highlight important facts about the genetic trait you selected. Discuss the innovative designs you incorporated into the display board. In your presentation, highlight the interactive part of your project.

Standardized Test Prep

Use the pedigree to answer Questions 3–4.

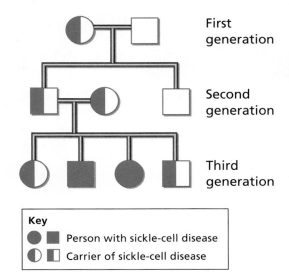

Key
- ● ■ Person with sickle-cell disease
- ◐ ◨ Carrier of sickle-cell disease

First generation

Second generation

Third generation

Test-Taking Tip
Interpreting Diagrams
If you are asked to interpret a pedigree diagram, first determine the trait that the pedigree shows. For example, the pedigree for Questions 3–4 shows the inheritance of sickle-cell disease. Remember that a circle represents a female and a square represents a male. Also look for a key that explains what the symbols in this particular pedigree show.

Use the pedigree for Questions 3–4 to answer the sample question below.

Sample Question
Which of the following is true for the first generation shown in the pedigree?
- **A** Both the man and the woman have sickle-cell disease.
- **B** Both the man and the woman are carriers of sickle-cell disease.
- **C** Only the woman is a carrier of sickle-cell disease.
- **D** Only the man is a carrier of sickle-cell disease.

Answer
The correct answer is **C**. Since the circle is half shaded, the woman is a carrier.

Choose the letter of the best answer.

1. A woman is heterozygous for the trait of hemophilia. Her husband does not have hemophilia. What is the probability that their son will have hemophilia?
   - **A** 0%
   - **B** 25%
   - **C** 50%
   - **D** 100%

2. Down syndrome is an example of a genetic disorder in which
   - **F** one DNA base has been added.
   - **G** one DNA base has been deleted.
   - **H** one chromosome is substituted for another.
   - **J** an extra chromosome is added to a pair.

3. How many people in the second generation have sickle-cell disease?
   - **A** none
   - **B** one person
   - **C** two people
   - **D** three people

4. Which statement is true about the third generation in the pedigree?
   - **F** No one has sickle-cell disease.
   - **G** Everyone has sickle-cell disease.
   - **H** Everyone has at least one allele for sickle-cell disease.
   - **J** No one has any alleles for sickle-cell disease.

5. To produce a human protein through genetic engineering, scientists use
   - **A** a bacterial gene inserted into a human chromosome.
   - **B** a human gene inserted into a plasmid.
   - **C** a bacterial gene inserted into a plasmid.
   - **D** a human gene inserted into a human chromosome.

Constructed Response

6. Explain why, for each pregnancy, human parents have a 50 percent probability of having a boy and a 50 percent probability of having a girl. Your answer should include the terms *X chromosome* and *Y chromosome*.

Changes Over Time

interactive Textbook

Darwin observed Sally light-foot crabs and iguanas on the Galápagos Islands. ▶

Lab zone™ Chapter **Project**

Life's Long Calendar

Earth's history goes back billions of years. This chapter project will help you understand this huge time span. In this project, you'll find a way to convert enormous time periods into a more familiar scale.

Your Goal To use a familiar measurement scale to create two timelines for Earth's history

To complete the project you must

- represent Earth's history using a familiar scale, such as months on a calendar or yards on a football field
- use your chosen scale twice, once to plot out 5 billion years of history, and once to focus on the past 600 million years
- include markers on both scales to show important events in the history of life

Plan It! Preview Figure 16 in this chapter to see what events occurred during the two time periods. In a small group, discuss some familiar scales you might use for your timelines. You could select a time interval such as a year or a day. Alternatively, you could choose a distance interval such as the length of your schoolyard or the walls in your classroom. Decide on the kind of timelines you will make. Then plan and construct your timelines.

Darwin's Theory

Reading Preview

Key Concepts
- What important observations did Darwin make on his voyage?
- What hypothesis did Darwin make to explain the differences between similar species?
- How does natural selection lead to evolution?

Key Terms
- species • fossil • adaptation
- evolution • scientific theory
- natural selection • variation

Target Reading Skill
Relating Cause and Effect In a graphic organizer, identify factors that cause natural selection.

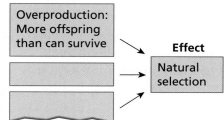

Causes

Overproduction: More offspring than can survive

Effect

Natural selection

Lab zone Discover **Activity**

How Do Living Things Vary?

1. Use a ruler to measure the length and width of 10 sunflower seeds. Record each measurement.
2. Now use a hand lens to carefully examine each seed. Record each seed's shape, color, and number of stripes.

Think It Over
Classifying In what ways are the seeds in your sample different from one another? In what ways are they similar? How could you group the seeds based on their similarities and differences?

In December 1831, the British ship HMS *Beagle* set sail from England on a five-year trip around the world. On board was a 22-year-old named Charles Darwin. Darwin eventually became the ship's naturalist—a person who studies the natural world. His job was to learn as much as he could about the living things he saw on the voyage. Darwin observed plants and animals he had never seen before. He wondered why they were so different from those in England. Darwin's observations led him to develop one of the most important scientific theories of all time: the theory of evolution by natural selection.

FIGURE 1

The Voyage of the *Beagle*

Charles Darwin sailed on the *Beagle* to the Galápagos Islands. He saw many unusual organisms on the islands, such as giant tortoises and the blue-footed booby.
Interpreting Maps *After leaving South America, where did the* Beagle *go?*

Replica of the *Beagle* ▶

Asia

Pacific Ocean

Australia

New Zealand

Darwin's Observations

As you can see in Figure 1, the *Beagle* made many stops along the coast of South America. From there, the ship traveled to the Galápagos Islands. Darwin observed living things as he traveled. He thought about relationships among those organisms. **Darwin's important observations included the diversity of living things, the remains of ancient organisms, and the characteristics of organisms on the Galápagos Islands.**

Diversity Darwin was amazed by the tremendous diversity of living things that he saw. In Brazil, he saw insects that looked like flowers and ants that marched across the forest floor like huge armies. In Argentina, he saw sloths, animals that moved very slowly and spent much of their time hanging in trees.

Today scientists know that organisms are even more diverse than Darwin could ever have imagined. Scientists have identified more than 1.7 million species of organisms on Earth. A **species** is a group of similar organisms that can mate with each other and produce fertile offspring.

Fossils Darwin saw the fossil bones of animals that had died long ago. A **fossil** is the preserved remains or traces of an organism that lived in the past. Darwin was puzzled by some of the fossils he observed. For example, he saw fossil bones that resembled the bones of living sloths. The fossil bones were much larger than those of the sloths that were alive in Darwin's time. He wondered what had happened to the giant creatures from the past.

Reading Checkpoint **What is a fossil?**

▲ **Giant tortoise**

▲ **Blue-footed booby**

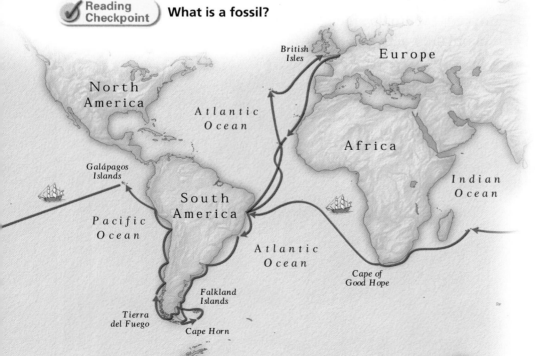

Galápagos Organisms

In 1835, the *Beagle* reached the Galápagos Islands. Darwin observed many unusual life forms on these small islands, such as giant tortoises, or land turtles. Some of these tortoises could look him in the eye! After returning to England, Darwin thought about the organisms he had seen. He compared Galápagos organisms to organisms that lived elsewhere. He also compared organisms on different islands in the Galápagos group. He was surprised by some of the similarities and differences he saw.

Comparisons to South American Organisms   Darwin found many similarities between Galápagos organisms and those in South America. Many of the birds on the islands, including hawks, mockingbirds, and finches, resembled those on the mainland. Many of the plants were similar to plants Darwin had collected on the mainland.

However, there were important differences between the organisms on the islands and those on the mainland. The iguanas on the Galápagos Islands had large claws that allowed them to grip slippery rocks, where they fed on seaweed. The iguanas on the mainland had smaller claws. Smaller claws allowed the mainland iguanas to climb trees, where they ate leaves. You can see these differences in Figure 2.

From his observations, Darwin hypothesized that a small number of different plant and animal species had come to the Galápagos Islands from the mainland. They might have been blown out to sea during a storm or set adrift on a fallen log. Once the plants and animals reached the islands, they reproduced. Eventually, their offspring became different from their mainland relatives.

FIGURE 2
Comparing Iguanas
Iguanas on mainland South America (above) have smaller claws than iguanas on the Galápagos Islands. Comparing and Contrasting *In what other ways are the iguanas different?*

FIGURE 3
Galápagos Finches
Darwin made these drawings of four species of Galápagos finches. The structure of each bird's beak is an adaptation related to the type of food the bird eats. **Comparing and Contrasting** *Identify some specific differences in these finches' beaks.*

1. Geospiza magnirostris
3. Geospiza parvula.
2. Geospiza fortis.
4. Certhidea olivasea.

Comparisons Among the Islands As he traveled from one Galápagos island to the next, Darwin also noticed many differences among organisms. For example, the tortoises on one island had dome-shaped shells. Those on another island had saddle-shaped shells. A government official in the islands told Darwin that he could tell which island a tortoise came from just by looking at its shell.

Adaptations Like the tortoises, the finches on the Galápagos were noticeably different from one island to the next. The most obvious differences were the varied sizes and shapes of the birds' beaks, as shown in Figure 3. An examination of the different finches showed that each species was well suited to the life it led. Finches that ate insects had narrow, needle-like beaks. Finches that ate seeds had strong, wide beaks.

Beak shape is an example of an **adaptation,** a trait that helps an organism survive and reproduce. The finches' beak structures help in obtaining food. Other adaptations help organisms avoid being eaten. For example, some plants, such as milkweed, are poisonous or have a bad taste. A variety of adaptations aid in reproduction. The bright colors of some flowers attract insects. When an insect lands on a flower, the insect may pick up pollen grains, which produce sperm. The insect then may carry the pollen grains to another flower, enabling fertilization to take place.

 **Reading Checkpoint** How did the beaks of Galápagos finches differ from one island to another?

Bird Beak Adaptations
Use this activity to explore adaptations in birds.

1. Scatter a small amount of bird seed on a paper plate. Scatter 20 raisins on the plate to represent insects.
2. Obtain a variety of objects such as tweezers, hair clips, and clothespins. Pick one object to use as a "beak."
3. See how many seeds you can pick up and drop into a cup in 10 seconds.
4. Now see how many "insects" you can pick up and drop into a cup in 10 seconds.
5. Use a different "beak" and repeat Steps 3 and 4.

Inferring What type of beak worked well for seeds? For insects? How are different-shaped beaks useful for eating different foods?

Evolution

After he returned to England, Darwin continued to think about what he had seen during his voyage on the *Beagle*. Darwin spent the next 20 years consulting with other scientists, gathering more information, and thinking through his ideas.

Darwin's Reasoning Darwin especially wanted to understand the different adaptations of organisms on the Galápagos Islands. **Darwin reasoned that plants or animals that arrived on the Galápagos Islands faced conditions that were different from those on the mainland. Perhaps, Darwin hypothesized, the species gradually changed over many generations and became better adapted to the new conditions.** The gradual change in a species over time is called **evolution**.

Darwin's ideas are often referred to as the theory of evolution. A **scientific theory** is a well-tested concept that explains a wide range of observations. From the evidence he collected, Darwin concluded that organisms on the Galápagos Islands had changed over time. However, Darwin did not know how the changes had happened.

Selective Breeding Darwin studied other examples of changes in living things to help him understand how evolution might occur. One example that Darwin studied was the offspring of animals produced by selective breeding. English farmers in Darwin's time used selective breeding to produce sheep with fine wool. Darwin himself had bred pigeons with large, fan-shaped tails. By repeatedly allowing only those pigeons with many tail feathers to mate, breeders had produced pigeons with two or three times the usual number of tail feathers. Darwin thought that a process similar to selective breeding might happen in nature. But he wondered what process selected certain traits.

Reading Checkpoint What is a scientific theory?

▲ Seattle Slew, great-grandfather of Funny Cide

Distorted Humor, ▲ father of Funny Cide

Funny Cide ▶

FIGURE 4
Selective Breeding
Race horses are selectively bred to obtain the trait of speed. Funny Cide's father, Distorted Humor, and great-grandfather, Seattle Slew, were known for their speed.

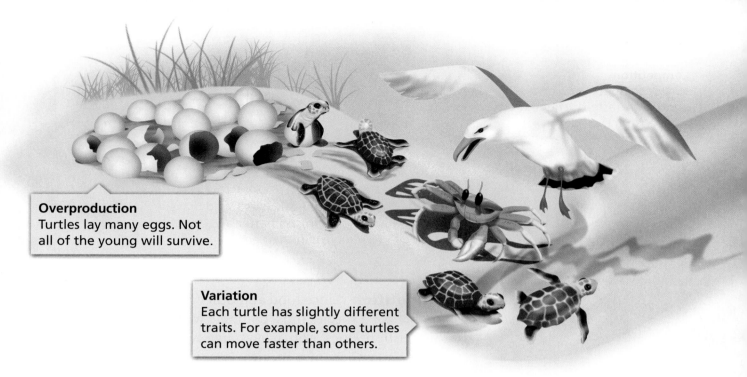

Overproduction
Turtles lay many eggs. Not all of the young will survive.

Variation
Each turtle has slightly different traits. For example, some turtles can move faster than others.

Natural Selection

In 1858, Darwin and another British biologist, Alfred Russel Wallace, each proposed an explanation for how evolution could occur in nature. The next year, Darwin described this mechanism in a book entitled *The Origin of Species*. In his book, Darwin proposed that evolution occurs by means of natural selection. **Natural selection** is the process by which individuals that are better adapted to their environment are more likely to survive and reproduce than other members of the same species. Darwin identified factors that affect the process of natural selection: overproduction, competition, and variations. Figure 5 and Figure 6 show how natural selection might happen in a group of turtles.

Overproduction Darwin knew that most species produce far more offspring than can possibly survive. In many species, so many offspring are produced that there are not enough resources—food, water, and living space—for all of them. Many female insects, for example, lay thousands of eggs. If all newly hatched insects survived, they would soon crowd out all other plants and animals. Darwin knew that this doesn't happen. Why not?

Variations As you learned in your study of genetics, members of a species differ from one another in many of their traits. Any difference between individuals of the same species is called a **variation.** For example, certain insects may be able to eat foods that other insects of their species avoid. The color of a few insects may be different from that of most other insects in their species.

FIGURE 5
Overproduction and Variation
Like actual sea turtles, the turtles in this illustration produce many more offspring than will survive. Some turtles are better adapted than others to survive in their environment.
Relating Cause and Effect What adaptations might help young sea turtles survive?

Lab zone Skills Activity

Making Models
Scatter 15 black buttons and 15 white buttons on a sheet of white paper. Have a partner time you to see how many buttons you can pick up in 10 seconds. Pick up the buttons one at a time. Did you collect more buttons of one color than the other? Why? How can a variation such as color affect the process of natural selection?

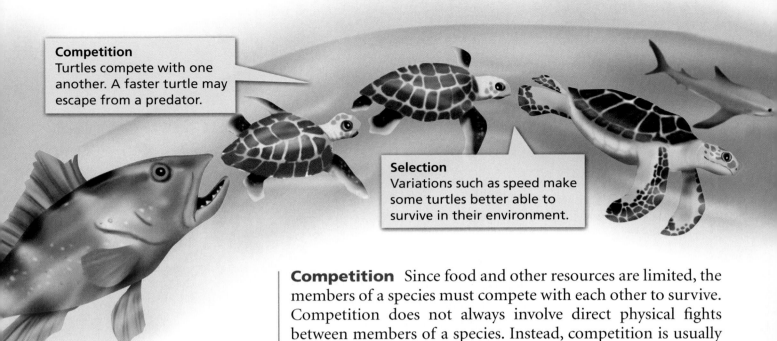

Competition
Turtles compete with one another. A faster turtle may escape from a predator.

Selection
Variations such as speed make some turtles better able to survive in their environment.

FIGURE 6
Competition and Selection
Variations among turtles make some of them better able to survive. Turtles that survive to become adults will be able to reproduce.
Applying Concepts *What are some variations that sea turtles might exhibit?*

For: Links on Charles Darwin
Visit: www.SciLinks.org
Web Code: scn-0351

Competition Since food and other resources are limited, the members of a species must compete with each other to survive. Competition does not always involve direct physical fights between members of a species. Instead, competition is usually indirect. For example, many insects do not find enough to eat. Others are caught by predators. Only a few insects will survive.

Selection Darwin observed that some variations make individuals better adapted to their environment. Those individuals are more likely to survive and reproduce. Their offspring may inherit the helpful characteristic. The offspring, in turn, will be more likely to survive and reproduce, and thus pass on the characteristic to their offspring. After many generations, more members of the species will have the helpful characteristic.

In effect, the environment has "selected" organisms with helpful traits to become parents of the next generation. **Darwin proposed that, over a long time, natural selection can lead to change. Helpful variations may gradually accumulate in a species, while unfavorable ones may disappear.**

Environmental Change A change in the environment can affect an organism's ability to survive. The environmental change can therefore lead to selection. For example, monkey flowers are a type of plant. Most monkey flowers cannot grow in soil that has a high concentration of copper. However, because of genetic variation, some varieties of monkey flower now grow near copper mines, in spite of the copper in the soil.

Here is how natural selection might have resulted in monkey flowers that can grow in copper-contaminated soil. When the soil around a mine first became contaminated, a small number of monkey-flower plants may have been able to survive in the high level of copper. These plants grew and reproduced. After many generations, most of the seeds that sprouted in the soil produced monkey flowers that could withstand the copper.

Survival and Reproduction Only a few turtles survive long enough to reproduce. The offspring may inherit the favorable traits of the parents.

Genes and Natural Selection Without variations, all the members of a species would have the same traits. Natural selection would not occur because all individuals would have an equal chance of surviving and reproducing. But where do variations come from? How are they passed on from parents to offspring?

Darwin could not explain what caused variations or how they were passed on. As scientists later learned, variations can result from mutation and the shuffling of alleles during meiosis. Genes are passed from parents to their offspring. Because of this, only traits that are inherited, or controlled by genes, can be acted upon by natural selection.

Section 1 Assessment

 **Target Reading Skill**
Relating Cause and Effect Work with a partner to check the information in your graphic organizer.

Reviewing Key Concepts

1. a. **Listing** List three general kinds of observations that Darwin made during the voyage of the *Beagle*.
   b. **Comparing and Contrasting** Contrast Galápagos iguanas to South American iguanas.
   c. **Applying Concepts** What is an adaptation? Explain how the claws of the Galápagos and South American iguanas are adaptations.
2. a. **Reviewing** How did Darwin explain why Galápagos species had different adaptations than similar South American species?
   b. **Developing Hypotheses** How does selective breeding support Darwin's hypothesis?

3. a. **Defining** What is variation? What is natural selection?
   b. **Relating Cause and Effect** How do variation and natural selection work together to help cause evolution?
   c. **Applying Concepts** Suppose the climate in an area becomes much drier than it was before. What kinds of variations in the area's plants might be acted on by natural selection?

Writing in Science

Interview You are a nineteenth-century reporter interviewing Charles Darwin about his theory of evolution. Write three questions you would ask him. Then write answers that Darwin might have given.

Nature at Work

Problem

How do species change over time?

Skills Focus

predicting, making models

Materials

- scissors
- marking pen
- construction paper, 2 colors

Procedure

1. Work on this lab with two other students. One student should choose construction paper of one color and make the team's 50 "mouse" cards, as described in Table 1. The second student should choose a different color construction paper and make the team's 25 "event" cards, as described in Table 2. The third student should copy the data table and record all the data.

PART 1   A White Sand Environment

2. Mix up the mouse cards.

3. Begin by using the cards to model what might happen to a group of mice in an environment of white sand dunes. Choose two mouse cards. Allele pairs *WW* and *Ww* produce a white mouse. Allele pair *ww* produces a brown mouse. Record the color of the mouse with a tally mark in the data table.

4. Choose an event card. An "S" card means the mouse survives. A "D" or a "P" card means the mouse dies. A "C" card means the mouse dies if its color contrasts with the white sand dunes. (Only brown mice will die when a "C" card is drawn.) Record each death with a tally mark in the data table.

5. If the mouse lives, put the two mouse cards in a "live mice" pile. If the mouse dies, put the cards in a "dead mice" pile. Put the event card at the bottom of its pack.

6. Repeat Steps 3 through 5 with the remaining mouse cards to study the first generation of mice. Record your results.

7. Leave the dead mice cards untouched. Mix up the cards from the live mice pile. Mix up the events cards.

8. Repeat Steps 3 through 7 for the second generation. Then repeat Steps 3 through 6 for the third generation.

PART 2   A Forest Floor Environment

9. How would the data differ if the mice in this model lived on a dark brown forest floor? Record your prediction in your notebook.

10. Make a new copy of the data table. Then use the cards to test your prediction. Remember that a "C" card now means that any mouse with white fur will die.

Data Table				
Type of Environment:				
Generation	Population		Deaths	
	White Mice	Brown Mice	White Mice	Brown Mice
1				
2				
3				

Table 1: Mouse Cards		
Number	**Label**	**Meaning**
25	*W*	Dominant allele for white fur
25	*w*	Recessive allele for brown fur

Table 2: Event Cards		
Number	**Label**	**Meaning**
5	S	Mouse survives.
1	D	Disease kills mouse.
1	P	Predator kills mice of all colors.
18	C	Predator kills mice that contrast with the environment.

Analyze and Conclude

1. **Calculating** In Part 1, how many white mice were there in each generation? How many brown mice? In each generation, which color mouse had the higher death rate? (*Hint:* To calculate the death rate for white mice, divide the number of white mice that died by the total number of white mice, then multiply by 100%.)

2. **Predicting** If the events in Part 1 occurred in nature, how would the group of mice change over time?

3. **Observing** How did the results in Part 2 differ from those in Part 1?

4. **Making Models** How would it affect your model if you increased the number of "C" cards? What would happen if you decreased the number of "C" cards?

5. **Communicating** Imagine that you are trying to explain the point of this lab to Charles Darwin. Write an explanation that you could give to him. To prepare to write, answer the following questions: What are some ways in which this investigation models natural selection? What are some ways in which natural selection differs from this model?

Design an Experiment

Choose a different species with a trait that interests you. Make a set of cards similar to these cards to investigate how natural selection might bring about the evolution of that species. *Obtain your teacher's permission before carrying out your investigation.*

Evidence of Evolution

Reading Preview

Key Concepts
- What evidence supports the theory of evolution?
- How do scientists infer evolutionary relationships among organisms?
- How do new species form?

Key Terms
- homologous structures
- branching tree

Target Reading Skill
Identifying Supporting Evidence Evidence consists of facts that can be confirmed by testing or observation. As you read, identify the evidence that supports the theory of evolution. Write the evidence in a graphic organizer like the one below.

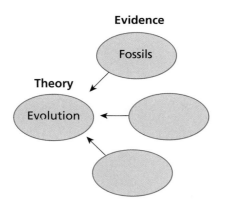

Evidence

Fossils

Theory

Evolution

Lab zone Discover Activity

How Can You Classify Species?
1. Collect six to eight different pens. Each pen will represent a different species of similar organisms.
2. Choose a trait that varies among your pen species, such as size or ink color. Using this trait, try to divide the pen species into two groups.
3. Now choose another trait. Divide each group into two smaller groups.

Think It Over
Classifying Which of the pen species share the most characteristics? What might the similarities suggest about how the pen species evolved?

Does natural selection occur today? Evidence indicates that the answer is yes. Consider, for example, what happens when chemicals called pesticides are used to kill harmful insects such as the cockroaches below. When a pesticide is first used in a building, it kills almost all the insects. But a few insects have traits that protect them from the pesticide. These insects survive.

The surviving insects reproduce. Some of their offspring inherit the pesticide protection. The surviving offspring, in turn, reproduce. Every time the pesticide is used, the only insects that survive are those that are resistant to the harmful effects of the pesticide. After many years, most of the cockroaches in the building are resistant to the pesticide. Therefore, the pesticide is no longer effective in controlling the insects. The development of pesticide resistance is one type of evidence that supports Darwin's theory of evolution.

FIGURE 7
Pesticide Resistance
Many insects, including cockroaches such as these, are no longer killed by some pesticides. Increased pesticide resistance is evidence that natural selection is happening.

Interpreting the Evidence

Since Darwin's time, scientists have found a great deal of evidence that supports the theory of evolution. **Fossils, patterns of early development, and similar body structures all provide evidence that organisms have changed over time.**

Fossils By examining fossils, scientists can infer the structures of ancient organisms. Fossils show that, in many cases, organisms that lived in the past were very different than organisms alive today. You will learn more about the importance of fossils in the next section.

Similarities in Early Development Scientists also make inferences about evolutionary relationships by comparing the early development of different organisms. Suppose you were asked to compare an adult fish, salamander, chicken, and opossum. You would probably say they look quite different from each other. However, during early development, these four organisms are similar, as you can see in Figure 8. For example, during the early stages of development all four organisms have a tail and a row of tiny slits along their throats. These similarities suggest that these vertebrate species are related and share a common ancestor.

Go Online

SciLINKS NSTA

For: Links on evolution
Visit: www.SciLinks.org
Web Code: scn-0352

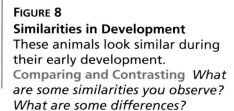

FIGURE 8
Similarities in Development
These animals look similar during their early development.
Comparing and Contrasting What are some similarities you observe? What are some differences?

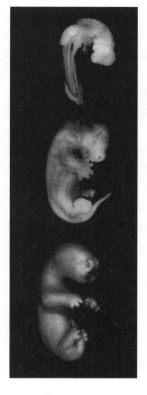
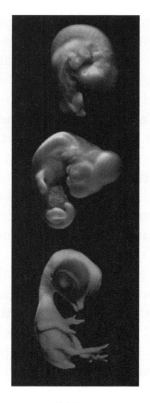
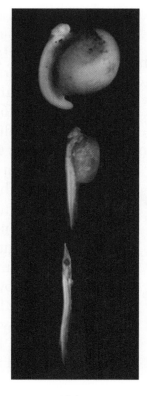

Opossum   **Chicken**   **Fish**   **Salamander**

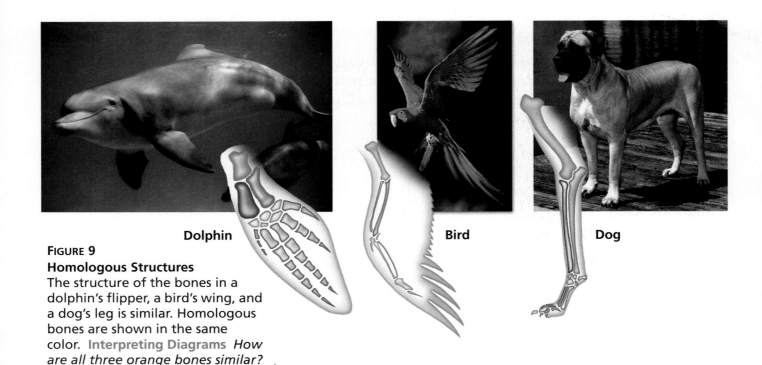

Dolphin   Bird   Dog

FIGURE 9
Homologous Structures
The structure of the bones in a
dolphin's flipper, a bird's wing, and
a dog's leg is similar. Homologous
bones are shown in the same
color. Interpreting Diagrams *How
are all three orange bones similar?*

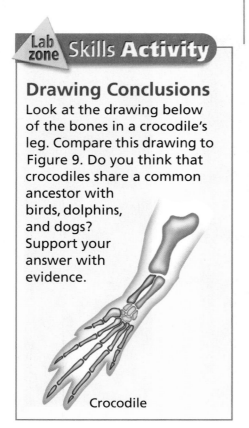

Lab zone Skills **Activity**

Drawing Conclusions
Look at the drawing below
of the bones in a crocodile's
leg. Compare this drawing to
Figure 9. Do you think that
crocodiles share a common
ancestor with
birds, dolphins,
and dogs?
Support your
answer with
evidence.

Crocodile

Similarities in Body Structure Long ago, scientists began
to compare the body structures of living species to look for
clues about evolution. In fact, this is how Darwin came to
understand that evolution had occurred on the Galápagos
Islands. An organism's body structure is its basic body plan,
such as how its bones are arranged. Fishes, amphibians, reptiles, birds, and mammals, for example, all have a similar body
structure—an internal skeleton with a backbone. This is why
scientists classify all five groups of animals together as verte-
brates. All of these groups probably inherited a similar structure from an early vertebrate ancestor that they shared.

Look closely at the structure of the bones in the bird's wing,
dolphin's flipper, and dog's leg that are shown in Figure 9.
Notice that the bones in the forelimbs of these three animals are
arranged in a similar way. These similarities provide evidence
that these three organisms all evolved from a common ancestor.
Similar structures that related species have inherited from a
common ancestor are known as **homologous structures** (hoh
MAHL uh gus).

Sometimes scientists find fossils that support the evidence
provided by homologous structures. For example, scientists
have recently found fossils of ancient whalelike creatures. The
fossils show that the ancestors of today's whales had legs and
walked on land. This evidence supports other evidence that
whales and humans share a common ancestor.

 **Reading Checkpoint** **In what way are the body structures of fishes,
amphibians, reptiles, and mammals similar?**

Inferring Species Relationships

Fossils, early development patterns, and body structure provide evidence that evolution has occurred. Scientists have also used these kinds of evidence to infer how organisms are related to one another. Not too long ago, fossils, embryos, and body structures were the only tools that scientists had to determine how species were related. Today, scientists can also compare the DNA and protein sequences of different species. **Scientists have combined the evidence from DNA, protein structure, fossils, early development, and body structure to determine the evolutionary relationships among species.**

Similarities in DNA Why do some species have similar body structures and development patterns? Scientists infer that the species inherited many of the same genes from a common ancestor. Recently, scientists have begun to compare the genes of different species to determine how closely related the species are.

Recall that genes are made of DNA. By comparing the sequence of nitrogen bases in the DNA of different species, scientists can infer how closely related the two species are. The more similar the DNA sequences, the more closely related the species are. For example, DNA analysis has shown that elephants and tiny elephant shrews, shown in Figure 10, are closely related.

The DNA bases along a gene specify what type of protein will be produced. Therefore, scientists can also compare the order of amino acids in a protein to see how closely related two species are.

Combining Evidence In most cases, evidence from DNA and protein structure has confirmed conclusions based on fossils, embryos, and body structure. For example, recent DNA comparisons show that dogs are more similar to wolves than they are to coyotes. Scientists had already reached this conclusion based on similarities in the structure and development of these three species.

FIGURE 10
DNA and Relationships
Because of its appearance, the tiny elephant shrew was thought to be closely related to mice and other rodents. However, DNA comparisons have shown that the elephant shrew is actually more closely related to elephants.

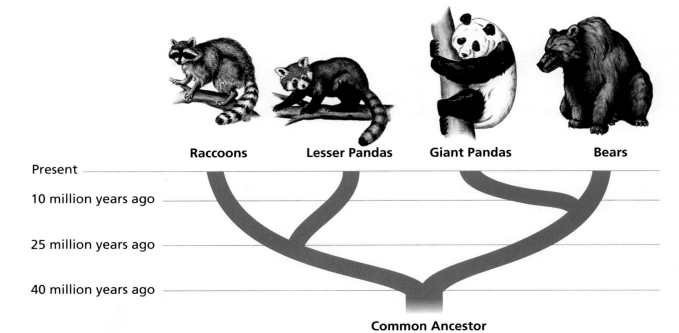

Raccoons   Lesser Pandas   Giant Pandas   Bears

Present

10 million years ago

25 million years ago

40 million years ago

Common Ancestor

FIGURE 11
A Branching Tree
This branching tree shows how scientists now think that raccoons, lesser pandas, giant pandas, and bears are related.
Interpreting Diagrams *Are giant pandas more closely related to lesser pandas or to bears?*

Sometimes, however, scientists have changed their hypotheses about species relationships. For example, lesser pandas were once thought to be closely related to giant pandas. Recently, however, DNA analysis and other methods have shown that giant pandas and lesser pandas are not closely related. Instead, giant pandas are more closely related to bears, while lesser pandas are more closely related to raccoons.

Branching Trees Scientists use the combined evidence of species relationships to draw branching trees. A **branching tree** is a diagram that shows how scientists think different groups of organisms are related. Figure 11 shows how raccoons, lesser pandas, giant pandas, and bears may be related.

 **Reading Checkpoint** **What is a branching tree?**

How Do New Species Form?

Natural selection explains how variations can lead to changes in a species. But how could an entirely new species form? **A new species can form when a group of individuals remains isolated from the rest of its species long enough to evolve different traits.** Isolation, or complete separation, occurs when some members of a species become cut off from the rest of the species. Group members may be separated by such things as a river, a volcano, or a mountain range.

Abert's squirrel and the Kaibab squirrel both live in forests in the Southwest. As you can see in Figure 12, the populations of the two kinds of squirrel are separated by the Grand Canyon. The Kaibab and Abert's squirrels belong to the same species, but they have slightly different characteristics. For example, the Kaibab squirrel has a black belly, while Abert's squirrel has a white belly. It is possible that one day Abert's squirrel and the Kaibab squirrel will become so different from each other that they will be separate species.

Kaibab squirrel ▼

Abert's squirrel ▼

FIGURE 12
Kaibab and Abert's Squirrels
These two kinds of squirrels have been isolated from one another for a long time. Eventually, this isolation may result in two different species.

Section 2 Assessment

Target Reading Skill

Identifying Supporting Evidence Refer to your graphic organizer about the theory of evolution as you answer Question 1 below.

Reviewing Key Concepts

1. a. Listing List three kinds of evidence that support the theory of evolution.
   b. Comparing and Contrasting What major difference have scientists discovered between today's whales and the fossils of whales' ancient ancestors?
   c. Drawing Conclusions How does this difference show that whales and animals with four legs are probably descended from a common ancestor?
2. a. Identifying When scientists try to determine how closely related species are, what evidence do they examine?
   b. Inferring Of the kinds of evidence you listed above, which are probably the most reliable? Explain your answer.

   c. Applying Concepts Insects and birds both have wings. What kinds of evidence might show whether or not insects and birds are closely related? Explain your answer.
3. a. Reviewing How can isolation lead to the formation of new species?
   b. Predicting A species of snake lives in a forest. A new road separates one group of the snakes from another. Is it likely that these two groups of snakes will become separate species? Why or why not?

Writing in Science

Explaining a Branching Tree Suppose the branching tree in Figure 11 is part of a museum exhibit. Write an explanation of the branching tree for museum visitors. Describe the relationships shown on the tree and identify evidence supporting the relationships.

Telltale Molecules

Problem

What information can protein structure reveal about evolutionary relationships among organisms?

Skills Focus

interpreting data, drawing conclusions

Procedure

1. Examine the table below. It shows the sequence of amino acids in one region of a protein, cytochrome c, for six different animals.

2. Predict which of the five other animals is most closely related to the horse. Which animal do you think is most distantly related?

3. Compare the amino acid sequence of the horse to that of the donkey. How many amino acids differ between the two species? Record that number in your notebook.

4. Compare the amino acid sequences of each of the other animals to that of the horse. Record the number of differences in your notebook.

Analyze and Conclude

1. **Interpreting Data** Which animal's amino acid sequence was most similar to that of the horse? What similarities and difference(s) did you observe?

2. **Drawing Conclusions** Based on these data, which species is most closely related to the horse? Which is most distantly related?

3. **Interpreting Data** For the entire protein, the horse's amino acid sequence differs from the other animals' as follows: donkey, 1 difference; rabbit, 6; snake, 22; turtle, 11; and whale, 5. How do the relationships indicated by the entire protein compare with those for the region you examined?

4. **Communicating** Write a paragraph explaining why data about amino acid sequences can provide information about evolutionary relationships among organisms.

More to Explore

Use the amino acid data to construct a branching tree that includes horses, donkeys, and snakes. The tree should show one way that the three species could have evolved from a common ancestor.

	Section of Cytochrome c Protein in Animals														
Animal	**Amino Acid Position**														
	39	**40**	**41**	**42**	**43**	**44**	**45**	**46**	**47**	**48**	**49**	**50**	**51**	**52**	**53**
Horse	A	B	C	D	E	F	G	H	I	J	K	L	M	N	O
Donkey	A	B	C	D	E	F	G	H	Z	J	K	L	M	N	O
Rabbit	A	B	C	D	E	Y	G	H	Z	J	K	L	M	N	O
Snake	A	B	C	D	E	Y	G	H	Z	J	K	W	M	N	O
Turtle	A	B	C	D	E	V	G	H	Z	J	K	U	M	N	O
Whale	A	B	C	D	E	Y	G	H	Z	J	K	L	M	N	O

The Fossil Record

Reading Preview

Key Concepts
- How do most fossils form?
- How can scientists determine a fossil's age?
- What is the Geologic Time Scale?
- What are some unanswered questions about evolution?

Key Terms
- petrified fossil
- mold
- cast
- relative dating
- radioactive dating
- radioactive element
- half-life
- fossil record
- extinct
- gradualism
- punctuated equilibria

Target Reading Skill
Building Vocabulary After you read the section, write a definition of each Key Term in your own words.

Lab zone Discover **Activity**

What Can You Learn From Fossils?

1. Look at the fossil in the photograph. Describe the fossil's characteristics in as much detail as you can.
2. From your description in Step 1, try to figure out how the organism lived. How did it move? Where did it live?

Think It Over
Inferring What type of present-day organism do you think is related to the fossil? Why?

The fossil dinosaur below has been nicknamed "Sue." If fossils could talk, Sue might say something like this: "I don't mind that museum visitors call me 'Sue,' but I do get annoyed when they refer to me as 'that old fossil.' I'm a 67-million-year old *Tyrannosaurus rex*, and I should get some respect. I was fearsome. My skull is one and a half meters long, and my longest tooth is more than 30 centimeters. Ah, the stories I could tell! But I'll have to let my bones speak for themselves. Scientists can learn a lot from studying fossils like me."

Of course, fossils can't really talk or think. But fossils such as Sue reveal life's history.

FIGURE 13 Dinosaur Fossil
The dinosaur nicknamed "Sue" was discovered in 1990 in South Dakota. Sue is now in the Field Museum in Chicago.

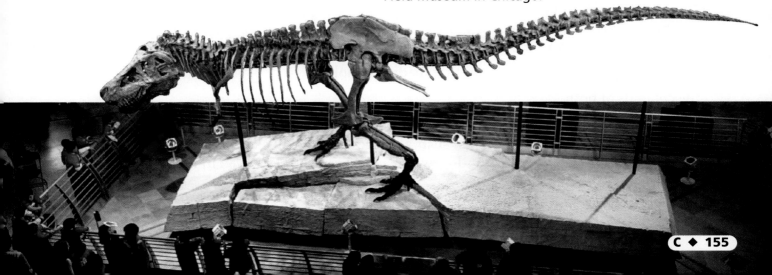

An ancient crocodile dies and sinks to the bottom of a river.

Layers of sediments cover the crocodile's body.

FIGURE 14
Fossil Formation
Most fossils, such as the fossil crocodile shown here, form in sedimentary rock. *Relating Cause and Effect In the process of fossil formation, what materials replace the crocodile's remains?*

How Do Fossils Form?

The formation of any fossil is a rare event. Usually only the hard parts of the organism, such as the bones or shells of animals, form fossils. **Most fossils form when organisms that die become buried in sediments.** Sediments are particles of soil and rock. When a river flows into a lake or ocean, the sediments that the river carries settle to the bottom. Layers of sediments may cover the dead organisms. Over millions of years, the layers may harden to become sedimentary rock. Figure 14 shows how a fossil can form.

Petrified Fossils Some remains that become buried in sediments are actually changed to rock. Minerals dissolved in the water soak into the buried remains. Gradually, the minerals replace the remains, changing them into rock. Fossils that form in this way are called **petrified fossils.**

Molds and Casts Sometimes shells or other hard parts buried by sediments gradually dissolve. An empty space remains in the place that the hard part once occupied. A hollow space in sediment in the shape of an organism or part of an organism is called a **mold.** A mold may become filled with hardened minerals, forming a cast. A **cast** is a copy of the shape of the organism that made the mold.

Preserved Remains Organisms can also be preserved in substances other than sediments. For example, entire organisms, such as huge elephant-like mammoths that lived thousands of years ago, have been preserved in ice.

 **Reading Checkpoint** What is the difference between a mold and a cast?

Lab zone Try This **Activity**

Preservation in Ice
1. Place fresh fruit, such as apple slices, strawberries, and blueberries, in an open plastic container.
2. Completely cover the fruit with water. Put the container in a freezer.
3. Place the same type and amount of fresh fruit in another open container. Leave it somewhere where no one will disturb it.
4. After three days, observe the contents of both containers.

Inferring Use your observations to explain why fossils preserved in ice can include soft, fleshy body parts.

Over millions of years, the sediments harden to become rock. The crocodile is preserved as a fossil.

The rock erodes. The fossil is exposed on the surface of a rock.

Go Online
active art

For: Fossil Formation activity
Visit: PHSchool.com
Web Code: cep-3053

Determining a Fossil's Age

To understand how living things have changed through time, scientists need to be able to determine the ages of fossils. They can then determine the order in which past events occurred. This information can be used to reconstruct the history of life on Earth.

For example, suppose a scientist is studying two fossils of ancient snails, Snail A and Snail B. The fossils are similar, but they are different enough that they are not the same species. Perhaps, the scientist hypothesizes, Snail A's species changed over time and eventually gave rise to Snail B's species. To help determine whether this hypothesis could be valid, the scientist must first learn which fossil—A or B—is older. **Scientists can determine a fossil's age in two ways: relative dating and radioactive dating.**

Relative Dating Scientists use **relative dating** to determine which of two fossils is older. To understand how relative dating works, imagine that a river has cut down through layers of sedimentary rock to form a canyon. If you look at the canyon walls, you can see the layers of sedimentary rock piled up one on top of another. The layers near the top of the canyon were formed most recently. These layers are the youngest rock layers. The lower down the canyon wall you go, the older the layers are. Therefore, fossils found in layers near the top of the canyon are younger than fossils found near the bottom of the canyon.

Relative dating can only be used when the rock layers have been preserved in their original sequence. Relative dating can help scientists determine whether one fossil is older than another. However, relative dating does not tell scientists the fossil's actual age.

Radioactive Decay

The half-life of potassium-40, a radioactive element, is 1.3 billion years. This means that half of the potassium-40 in a sample will break down into argon-40 every 1.3 billion years. The graph shows the breakdown of a 1-gram sample of potassium-40 into argon-40 over billions of years.

1. **Reading Graphs** What does the red line represent? What does the blue line represent?

2. **Reading Graphs** At 2.6 billion years ago, how much of the sample consisted of potassium 40? How much of the sample consisted of argon-40?

3. **Reading Graphs** At what point in time do the two graph lines cross?

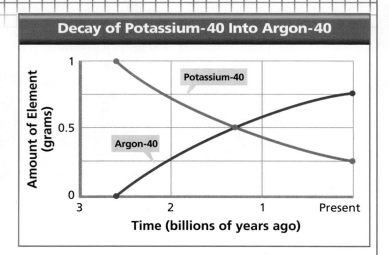

Decay of Potassium-40 Into Argon-40

4. **Interpreting Data** At the point where the graph lines cross, how much of the sample consisted of potassium-40? How much consisted of argon-40? Explain why this is the case.

Radioactive Dating A technique called **radioactive dating** allows scientists to determine the actual age of fossils. The rocks that fossils are found near contain **radioactive elements,** which are unstable elements that decay, or break down, into different elements. The **half-life** of a radioactive element is the time it takes for half of the atoms in a sample to decay. The graph in Analyzing Data shows how a sample of potassium-40, a radioactive element, breaks down into argon-40 over time.

Scientists can compare the amount of a radioactive element in a sample to the amount of the element into which it breaks down. This information can be used to calculate the age of the rock, and thus the age of the fossil.

 **What is a half-life?**

What Do Fossils Reveal?

Like pieces in a jigsaw puzzle, fossils can help scientists piece together information about Earth's past. From the fossil record, scientists have learned information about the history of life on Earth. The millions of fossils that scientists have collected are called the **fossil record.**

Extinct Organisms Almost all of the species preserved as fossils are now extinct. A species is **extinct** if no members of that species are still alive. Most of what scientists know about extinct species is based on the fossil record.

The Geologic Time Scale The fossil record provides clues about how and when new groups of organisms evolved. Using radioactive dating, scientists have calculated the ages of many different fossils and rocks. From this information, scientists have created a "calendar" of Earth's history that spans more than 4.6 billion years. Scientists have divided this large time span into smaller units called eras and periods. **This calendar of Earth's history is sometimes called the Geologic Time Scale.**

The largest span of time in the Geologic Time Scale is Precambrian Time, also called the Precambrian (pree KAM bree un). It covers the first 4 billion years of Earth's history. Scientists know very little about the Precambrian because there are few fossils from these ancient times. After the Precambrian, the Geologic Time Scale is divided into three major blocks of time, or eras. Each era is further divided into shorter periods. In Figure 16 on the next two pages, you can see the events that occurred during each time period.

 Reading Checkpoint) **What is the largest span in the Geologic Time Scale?**

FIGURE 15
Earth's History as a Clock
Fossils found in rock layers tell the history of life on Earth. The history of life can be compared to 12 hours on a clock.
Interpreting Diagrams *At what time on a 12-hour time scale did plants appear on land?*

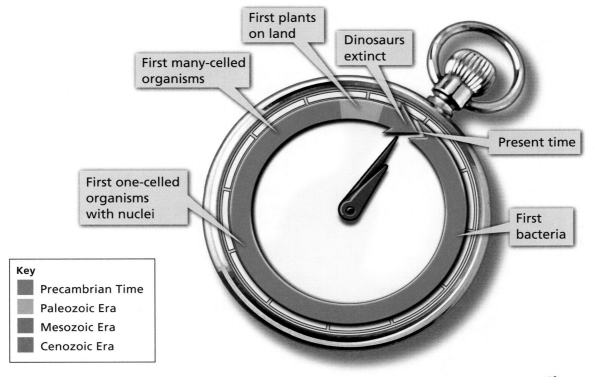

First plants on land

Dinosaurs extinct

First many-celled organisms

Present time

First one-celled organisms with nuclei

First bacteria

Key
- Precambrian Time
- Paleozoic Era
- Mesozoic Era
- Cenozoic Era

FIGURE 16
The Geologic Time Scale

Sequencing *Which organisms appeared first—amphibians or fishes?*

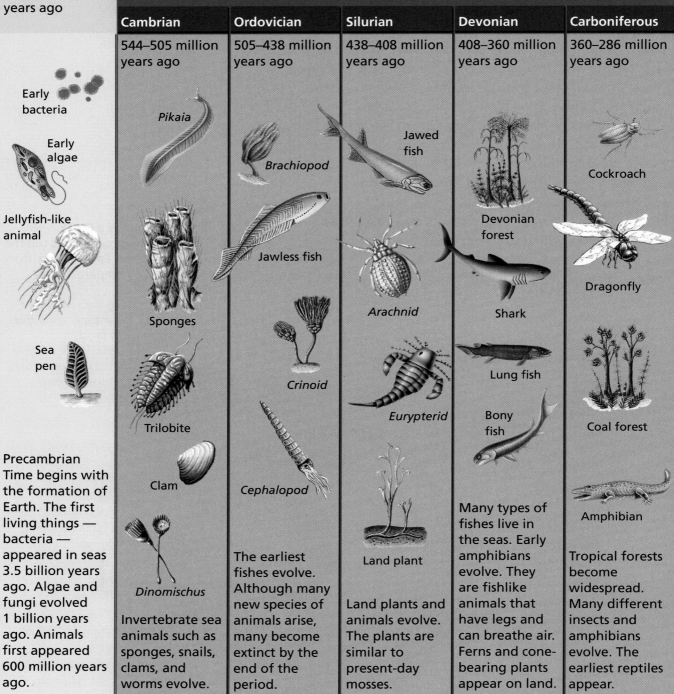

Precambrian Time
4.6 billion–544 million years ago

Early bacteria

Early algae

Jellyfish-like animal

Sea pen

Precambrian Time begins with the formation of Earth. The first living things — bacteria — appeared in seas 3.5 billion years ago. Algae and fungi evolved 1 billion years ago. Animals first appeared 600 million years ago.

Paleozoic Era
544–245 million years ago

Cambrian
544–505 million years ago

Pikaia

Sponges

Trilobite

Clam

Dinomischus

Invertebrate sea animals such as sponges, snails, clams, and worms evolve.

Ordovician
505–438 million years ago

Brachiopod

Jawless fish

Crinoid

Cephalopod

The earliest fishes evolve. Although many new species of animals arise, many become extinct by the end of the period.

Silurian
438–408 million years ago

Jawed fish

Arachnid

Eurypterid

Land plant

Land plants and animals evolve. The plants are similar to present-day mosses.

Devonian
408–360 million years ago

Devonian forest

Shark

Lung fish

Bony fish

Many types of fishes live in the seas. Early amphibians evolve. They are fishlike animals that have legs and can breathe air. Ferns and cone-bearing plants appear on land.

Carboniferous
360–286 million years ago

Cockroach

Dragonfly

Coal forest

Amphibian

Tropical forests become widespread. Many different insects and amphibians evolve. The earliest reptiles appear.

Mesozoic Era
245–66 million years ago

Cenozoic Era
66 million years ago to the present

Permian	Triassic	Jurassic	Cretaceous	Tertiary	Quaternary
286–245 million years ago	245–208 million years ago	208–144 million years ago	144–66 million years ago	66–1.8 million years ago	1.8 million years ago to the present

Conifer

Dimetrodon

Dicynodon

Cycad

Early mammal

Coelophysis

Morganucodon

Diplodocus

Archaeopteryx

Triceratops

Magnolia

Tyrannosaurus rex

Creodont

Uintatherium

Plesiadapis

Hyracotherium

Saber-toothed cat

Megatherium

Homo sapiens

Permian	Triassic	Jurassic	Cretaceous	Tertiary	Quaternary
Seed plants, insects, and reptiles become common. Reptile-like mammals appear. At the end of the period, most sea animals and amphibians become extinct.	The first dinosaurs evolve. First turtles and crocodiles appear. Mammals first appear. Cone-bearing trees and palmlike trees dominate forests.	Large dinosaurs roam the world. The first birds appear. Mammals become more common and varied.	The first flowering plants appear. At the end of the period, a mass extinction causes the disappearance of many organisms, including the dinosaurs.	New groups of animals, including the first monkeys and apes, appear. Flowering plants become the most common kinds of plants. First grasses appear.	Mammals, flowering plants, and insects dominate land. Humans appear. Later in the period, many large mammals, including mammoths, become extinct.

FIGURE 17
Mass Extinctions

An asteroid may have caused the mass extinction that occurred about 65 million years ago.
Relating Cause and Effect How could an asteroid have caused climate change?

▲ An asteroid zooms toward Earth.

Unanswered Questions

The fossil record has provided scientists with a lot of important information about past life on Earth. The fossil record, however, is incomplete, because most organisms died without leaving fossils behind. These gaps in the fossil record leave many questions unanswered. **Two unanswered questions about evolution involve the causes of mass extinctions and the rate at which evolution occurs.**

Mass Extinctions When many types of organisms become extinct at the same time, a mass extinction has occurred. Several mass extinctions have taken place during the history of life. One mass extinction, for example, occurred at the end of the Cretaceous Period, about 65 million years ago. During the Cretaceous mass extinction, many kinds of plants and animals, including the dinosaurs, disappeared forever.

Scientists are not sure what causes mass extinctions, but they hypothesize that major climate changes may be responsible. For example, a climate change may have caused the mass extinction at the end of the Cretaceous Period. An asteroid, which is a rocky mass from space, may have hit Earth, throwing huge clouds of dust and other materials into the air. The dust clouds would have blocked sunlight, making the climate cooler, and killing plants. If there were fewer plants, many animals would have starved. Some scientists, however, think volcanic eruptions, not an asteroid, caused the climate change.

The asteroid ▲
hits Earth.

▼ **Many plants and animals die.**

Gradualism Scientists also are not sure how rapidly species change. One theory, called **gradualism,** proposes that evolution occurs slowly but steadily. According to this theory, tiny changes in a species gradually add up to major changes over very long periods of time. This is how Darwin thought evolution occurred.

If the theory of gradualism is correct, the fossil record should include intermediate forms between a fossil organism and its descendants. However, there are often long periods of time in which fossils show little or no change. Then, quite suddenly, fossils appear that are distinctly different. One possible explanation for the lack of intermediate forms is that the fossil record is incomplete. Scientists may eventually find more fossils to fill the gaps.

Punctuated Equilibria A theory that accounts for the gaps in the fossil record is called **punctuated equilibria.** According to this theory, species evolve quickly during relatively short periods. These periods of rapid change are separated by long periods of little or no change. Today most scientists think that evolution can occur gradually at some times and more rapidly at others.

FIGURE 18
Trilobite
Trilobites were once common in Earth's oceans, but they were destroyed in a mass extinction.

 **Reading Checkpoint** **What theory proposes that evolution occurs slowly but steadily?**

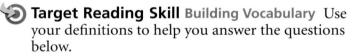

Section 3 Assessment

 **Target Reading Skill** Building Vocabulary Use your definitions to help you answer the questions below.

Reviewing Key Concepts

1. a. **Reviewing** What are sediments? How are they involved in the formation of fossils?
   b. **Classifying** Identify the types of fossils.
   c. **Comparing and Contrasting** Which of the major types of fossils do not form in sediments? Describe how this type can form.
2. a. **Identifying** What are the two methods of determining a fossil's age?
   b. **Describing** Describe each method.
   c. **Applying Concepts** Some fossil organisms are frozen rather than preserved in sediment. Which method of dating would you use with frozen fossils? Why?
3. a. **Defining** What is the Geologic Time Scale? Into what smaller units is it divided?
   b. **Interpreting Diagrams** Look at Figure 16. Did the organisms during Precambrian Time have hard body parts?
   c. **Relating Cause and Effect** Give one reason why there are few Precambrian fossils.
4. a. **Reviewing** What are two unanswered questions about evolution?
   b. **Comparing and Contrasting** How are the theories of gradualism and punctuated equilibria different? How are they similar?

Lab zone **At-Home Activity**

Modeling Fossil Formation With an adult family member, spread some mud in a shallow pan. Use your fingertips to make "footprints" across the mud. Let the mud dry and harden. Explain how this is similar to fossil formation.

① Darwin's Theory

Key Concepts

- Darwin's important observations included the diversity of living things, the remains of ancient organisms, and the characteristics of organisms on the Galápagos Islands.

- Darwin reasoned that plants or animals that arrived on the Galápagos Islands faced conditions that were different from those on the mainland. Perhaps, Darwin hypothesized, the species gradually changed over many generations and became better adapted to the new conditions.

- Darwin proposed that, over a long period of time, natural selection can lead to change. Helpful variations may gradually accumulate in a species, while unfavorable ones may disappear.

Key Terms

species
fossil
adaptation
evolution
scientific theory
natural selection
variation

② Evidence of Evolution

Key Concepts

- Fossils, patterns of early development, and similar body structures all provide evidence that organisms have changed over time.

- Scientists have combined the evidence from DNA, protein structure, fossils, early development, and body structure to determine the evolutionary relationships among species.

- A new species can form when a group of individuals remains separated from the rest of its species long enough to evolve different traits.

Key Terms

homologous structures
branching tree

③ The Fossil Record

Key Concepts

- Most fossils form when organisms that die become buried in sediments.

- Scientists can determine a fossil's age in two ways: relative dating and radioactive dating.

- The calendar of Earth's history is sometimes called the Geologic Time Scale.

- Two unanswered questions about evolution involve mass extinctions and the rate at which evolution occurs.

Key Terms

petrified fossil
mold
cast
relative dating
radioactive dating
radioactive element
half-life
fossil record
extinct
gradualism
punctuated equilibria

Review and Assessment

Go Online
PHSchool.com

For: Self-Assessment
Visit: PHSchool.com
Web Code: cea-3050

Organizing Information

Sequencing Copy the flowchart about fossil formation onto a separate sheet of paper. Complete the flowchart by writing a sentence describing each stage in the process of fossil formation. Then add a title. (For more on Sequencing, see the Skills Handbook.)

An organism dies in water.

a. _____ ?

b. _____ ?

c. _____ ?

Reviewing Key Terms

Choose the letter of the best answer.

1. Changes in a species over long periods of time are called
   a. half-life.
   b. evolution.
   c. homologous structures.
   d. developmental stages.

2. A trait that helps an organism survive and reproduce is called a(n)
   a. variation.
   b. adaptation.
   c. species.
   d. selection.

3. Similar structures that related species have inherited from a common ancestor are called
   a. adaptations.
   b. punctuated equilibria.
   c. ancestral structures.
   d. homologous structures.

4. Fossils formed when an organism dissolves and leaves an empty space in a rock are called
   a. casts.
   b. mold.
   c. preserved remains.
   d. petrified fossils.

5. The rate of decay of a radioactive element is measured by its
   a. year.
   b. era.
   c. period.
   d. half-life.

If the statement is true, write _true_. If it is false, change the underlined word or words to make the statement true.

6. Darwin's idea about how evolution occurs is called <u>natural selection</u>.

7. Most members of a species show differences, or <u>variations</u>.

8. A diagram that shows how organisms might be related is called <u>gradualism</u>.

9. The technique of <u>relative dating</u> can be used to determine the actual age of a fossil.

10. According to the theory of <u>punctuated equilibria</u>, evolution occurs slowly but steadily.

Writing in Science

Notebook Entry Imagine that you are a biologist exploring the Galápagos Islands. Write a notebook entry on one of the unusual species you have found on the islands. Include a description of how it is adapted to its environment.

DISCOVERY
CHANNEL
SCHOOL™

Changes Over Time
Video Preview
Video Field Trip
▶ Video Assessment

Review and Assessment

Checking Concepts

11. What role does the overproduction of organisms play in natural selection?

12. Use an example to explain how natural selection can lead to evolution.

13. Explain how geographic isolation can result in the formation of a new species.

14. On the basis of similar body structures, scientists hypothesize that two species are closely related. What other evidence would the scientists look for to support their hypothesis?

15. Explain why similarities in the early development of different species suggest that the species are related.

16. What is meant by *extinct?* How do scientists obtain information about extinct species?

17. What are mass extinctions? What may cause mass extinction?

Thinking Critically

18. **Relating Cause and Effect** Why did Darwin's visit to the Galápagos Islands have such an important influence on his development of the theory of evolution?

19. **Applying Concepts** Some insects look just like sticks. How could this be an advantage to the insects? How could this trait have evolved through natural selection?

20. **Predicting** Which of the organisms shown below is least likely to become a fossil? Explain your answer.

Snail   Dandelion   Squirrel

21. **Making Judgments** What type of evidence is the best indicator of how closely two species are related? Explain your anwer.

22. **Comparing and Contrasting** How are selective breeding and natural selection similar? How are they different?

Applying Skills

Use the data in the table below to answer Questions 23–25.

Radioactive carbon-14 decays to nitrogen with a half-life of 5,730 years. The table contains information about the amounts of carbon-14 and nitrogen in three fossils. The table also gives information about the position of each fossil in rock layers.

Fossil	Amount of Carbon-14 in Fossil	Amount of Nitrogen in Fossil	Position of Fossil in Rock Layers
A	1 gram	7 grams	Bottom layer
B	4 grams	4 grams	Top layer
C	2 grams	6 grams	Middle layer

23. **Inferring** Use the positions of the fossils in the rock layers to put the fossils in their probable order from the youngest to the oldest.

24. **Calculating** Calculate the age of each fossil using the data about carbon-14 and nitrogen.

25. **Drawing Conclusions** Do your answers to Questions 23 and 24 agree or disagree with each other? Explain.

Lab zone Chapter **Project**

Performance Assessment Complete both your timelines. Display your completed timelines for the class. Be prepared to explain why you chose the scale that you did. Also, describe how your timelines are related to each other.

Standardized Test Prep

Choose the letter of the best answer.

1. The process by which individuals that are better adapted to their environment are more likely to survive and reproduce than other members of the same species is called
   A natural selection.
   B evolution.
   C competition.
   D overproduction.

2. Which of the following is the best example of an adaptation that helps an organism survive in its environment?
   F green coloring in a lizard living on gray rocks
   G a thick coat of fur on an animal that lives in the desert
   H extensive root system in a desert plant
   J thin, delicate leaves on a plant in a cold climate

3. Which of the following is the weakest evidence supporting a close evolutionary relationship between two animals?
   A The bones of a bird's wings are similar to the bones of a dog's legs.
   B Human embryos look like turtle embryos in their early development.
   C Lesser pandas look like bears.
   D The amino acid sequence in mouse hemoglobin is similar to the amino acid sequence in chimpanzee hemoglobin.

Use the diagram below and your knowledge of science to answer Questions 4–5.

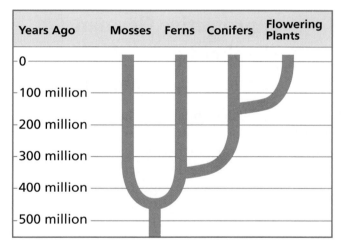

4. About how long ago did mosses first appear?
   F 100 million years ago
   G 150 million years ago
   H 350 million years ago
   J 450 million years ago

5. Which group of plants would have DNA that is most similar to the DNA of flowering plants?
   A mosses
   B ferns
   C conifers
   D They would all be equally alike.

Constructed Response

6. Relative dating and radioactive dating are two methods for determining the age of a fossil. Compare and contrast these two methods.

Egyptian Art
More than 3,000 years ago, an artist drew three dogs chasing a hyena.

Dogs— Loyal Companions

What's your image of a dog?

- **A powerful Great Dane?**
- **A tiny, lively Chihuahua?**
- **A protective German shepherd guide dog?**
- **A friendly, lovable mutt?**

Most dogs are descendants of the gray wolf, which was originally found throughout Europe, Asia, and North America. Dogs were the first animals to be domesticated, or tamed. As far back as 9,000 years ago, farmers who raised sheep, cattle, and goats tamed dogs to herd and guard the livestock.

After taming dogs, people began to breed them for traits that people valued. Early herding dogs helped shepherds. Speedy hunting dogs learned to chase deer and other game. Strong, sturdy working dogs pulled sleds and even rescued people. Small, quick terriers hunted animals, such as rats. "Toy" dogs were companions to people of wealth and leisure. More recently, sporting dogs were trained to flush out and retrieve birds. Still others were bred to be guard dogs. But perhaps the real reasons people bred dogs were for loyalty and companionship.

Girl with dalmatian

From Wolf to Purebred

About 10,000 years ago, some wolves may have been attracted to human settlements. They may have found it easier to feed on food scraps than to hunt for themselves. Gradually the wolves came to depend on people for food. The wolves, in turn, kept the campsites clean and safe. They ate the garbage and barked to warn of approaching strangers. These wolves were the ancestors of the dogs you know today.

Over time, dogs became more and more a part of human society. People began to breed dogs for the traits needed for tasks such as herding sheep and hunting. Large, aggressive dogs, for example, were bred to be herding dogs, while fast dogs with a keen sense of smell were bred to be hunting dogs. Today, there are hundreds of breeds. They range from the tiny Chihuahua to the massive Saint Bernard, one of which can weigh as much as 50 Chihuahuas.

Today, people breed dogs mostly for their appearance and personality. Physical features such as long ears or a narrow snout are valued in particular breeds of dogs. To create "pure" breeds of dogs, breeders use a method known as inbreeding. Inbreeding involves mating dogs that are genetically very similar. Inbreeding is the surest way to produce dogs with a uniform physical appearance.

One undesirable result of inbreeding is an increase in genetic disorders. Experts estimate that 25 percent of all purebred dogs have a genetic disorder. Dalmatians, for example, often inherit deafness. German shepherds may develop severe hip problems. Mixed-breed dogs, in contrast, are less likely to inherit genetic disorders.

Fur Color in Retrievers
In Labrador retrievers, the allele for dark-colored fur is dominant over the allele for yellow fur.

Science Activity

Most traits that dogs are bred for are controlled by more than one gene. A few traits, however, show simpler inheritance patterns. For example, in Labrador retrievers, a single gene with one dominant and one recessive allele determines whether the dog's fur will be dark or yellow. The allele for dark fur (D) is dominant over the allele for yellow fur (d).

- Construct a Punnett square for a cross between two Labrador retrievers that are both heterozygous for dark fur (Dd).

- Suppose there were eight puppies in the litter. Predict how many would have dark fur and how many would have yellow fur.

- Construct a second Punnett square for a cross between a Labrador retriever with yellow fur (dd) and one with dark fur (Dd). In a litter with six puppies, predict how many would have dark fur and how many would have yellow fur.

Dogs and People

Over thousands of years, people have developed many different breeds of dogs. Each of the dogs shown on the map was bred for a purpose—hunting, herding, guarding, pulling sleds—as well as companionship. Every breed has its own story.

Border Collie
Great Britain, after A.D. 1100
This breed was developed in the counties near the border between England and Scotland for herding sheep. The border collie's ancestors were crossbreeds of local sheepdogs and dogs brought to Scotland by the Vikings.

Russia

Dachshund
Germany, A.D. 1600s
These dogs were bred to catch badgers or rats. Their short legs and long body can fit into a badger's burrow. In fact, in German the word *Dachshund* means "badger dog."

EUROPE

Golden Retriever
Great Britain, A.D. 1870s
Lord Tweedmouth developed this breed to help hunters retrieve waterfowl and other small animals.

Basset Hound
France, A.D. 1500s
Second only to the bloodhound at following a scent, the basset hound has short legs and a compact body that help it run through underbrush.

AFRICA

Greyhound
Egypt, 3000 B.C.
These speedy, slender hounds were bred for chasing prey. Today, greyhounds are famous as racers.

Siberian Husky
Siberia, 1000 B.C.
The Chukchi people of northeastern Siberia used these strong working dogs to pull sleds long distances across the snow.

Pekingese
China, A.D. 700s
These lapdogs were bred as pets in ancient China. One Chinese name for a Pekingese means "lion dog," which refers to the dog's long, golden mane.

Chow Chow
China, 150 B.C.
Chow chows, the working dogs of ancient China, worked as hunters, herders, and guard dogs.

China

Japan

Akita
Japan, A.D. 1600s
This breed was developed in the cold mountains of northern Japan as a guard dog and hunting dog. The Akita is able to hunt in deep snow and is also a powerful swimmer.

Lhasa Apso
Tibet, A.D. 1100
This breed has a long, thick coat that protects it from the cold air of the high Tibetan plateau. In spite of its small size, the Lhasa apso guarded homes and temples.

Social Studies Activity

Draw a timeline that shows the approximate date of origin of different breeds of domestic dogs from 3000 B.C. to the present. Use the information on the map to fill out your timeline. Include information about where each breed was developed.

Picking a Puppy

People look for different traits in the dogs they choose. Here is how one expert selected his dog based on good breeding and personality.

James Herriot, a country veterinarian in Yorkshire, England, had owned several dogs during his lifetime. But he had always wanted a Border terrier. These small, sturdy dogs are descendants of working terrier breeds that lived on the border of England and Scotland. For centuries they were used to hunt foxes, rats, and other small animals. In this story, Herriot and his wife, Helen, follow up on an advertisement for Border terrier puppies.

James Herriot
In several popular books published in the 1970s and 1980s, James Herriot wrote warm, humorous stories about the animals he cared for.

◀ **Border terriers**

She [Helen, his wife] turned to me and spoke agitatedly, "I've got Mrs. Mason on the line now. There's only one pup left out of the litter and there are people coming from as far as eighty miles away to see it. We'll have to hurry. What a long time you've been out there!"

We bolted our lunch and Helen, Rosie, granddaughter Emma and I drove out to Bedale. Mrs. Mason led us into the kitchen and pointed to a tiny brindle creature twisting and writhing under the table.

"That's him," she said.

I reached down and lifted the puppy as he curled his little body round, apparently trying to touch his tail with his nose. But that tail wagged furiously and the pink tongue was busy at my hand. I knew he was ours before my quick examination for hernia and overshot jaw.

The deal was quickly struck and we went outside to inspect the puppy's relations. His mother and grandmother were out there.

They lived in little barrels which served as kennels and both of them darted out and stood up at our legs, tails lashing, mouths panting in delight. I felt vastly reassured. With happy, healthy ancestors like those I knew we had every chance of a first rate dog.

As we drove home with the puppy in Emma's arms, the warm thought came to me. The wheel had indeed turned. After nearly fifty years I had my Border terrier.

Language Arts Activity

James Herriot describes this scene using dialog and first-person narrative. The narrative describes Herriot's feelings about a memorable event—finally finding the dog he had wanted for so long. Write a first-person narrative describing a memorable event in your life. You might choose a childhood memory or a personal achievement at school. What emotions did you feel? How did you make your decision? If possible, use dialog in your writing.

Popular Breeds

The popularity of different breeds of dogs changes over time. For example, the line graph shows how the number of poodles registered with the American Kennel Club changed between 1970 and 2000.

Standard poodle and puppy ▶

Math Activity

Use the table below to create your own line graph for Labrador retrievers and cocker spaniels. Which breed was more popular in 1980, Labrador retrievers or cocker spaniels?

How has the number of Labrador retrievers changed from 1970 to 2000? How has the number of cocker spaniels changed over the same time?

Dog Populations				
Breed	**1970**	**1980**	**1990**	**2000**
Poodle	265,879	92,250	71,757	45,868
Labrador Retriever	25,667	52,398	95,768	172,841
Cocker Spaniel	21,811	76,113	105,642	29,393

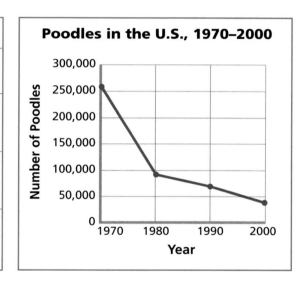

Poodles in the U.S., 1970–2000

Tie It Together

Best-of-Breed Show

In many places, proud dog owners of all ages bring their animals to compete in dog shows.

Organize your own dog show.

With a partner, choose one specific breed of dog. Pick a breed shown on the map on pages 170–171, or use library resources to research another breed.

- Find out what the breed looks like, the time and place where it originated, and what traits it was first bred for.

- List your breed's characteristics, height, weight, and coloring.

- Research the breed's personality and behavior.

- Find out your breed's strengths. Learn what weaknesses may develop as a result of inbreeding.

- Make a poster for your breed. Include a drawing or photo and the information that you researched.

- With your class, organize the dog displays into categories of breeds, such as hunting dogs, herding dogs, and toy dogs.

Think Like a Scientist

Scientists have a particular way of looking at the world, or scientific habits of mind. Whenever you ask a question and explore possible answers, you use many of the same skills that scientists do. Some of these skills are described on this page.

Observing

When you use one or more of your five senses to gather information about the world, you are **observing.** Hearing a dog bark, counting twelve green seeds, and smelling smoke are all observations. To increase the power of their senses, scientists sometimes use microscopes, telescopes, or other instruments that help them make more detailed observations.

An observation must be an accurate report of what your senses detect. It is important to keep careful records of your observations in science class by writing or drawing in a notebook. The information collected through observations is called evidence, or data.

Inferring

When you interpret an observation, you are **inferring,** or making an inference. For example, if you hear your dog barking, you may infer that someone is at your front door. To make this inference, you combine the evidence— the barking dog—and your experience or knowledge—you know that your dog barks when strangers approach—to reach a logical conclusion.

Notice that an inference is not a fact; it is only one of many possible interpretations for an observation. For example, your dog may be barking because it wants to go for a walk. An inference may turn out to be incorrect even if it is based on accurate observations and logical reasoning. The only way to find out if an inference is correct is to investigate further.

Predicting

When you listen to the weather forecast, you hear many predictions about the next day's weather—what the temperature will be, whether it will rain, and how windy it will be. Weather forecasters use observations and knowledge of weather patterns to predict the weather. The skill of **predicting** involves making an inference about a future event based on current evidence or past experience.

Because a prediction is an inference, it may prove to be false. In science class, you can test some of your predictions by doing experiments. For example, suppose you predict that larger paper airplanes can fly farther than smaller airplanes. How could you test your prediction?

Activity

Use the photograph to answer the questions below.

Observing Look closely at the photograph. List at least three observations.

Inferring Use your observations to make an inference about what has happened. What experience or knowledge did you use to make the inference?

Predicting Predict what will happen next. On what evidence or experience do you base your prediction?

Classifying

Could you imagine searching for a book in the library if the books were shelved in no particular order? Your trip to the library would be an all-day event! Luckily, librarians group together books on similar topics or by the same author. Grouping together items that are alike in some way is called **classifying.** You can classify items in many ways: by size, by shape, by use, and by other important characteristics.

Like librarians, scientists use the skill of classifying to organize information and objects. When things are sorted into groups, the relationships among them become easier to understand.

Activity

Classify the objects in the photograph into two groups based on any characteristic you choose. Then use another characteristic to classify the objects into three groups.

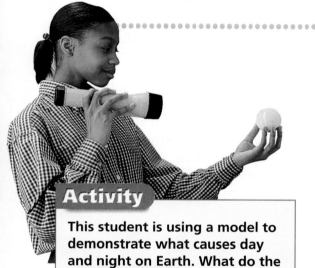

Activity

This student is using a model to demonstrate what causes day and night on Earth. What do the flashlight and the tennis ball in the model represent?

Making Models

Have you ever drawn a picture to help someone understand what you were saying? Such a drawing is one type of model. A model is a picture, diagram, computer image, or other representation of a complex object or process. **Making models** helps people understand things that they cannot observe directly.

Scientists often use models to represent things that are either very large or very small, such as the planets in the solar system, or the parts of a cell. Such models are physical models—drawings or three-dimensional structures that look like the real thing. Other models are mental models—mathematical equations or words that describe how something works.

Communicating

Whenever you talk on the phone, write a report, or listen to your teacher at school, you are communicating. **Communicating** is the process of sharing ideas and information with other people. Communicating effectively requires many skills, including writing, reading, speaking, listening, and making models.

Scientists communicate to share results, information, and opinions. Scientists often communicate about their work in journals, over the telephone, in letters, and on the Internet.

They also attend scientific meetings where they share their ideas with one another in person.

Activity

On a sheet of paper, write out clear, detailed directions for tying your shoe. Then exchange directions with a partner. Follow your partner's directions exactly. How successful were you at tying your shoe? How could your partner have communicated more clearly?

Making Measurements

By measuring, scientists can express their observations more precisely and communicate more information about what they observe.

Measuring in SI

The standard system of measurement used by scientists around the world is known as the International System of Units, which is abbreviated as SI (**Système International d'Unités,** in French). SI units are easy to use because they are based on multiples of 10. Each unit is ten times larger than the next smallest unit and one tenth the size of the next largest unit. The table lists the prefixes used to name the most common SI units.

Common SI Prefixes		
Prefix	**Symbol**	**Meaning**
kilo-	k	1,000
hecto-	h	100
deka-	da	10
deci-	d	0.1 (one tenth)
centi-	c	0.01 (one hundredth)
milli-	m	0.001 (one thousandth)

Length To measure length, or the distance between two points, the unit of measure is the **meter (m).** The distance from the floor to a doorknob is approximately one meter. Long distances, such as the distance between two cities, are measured in kilometers (km). Small lengths are measured in centimeters (cm) or millimeters (mm). Scientists use metric rulers and meter sticks to measure length.

Common Conversions	
1 km	=	1,000 m
1 m	=	100 cm
1 m	=	1,000 mm
1 cm	=	10 mm

Liquid Volume To measure the volume of a liquid, or the amount of space it takes up, you will use a unit of measure known as the **liter (L).** One liter is the approximate volume of a medium-size carton of milk. Smaller volumes are measured in milliliters (mL). Scientists use graduated cylinders to measure liquid volume.

Activity

The larger lines on the metric ruler in the picture show centimeter divisions, while the smaller, unnumbered lines show millimeter divisions. How many centimeters long is the shell? How many millimeters long is it?

Activity

The graduated cylinder in the picture is marked in milliliter divisions. Notice that the water in the cylinder has a curved surface. This curved surface is called the *meniscus.* To measure the volume, you must read the level at the lowest point of the meniscus. What is the volume of water in this graduated cylinder?

Common Conversion
1 L = 1,000 mL

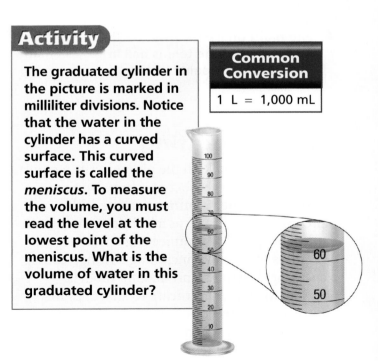

Mass To measure mass, or the amount of matter in an object, you will use a unit of measure known as the **gram (g).** One gram is approximately the mass of a paper clip. Larger masses are measured in kilograms (kg). Scientists use a balance to find the mass of an object.

Common Conversion

1 kg = 1,000 g

Activity

The mass of the potato in the picture is measured in kilograms. What is the mass of the potato? Suppose a recipe for potato salad called for one kilogram of potatoes. About how many potatoes would you need?

`0.25 KG`

Temperature To measure the temperature of a substance, you will use the **Celsius scale.** Temperature is measured in degrees Celsius (°C) using a Celsius thermometer. Water freezes at 0°C and boils at 100°C.

Time The unit scientists use to measure time is the **second (s).**

Activity

What is the temperature of the liquid in degrees Celsius?

Converting SI Units

To use the SI system, you must know how to convert between units. Converting from one unit to another involves the skill of **calculating,** or using mathematical operations. Converting between SI units is similar to converting between dollars and dimes because both systems are based on multiples of ten.

Suppose you want to convert a length of 80 centimeters to meters. Follow these steps to convert between units.

1. Begin by writing down the measurement you want to convert—in this example, 80 centimeters.

2. Write a conversion factor that represents the relationship between the two units you are converting. In this example, the relationship is 1 meter = 100 centimeters. Write this conversion factor as a fraction, making sure to place the units you are converting from (centimeters, in this example) in the denominator.

3. Multiply the measurement you want to convert by the fraction. When you do this, the units in the first measurement will cancel out with the units in the denominator. Your answer will be in the units you are converting to (meters, in this example).

Example

80 centimeters = ■ meters

$$80 \text{ centimeters} \times \frac{1 \text{ meter}}{100 \text{ centimeters}} = \frac{80 \text{ meters}}{100}$$

$$= 0.8 \text{ meters}$$

Activity

Convert between the following units.
1. 600 millimeters = ■ meters
2. 0.35 liters = ■ milliliters
3. 1,050 grams = ■ kilograms

Conducting a Scientific Investigation

In some ways, scientists are like detectives, piecing together clues to learn about a process or event. One way that scientists gather clues is by carrying out experiments. An experiment tests an idea in a careful, orderly manner. Although experiments do not all follow the same steps in the same order, many follow a pattern similar to the one described here.

Posing Questions

Experiments begin by asking a scientific question. A scientific question is one that can be answered by gathering evidence. For example, the question "Which freezes faster—fresh water or salt water?" is a scientific question because you can carry out an investigation and gather information to answer the question.

Developing a Hypothesis

The next step is to form a hypothesis. A **hypothesis** is a possible explanation for a set of observations or answer to a scientific question. In science, a hypothesis must be something that can be tested. A hypothesis can be worded as an *If . . . then . . .* statement. For example, a hypothesis might be *"If I add salt to fresh water, then the water will take longer to freeze."* A hypothesis worded this way serves as a rough outline of the experiment you should perform.

Designing an Experiment

Next you need to plan a way to test your hypothesis. Your plan should be written out as a step-by-step procedure and should describe the observations or measurements you will make.

Two important steps involved in designing an experiment are controlling variables and forming operational definitions.

Controlling Variables In a well-designed experiment, you need to keep all variables the same except for one. A **variable** is any factor that can change in an experiment. The factor that you change is called the **manipulated variable**. In this experiment, the manipulated variable is the amount of salt added to the water. Other factors, such as the amount of water or the starting temperature, are kept constant.

The factor that changes as a result of the manipulated variable is called the **responding variable.** The responding variable is what you measure or observe to obtain your results. In this experiment, the responding variable is how long the water takes to freeze.

An experiment in which all factors except one are kept constant is called a **controlled experiment.** Most controlled experiments include a test called the control. In this experiment, Container 3 is the control. Because no salt is added to Container 3, you can compare the results from the other containers to it. Any difference in results must be due to the addition of salt alone.

Forming Operational Definitions Another important aspect of a well-designed experiment is having clear operational definitions. An **operational definition** is a statement that describes how a particular variable is to be measured or how a term is to be defined. For example, in this experiment, how will you determine if the water has frozen? You might decide to insert a stick in each container at the start of the experiment. Your operational definition of "frozen" would be the time at which the stick can no longer move.

Experimental Procedure
1. Fill 3 containers with 300 milliliters of cold tap water.
2. Add 10 grams of salt to Container 1; stir. Add 20 grams of salt to Container 2; stir. Add no salt to Container 3.
3. Place the 3 containers in a freezer.
4. Check the containers every 15 minutes. Record your observations.

Interpreting Data

The observations and measurements you make in an experiment are called **data.** At the end of an experiment, you need to analyze the data to look for any patterns or trends. Patterns often become clear if you organize your data in a data table or graph. Then think through what the data reveal. Do they support your hypothesis? Do they point out a flaw in your experiment? Do you need to collect more data?

Drawing Conclusions

A **conclusion** is a statement that sums up what you have learned from an experiment. When you draw a conclusion, you need to decide whether the data you collected support your hypothesis or not. You may need to repeat an experiment several times before you can draw any conclusions from it. Conclusions often lead you to pose new questions and plan new experiments to answer them.

Activity

Is a ball's bounce affected by the height from which it is dropped? Using the steps just described, plan a controlled experiment to investigate this problem.

Technology Design Skills

Engineers are people who use scientific and technological knowledge to solve practical problems. To design new products, engineers usually follow the process described here, even though they may not follow these steps in the exact order. As you read the steps, think about how you might apply them in technology labs.

Identify a Need

Before engineers begin designing a new product, they must first identify the need they are trying to meet. For example, suppose you are a member of a design team in a company that makes toys. Your team has identified a need: a toy boat that is inexpensive and easy to assemble.

Research the Problem

Engineers often begin by gathering information that will help them with their new design. This research may include finding articles in books, magazines, or on the Internet. It may also include talking to other engineers who have solved similar problems. Engineers often perform experiments related to the product they want to design.

For your toy boat, you could look at toys that are similar to the one you want to design. You might do research on the Internet. You could also test some materials to see whether they will work well in a toy boat.

Drawing for a boat design ▼

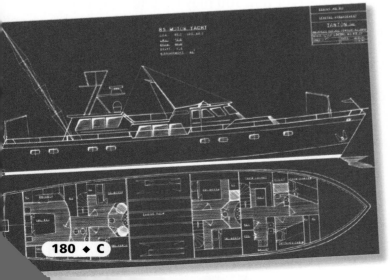

Design a Solution

Research gives engineers information that helps them design a product. When engineers design new products, they usually work in teams.

Generating Ideas Often design teams hold brainstorming meetings in which any team member can contribute ideas. **Brainstorming** is a creative process in which one team member's suggestions often spark ideas in other group members. Brainstorming can lead to new approaches to solving a design problem.

Evaluating Constraints During brainstorming, a design team will often come up with several possible designs. The team must then evaluate each one.

As part of their evaluation, engineers consider constraints. **Constraints** are factors that limit or restrict a product design. Physical characteristics, such as the properties of materials used to make your toy boat, are constraints. Money and time are also constraints. If the materials in a product cost a lot, or if the product takes a long time to make, the design may be impractical.

Making Trade-offs Design teams usually need to make trade-offs. In a **trade-off,** engineers give up one benefit of a proposed design in order to obtain another. In designing your toy boat, you will have to make trade-offs. For example, suppose one material is sturdy but not fully waterproof. Another material is more waterproof, but breakable. You may decide to give up the benefit of sturdiness in order to obtain the benefit of waterproofing.

Build and Evaluate a Prototype

Once the team has chosen a design plan, the engineers build a prototype of the product. A **prototype** is a working model used to test a design. Engineers evaluate the prototype to see whether it works well, is easy to operate, is safe to use, and holds up to repeated use.

Think of your toy boat. What would the prototype be like? Of what materials would it be made? How would you test it?

Troubleshoot and Redesign

Few prototypes work perfectly, which is why they need to be tested. Once a design team has tested a prototype, the members analyze the results and identify any problems. The team then tries to **troubleshoot,** or fix the design problems. For example, if your toy boat leaks or wobbles, the boat should be redesigned to eliminate those problems.

Communicate the Solution

A team needs to communicate the final design to the people who will manufacture and use the product. To do this, teams may use sketches, detailed drawings, computer simulations, and word descriptions.

Activity

You can use the technology design process to design and build a toy boat.

Research and Investigate

1. Visit the library or go online to research toy boats.

2. Investigate how a toy boat can be powered, including wind, rubber bands, or baking soda and vinegar.

3. Brainstorm materials, shapes, and steering for your boat.

Design and Build

4. Based on your research, design a toy boat that
   - is made of readily available materials
   - is no larger than 15 cm long and 10 cm wide
   - includes a power system, a rudder, and an area for cargo
   - travels 2 meters in a straight line carrying a load of 20 pennies

5. Sketch your design and write a step-by-step plan for building your boat. After your teacher approves your plan, build your boat.

Evaluate and Redesign

6. Test your boat, evaluate the results, and troubleshoot any problems.

7. Based on your evaluation, redesign your toy boat so it performs better.

Creating Data Tables and Graphs

How can you make sense of the data in a science experiment? The first step is to organize the data to help you understand them. Data tables and graphs are helpful tools for organizing data.

Data Tables

You have gathered your materials and set up your experiment. But before you start, you need to plan a way to record what happens during the experiment. By creating a data table, you can record your observations and measurements in an orderly way.

Suppose, for example, that a scientist conducted an experiment to find out how many Calories people of different body masses burn while doing various activities. The data table shows the results.

Notice in this data table that the manipulated variable (body mass) is the heading of one column. The responding variable (for

Calories Burned in 30 Minutes			
Body Mass	Experiment 1: Bicycling	Experiment 2: Playing Basketball	Experiment 3: Watching Television
30 kg	60 Calories	120 Calories	21 Calories
40 kg	77 Calories	164 Calories	27 Calories
50 kg	95 Calories	206 Calories	33 Calories
60 kg	114 Calories	248 Calories	38 Calories

Experiment 1, the number of Calories burned while bicycling) is the heading of the next column. Additional columns were added for related experiments.

Bar Graphs

To compare how many Calories a person burns doing various activities, you could create a bar graph. A bar graph is used to display data in a number of separate, or distinct, categories. In this example, bicycling, playing basketball, and watching television are the three categories.

To create a bar graph, follow these steps.

1. On graph paper, draw a horizontal, or *x*-, axis and a vertical, or *y*-, axis.

2. Write the names of the categories to be graphed along the horizontal axis. Include an overall label for the axis as well.

3. Label the vertical axis with the name of the responding variable. Include units of measurement. Then create a scale along the axis by marking off equally spaced numbers that cover the range of the data collected.

4. For each category, draw a solid bar using the scale on the vertical axis to determine the height. Make all the bars the same width.

5. Add a title that describes the graph.

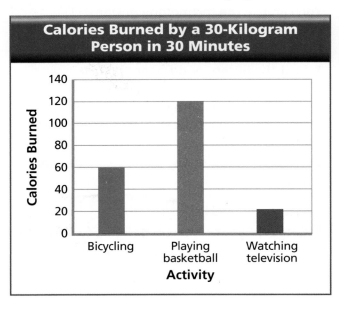

Line Graphs

To see whether a relationship exists between body mass and the number of Calories burned while bicycling, you could create a line graph. A line graph is used to display data that show how one variable (the responding variable) changes in response to another variable (the manipulated variable). You can use a line graph when your manipulated variable is **continuous,** that is, when there are other points between the ones that you tested. In this example, body mass is a continuous variable because there are other body masses between 30 and 40 kilograms (for example, 31 kilograms). Time is another example of a continuous variable.

Line graphs are powerful tools because they allow you to estimate values for conditions that you did not test in the experiment. For example, you can use the line graph to estimate that a 35-kilogram person would burn 68 Calories while bicycling.

To create a line graph, follow these steps.

1. On graph paper, draw a horizontal, or *x*-, axis and a vertical, or *y*-, axis.

2. Label the horizontal axis with the name of the manipulated variable. Label the vertical axis with the name of the responding variable. Include units of measurement.

3. Create a scale on each axis by marking off equally spaced numbers that cover the range of the data collected.

4. Plot a point on the graph for each piece of data. In the line graph above, the dotted lines show how to plot the first data point (30 kilograms and 60 Calories). Follow an imaginary vertical line extending up from the horizontal axis at the 30-kilogram mark. Then follow an imaginary horizontal line extending across from the vertical axis at the 60-Calorie mark. Plot the point where the two lines intersect.

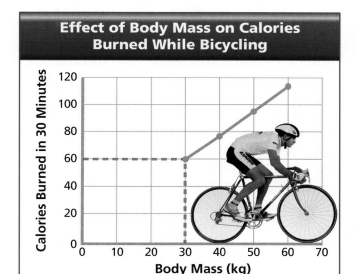

5. Connect the plotted points with a solid line. (In some cases, it may be more appropriate to draw a line that shows the general trend of the plotted points. In those cases, some of the points may fall above or below the line. Also, not all graphs are linear. It may be more appropriate to draw a curve to connect the points.)

6. Add a title that identifies the variables or relationship in the graph.

Activity

Create line graphs to display the data from Experiment 2 and Experiment 3 in the data table.

Activity

You read in the newspaper that a total of 4 centimeters of rain fell in your area in June, 2.5 centimeters fell in July, and 1.5 centimeters fell in August. What type of graph would you use to display these data? Use graph paper to create the graph.

Circle Graphs

Like bar graphs, circle graphs can be used to display data in a number of separate categories. Unlike bar graphs, however, circle graphs can only be used when you have data for *all* the categories that make up a given topic. A circle graph is sometimes called a pie chart. The pie represents the entire topic, while the slices represent the individual categories. The size of a slice indicates what percentage of the whole a particular category makes up.

The data table below shows the results of a survey in which 24 teenagers were asked to identify their favorite sport. The data were then used to create the circle graph at the right.

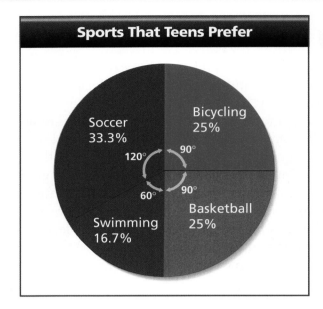

Sports That Teens Prefer

Favorite Sports	
Sport	**Students**
Soccer	8
Basketball	6
Bicycling	6
Swimming	4

To create a circle graph, follow these steps.

1. Use a compass to draw a circle. Mark the center with a point. Then draw a line from the center point to the top of the circle.

2. Determine the size of each "slice" by setting up a proportion where *x* equals the number of degrees in a slice. (*Note:* A circle contains 360 degrees.) For example, to find the number of degrees in the "soccer" slice, set up the following proportion:

$$\frac{\text{Students who prefer soccer}}{\text{Total number of students}} = \frac{x}{\text{Total number of degrees in a circle}}$$

$$\frac{8}{24} = \frac{x}{360}$$

Cross-multiply and solve for x.

$$24x = 8 \times 360$$
$$x = 120$$

The "soccer" slice should contain 120 degrees.

3. Use a protractor to measure the angle of the first slice, using the line you drew to the top of the circle as the 0° line. Draw a line from the center of the circle to the edge for the angle you measured.

4. Continue around the circle by measuring the size of each slice with the protractor. Start measuring from the edge of the previous slice so the wedges do not overlap. When you are done, the entire circle should be filled in.

5. Determine the percentage of the whole circle that each slice represents. To do this, divide the number of degrees in a slice by the total number of degrees in a circle (360), and multiply by 100%. For the "soccer" slice, you can find the percentage as follows:

$$\frac{120}{360} \times 100\% = 33.3\%$$

6. Use a different color for each slice. Label each slice with the category and with the percentage of the whole it represents.

7. Add a title to the circle graph.

Activity

In a class of 28 students, 12 students take the bus to school, 10 students walk, and 6 students ride their bicycles. Create a circle graph to display these data.

Math Review

Scientists use math to organize, analyze, and present data. This appendix will help you review some basic math skills.

Mean, Median, and Mode

The **mean** is the average, or the sum of the data divided by the number of data items. The middle number in a set of ordered data is called the **median**. The **mode** is the number that appears most often in a set of data.

Example

A scientist counted the number of distinct songs sung by seven different male birds and collected the data shown below.

Male Bird Songs							
Bird	A	B	C	D	E	F	G
Number of Songs	36	29	40	35	28	36	27

To determine the mean number of songs, add the total number of songs and divide by the number of data items—in this case, the number of male birds.

$$\text{Mean} = \frac{231}{7} = 33 \text{ songs}$$

To find the median number of songs, arrange the data in numerical order and find the number in the middle of the series.

27 28 29 35 36 36 40

The number in the middle is 35, so the median number of songs is 35.

The mode is the value that appears most frequently. In the data, 36 appears twice, while each other item appears only once. Therefore, 36 songs is the mode.

Practice

Find out how many minutes it takes each student in your class to get to school. Then find the mean, median, and mode for the data.

Probability

Probability is the chance that an event will occur. Probability can be expressed as a ratio, a fraction, or a percentage. For example, when you flip a coin, the probability that the coin will land heads up is 1 in 2, or $\frac{1}{2}$, or 50 percent.

The probability that an event will happen can be expressed in the following formula.

$$P(\text{event}) = \frac{\text{Number of times the event can occur}}{\text{Total number of possible events}}$$

Example

A paper bag contains 25 blue marbles, 5 green marbles, 5 orange marbles, and 15 yellow marbles. If you close your eyes and pick a marble from the bag, what is the probability that it will be yellow?

$$P(\text{yellow marbles}) = \frac{15 \text{ yellow marbles}}{50 \text{ marbles total}}$$

$$P = \frac{15}{50}, \text{ or } \frac{3}{10}, \text{ or } 30\%$$

Practice

Each side of a cube has a letter on it. Two sides have A, three sides have B, and one side has C. If you roll the cube, what is the probability that A will land on top?

Area

The **area** of a surface is the number of square units that cover it. The front cover of your textbook has an area of about 600 cm².

Area of a Rectangle and a Square To find the area of a rectangle, multiply its length times its width. The formula for the area of a rectangle is

$$A = \ell \times w, \text{ or } A = \ell w$$

Since all four sides of a square have the same length, the area of a square is the length of one side multiplied by itself, or squared.

$$A = s \times s, \text{ or } A = s^2$$

Example

A scientist is studying the plants in a field that measures 75 m × 45 m. What is the area of the field?

$$A = \ell \times w$$
$$A = 75 \text{ m} \times 45 \text{ m}$$
$$A = 3,375 \text{ m}^2$$

Area of a Circle The formula for the area of a circle is

$$A = \pi \times r \times r, \text{ or } A = \pi r^2$$

The length of the radius is represented by r, and the value of π is approximately $\frac{22}{7}$.

Example

Find the area of a circle with a radius of 14 cm.

$$A = \pi r^2$$
$$A = 14 \times 14 \times \frac{22}{7}$$
$$A = 616 \text{ cm}^2$$

Practice

Find the area of a circle that has a radius of 21 m.

Circumference

The distance around a circle is called the circumference. The formula for finding the circumference of a circle is

$$C = 2 \times \pi \times r, \text{ or } C = 2\pi r$$

Example

The radius of a circle is 35 cm. What is its circumference?

$$C = 2\pi r$$
$$C = 2 \times 35 \times \frac{22}{7}$$
$$C = 220 \text{ cm}$$

Practice

What is the circumference of a circle with a radius of 28 m?

Volume

The volume of an object is the number of cubic units it contains. The volume of a wastebasket, for example, might be about 26,000 cm³.

Volume of a Rectangular Object To find the volume of a rectangular object, multiply the object's length times its width times its height.

$$V = \ell \times w \times h, \text{ or } V = \ell w h$$

Example

Find the volume of a box with length 24 cm, width 12 cm, and height 9 cm.

$$V = \ell w h$$
$$V = 24 \text{ cm} \times 12 \text{ cm} \times 9 \text{ cm}$$
$$V = 2,592 \text{ cm}^3$$

Practice

What is the volume of a rectangular object with length 17 cm, width 11 cm, and height 6 cm?

Fractions

A **fraction** is a way to express a part of a whole. In the fraction $\frac{4}{7}$, 4 is the numerator and 7 is the denominator.

Adding and Subtracting Fractions To add or subtract two or more fractions that have a common denominator, first add or subtract the numerators. Then write the sum or difference over the common denominator.

To find the sum or difference of fractions with different denominators, first find the least common multiple of the denominators. This is known as the least common denominator. Then convert each fraction to equivalent fractions with the least common denominator. Add or subtract the numerators. Then write the sum or difference over the common denominator.

> **Example**
>
> $\frac{5}{6} - \frac{3}{4} = \frac{10}{12} - \frac{9}{12} = \frac{10-9}{12} = \frac{1}{12}$

Multiplying Fractions To multiply two fractions, first multiply the two numerators, then multiply the two denominators.

> **Example**
>
> $\frac{5}{6} \times \frac{2}{3} = \frac{5 \times 2}{6 \times 3} = \frac{10}{18} = \frac{5}{9}$

Dividing Fractions Dividing by a fraction is the same as multiplying by its reciprocal. Reciprocals are numbers whose numerators and denominators have been switched. To divide one fraction by another, first invert the fraction you are dividing by—in other words, turn it upside down. Then multiply the two fractions.

> **Example**
>
> $\frac{2}{5} \div \frac{7}{8} = \frac{2}{5} \times \frac{8}{7} = \frac{2 \times 8}{5 \times 7} = \frac{16}{35}$

> **Practice**
>
> Solve the following: $\frac{3}{7} \div \frac{4}{5}$.

Decimals

Fractions whose denominators are 10, 100, or some other power of 10 are often expressed as decimals. For example, the fraction $\frac{9}{10}$ can be expressed as the decimal 0.9, and the fraction $\frac{7}{100}$ can be written as 0.07.

Adding and Subtracting With Decimals To add or subtract decimals, line up the decimal points before you carry out the operation.

> **Example**
>
> $\begin{array}{r} 27.4 \\ + \ 6.19 \\ \hline 33.59 \end{array}$ $\qquad$ $\begin{array}{r} 278.635 \\ - \ 191.4 \\ \hline 87.235 \end{array}$

Multiplying With Decimals When you multiply two numbers with decimals, the number of decimal places in the product is equal to the total number of decimal places in each number being multiplied.

> **Example**
>
> $\begin{array}{r} 46.2 \ \textbf{(one decimal place)} \\ \times \ 2.37 \ \textbf{(two decimal places)} \\ \hline 109.494 \ \textbf{(three decimal places)} \end{array}$

Dividing With Decimals To divide a decimal by a whole number, put the decimal point in the quotient above the decimal point in the dividend.

> **Example**
>
> $15.5 \div 5$
>
> $\begin{array}{r} 3.1 \\ 5 \overline{)15.5} \end{array}$

To divide a decimal by a decimal, you need to rewrite the divisor as a whole number. Do this by multiplying both the divisor and dividend by the same multiple of 10.

> **Example**
>
> $1.68 \div 4.2 = 16.8 \div 42$
>
> $\begin{array}{r} 0.4 \\ 42 \overline{)16.8} \end{array}$

> **Practice**
>
> Multiply 6.21 by 8.5.

Ratio and Proportion

A **ratio** compares two numbers by division. For example, suppose a scientist counts 800 wolves and 1,200 moose on an island. The ratio of wolves to moose can be written as a fraction, $\frac{800}{1,200}$, which can be reduced to $\frac{2}{3}$. The same ratio can also be expressed as 2 to 3 or 2 : 3.

A **proportion** is a mathematical sentence saying that two ratios are equivalent. For example, a proportion could state that $\frac{800 \text{ wolves}}{1,200 \text{ moose}} = \frac{2 \text{ wolves}}{3 \text{ moose}}$. You can sometimes set up a proportion to determine or estimate an unknown quantity. For example, suppose a scientist counts 25 beetles in an area of 10 square meters. The scientist wants to estimate the number of beetles in 100 square meters.

> **Example**
>
> 1. Express the relationship between beetles and area as a ratio: $\frac{25}{10}$, simplified to $\frac{5}{2}$.
> 2. Set up a proportion, with x representing the number of beetles. The proportion can be stated as $\frac{5}{2} = \frac{x}{100}$.
> 3. Begin by cross-multiplying. In other words, multiply each fraction's numerator by the other fraction's denominator.
>
> $5 \times 100 = 2 \times x$, or $500 = 2x$
>
> 4. To find the value of x, divide both sides by 2. The result is 250, or 250 beetles in 100 square meters.

> **Practice**
>
> Find the value of x in the following proportion: $\frac{6}{7} = \frac{x}{49}$.

Percentage

A **percentage** is a ratio that compares a number to 100. For example, there are 37 granite rocks in a collection that consists of 100 rocks. The ratio $\frac{37}{100}$ can be written as 37%. Granite rocks make up 37% of the rock collection.

You can calculate percentages of numbers other than 100 by setting up a proportion.

> **Example**
>
> Rain falls on 9 days out of 30 in June. What percentage of the days in June were rainy?
>
> $$\frac{9 \text{ days}}{30 \text{ days}} = \frac{d\%}{100\%}$$
>
> To find the value of d, begin by cross-multiplying, as for any proportion:
>
> $9 \times 100 = 30 \times d \qquad d = \frac{900}{30} \qquad d = 30$

> **Practice**
>
> There are 300 marbles in a jar, and 42 of those marbles are blue. What percentage of the marbles are blue?

Significant Figures

The **precision** of a measurement depends on the instrument you use to take the measurement. For example, if the smallest unit on the ruler is millimeters, then the most precise measurement you can make will be in millimeters.

The sum or difference of measurements can only be as precise as the least precise measurement being added or subtracted. Round your answer so that it has the same number of digits after the decimal as the least precise measurement. Round up if the last digit is 5 or more, and round down if the last digit is 4 or less.

Example

Subtract a temperature of 5.2°C from the temperature 75.46°C.

75.46 − 5.2 = 70.26

5.2 has the fewest digits after the decimal, so it is the least precise measurement. Since the last digit of the answer is 6, round up to 3. The most precise difference between the measurements is 70.3°C.

Practice

Add 26.4 m to 8.37 m. Round your answer according to the precision of the measurements.

Significant figures are the number of nonzero digits in a measurement. Zeroes between nonzero digits are also significant. For example, the measurements 12,500 L, 0.125 cm, and 2.05 kg all have three significant figures. When you multiply and divide measurements, the one with the fewest significant figures determines the number of significant figures in your answer.

Example

Multiply 110 g by 5.75 g.

110 × 5.75 = 632.5

Because 110 has only two significant figures, round the answer to 630 g.

Scientific Notation

A **factor** is a number that divides into another number with no remainder. In the example, the number 3 is used as a factor four times.

An **exponent** tells how many times a number is used as a factor. For example, $3 \times 3 \times 3 \times 3$ can be written as 3^4. The exponent 4 indicates that the number 3 is used as a factor four times. Another way of expressing this is to say that 81 is equal to 3 to the fourth power.

Example

$$3^4 = 3 \times 3 \times 3 \times 3 = 81$$

Scientific notation uses exponents and powers of ten to write very large or very small numbers in shorter form. When you write a number in scientific notation, you write the number as two factors. The first factor is any number between 1 and 10. The second factor is a power of 10, such as 10^3 or 10^6.

Example

The average distance between the planet Mercury and the sun is 58,000,000 km. To write the first factor in scientific notation, insert a decimal point in the original number so that you have a number between 1 and 10. In the case of 58,000,000, the number is 5.8.

To determine the power of 10, count the number of places that the decimal point moved. In this case, it moved 7 places.

58,000,000 km = 5.8×10^7 km

Practice

Express 6,590,000 in scientific notation.

Reading Comprehension Skills

Your textbook is an important source of science information. As you read your science textbook, you will find that the book has been written to assist you in understanding the science concepts.

Learning From Science Textbooks

As you study science in school, you will learn science concepts in a variety of ways. Sometimes you will do interesting activities and experiments to explore science ideas. To fully understand what you observe in experiments and activities, you will need to read your science textbook. To help you read, some of the important ideas are highlighted so that you can easily recognize what they are. In addition, a target reading skill in each section will help you understand what you read.

By using the target reading skills, you will improve your reading comprehension—that is, you will improve your ability to understand what you read. As you learn science, you will build knowledge that will help you understand even more of what you read. This knowledge will help you learn about all the topics presented in this textbook.

And—guess what?—these reading skills can be useful whenever you are reading. Reading to learn is important for your entire life. You have an opportunity to begin that process now.

The target reading skills that will improve your reading comprehension are described below.

Building Vocabulary

To understand the science concepts taught in this textbook, you need to remember the meanings of the Key Terms. One strategy consists of writing the definitions of these terms in your own words. You can also practice using the terms in sentences and make lists of words or phrases you associate with each term.

Using Prior Knowledge

Your prior knowledge is what you already know before you begin to read about a topic. Building on what you already know gives you a head start on learning new information. Before you begin a new assignment, think about what you know. You might page through your reading assignment, looking at the headings and the visuals to spark your memory. You can list what you know in the graphic organizer provided in the section opener. Then, as you read, consider questions like the ones below to connect what you learn to what you already know.

- How does what you learn relate to what you know?
- How did something you already know help you learn something new?
- Did your original ideas agree with what you have just learned? If not, how would you revise your original ideas?

Asking Questions

Asking yourself questions is an excellent way to focus on and remember new information in your textbook. You can learn how to ask good questions.

One way is to turn the text headings into questions. Then your questions can guide you to identify and remember the important information as you read. Look at these examples:

Heading: Using Seismographic Data
Question: How are seismographic data used?
Heading: Kinds of Faults
Question: What are the kinds of faults?

You do not have to limit your questions to the text headings. Ask questions about anything that you need to clarify or that will help you understand the content. *What* and *how* are probably the most common question words, but you may also ask *why*, *who*, *when*, or *where* questions. Here is an example:

Properties of Waves

Question	Answer
What is amplitude?	Amplitude is . . .

Previewing Visuals

Visuals are photographs, graphs, tables, diagrams, and illustrations. Visuals, such as this diagram of a normal fault, contain important information. Look at visuals and their captions before you read. This will help you prepare for what you will be reading about.

Often you will be asked what you want to learn about a visual. For example, after you look at the normal fault diagram, you might ask: What is the movement along a normal fault? Questions about visuals give you a purpose for reading—to answer your questions. Previewing visuals also helps you see what you already know.

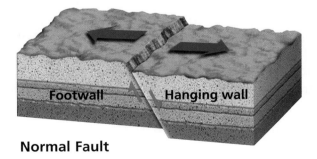

Footwall   **Hanging wall**

Normal Fault

Outlining

An outline shows the relationship between main ideas and supporting ideas. An outline has a formal structure. You write the main ideas, called topics, next to Roman numerals. The supporting ideas, sometimes called subtopics, are written under the main ideas and labeled A, B, C, and so on. An outline looks like this:

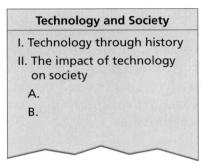

Technology and Society

I. Technology through history
II. The impact of technology on society
   A.
   B.

When you have completed an outline like this, you can see at a glance the structure of the section. You can use this outline as a study tool.

Identifying Main Ideas

When you are reading, it is important to try to understand the ideas and concepts that are in a passage. As you read science material, you will recognize that each paragraph has a lot of information and detail. Good readers try to identify the most important—or biggest—idea in every paragraph or section. That's the main idea. The other information in the paragraph supports or further explains the main idea.

Sometimes main ideas are stated directly. In this book, some main ideas are identified for you as key concepts. These are printed in boldface type. However, you must identify other main ideas yourself. In order to do this, you must identify all the ideas within a paragraph or section. Then ask yourself which idea is big enough to include all the other ideas.

Comparing and Contrasting

When you compare and contrast, you examine the similarities and differences between things. You can compare and contrast in a Venn diagram or in a table. Your completed diagram or table shows you how the items are alike and how they are different.

Venn Diagram A Venn diagram consists of two overlapping circles. In the space where the circles overlap, you write the characteristics that the two items have in common. In one of the circles outside the area of overlap, you write the differing features or characteristics of one of the items. In the other circle outside the area of overlap, you write the differing characteristics of the other item.

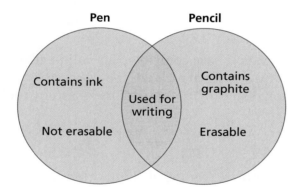

Table In a compare/contrast table, you list the items to be compared across the top of the table. Then list the characteristics or features to be compared in the left column. Complete the table by filling in information about each characteristic or feature.

Blood Vessel	Function	Structure of Wall
Artery	Carries blood away from heart	
Capillary		
Vein		

Sequencing

A sequence is the order in which a series of events occurs. Recognizing and remembering the sequence of events is important to understanding many processes in science. Sometimes the text uses words like *first, next, during,* and *after* to signal a sequence. A flowchart or a cycle diagram can help you visualize a sequence.

Flowchart To make a flowchart, write a brief description of each step or event in a box. Place the boxes in order, with the first event at the top of the page. Then draw an arrow to connect each step or event to the next.

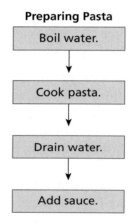

Cycle Diagram A cycle diagram shows a sequence that is continuous, or cyclical. A continuous sequence does not have an end because when the final event is over, the first event begins again. To create a cycle diagram, write the starting event in a box placed at the top of a page in the center. Then, moving in a clockwise direction around an imaginary circle, write each event in a box in its proper sequence. Draw arrows that connect each event to the one that occurs next, forming a continuous circle.

Identifying Supporting Evidence

A hypothesis is a possible explanation for observations made by scientists or an answer to a scientific question. A hypothesis is tested over and over again. The tests may produce evidence that supports the hypothesis. When enough supporting evidence is collected, a hypothesis may become a theory.

Identifying the supporting evidence for a hypothesis or theory can help you understand the hypothesis or theory. Evidence consists of facts—information whose accuracy can be confirmed by testing or observation.

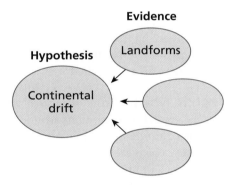

Relating Cause and Effect

Identifying causes and effects helps you understand relationships among events. A cause makes something happen. An effect is what happens. When you recognize that one event causes another, you are relating cause and effect. Words like *cause, because, effect, affect,* and *result* often signal a cause or an effect.

Sometimes an effect can have more than one cause, or a cause can produce several effects. For example, car exhaust and smoke from industrial plants are two causes of air pollution. Some effects of air pollution include breathing difficulties for some people, death of plants along some highways, and damage to some building surfaces.

Science involves many cause-and-effect relationships. Seeing and understanding these relationships helps you understand science processes.

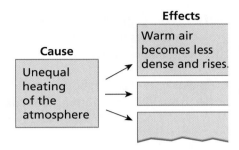

Concept Mapping

Concept maps are useful tools for organizing information on any topic. A concept map begins with a main idea or core concept and shows how the idea can be subdivided into related subconcepts or smaller ideas. In this way, relationships between concepts become clearer and easier to understand.

You construct a concept map by placing concepts (usually nouns) in ovals and connecting them with linking words. The biggest concept or idea is placed in an oval at the top of the map. Related concepts are arranged in ovals below the big idea. The linking words are often verbs and verb phrases and are written on the lines that connect the ovals.

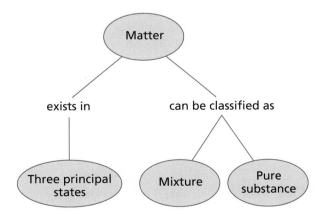

Safety Symbols

These symbols warn of possible dangers in the laboratory and remind you to work carefully.

 Safety Goggles Wear safety goggles to protect your eyes in any activity involving chemicals, flames or heating, or glassware.

 Lab Apron Wear a laboratory apron to protect your skin and clothing from damage.

 Breakage Handle breakable materials, such as glassware, with care. Do not touch broken glassware.

 Heat-Resistant Gloves Use an oven mitt or other hand protection when handling hot materials such as hot plates or hot glassware.

 Plastic Gloves Wear disposable plastic gloves when working with harmful chemicals and organisms. Keep your hands away from your face, and dispose of the gloves according to your teacher's instructions.

 Heating Use a clamp or tongs to pick up hot glassware. Do not touch hot objects with your bare hands.

 Flames Before you work with flames, tie back loose hair and clothing. Follow instructions from your teacher about lighting and extinguishing flames.

 No Flames When using flammable materials, make sure there are no flames, sparks, or other exposed heat sources present.

 Corrosive Chemical Avoid getting acid or other corrosive chemicals on your skin or clothing or in your eyes. Do not inhale the vapors. Wash your hands after the activity.

 Poison Do not let any poisonous chemical come into contact with your skin, and do not inhale its vapors. Wash your hands when you are finished with the activity.

 Fumes Work in a ventilated area when harmful vapors may be involved. Avoid inhaling vapors directly. Only test an odor when directed to do so by your teacher, and use a wafting motion to direct the vapor toward your nose.

 Sharp Object Scissors, scalpels, knives, needles, pins, and tacks can cut your skin. Always direct a sharp edge or point away from yourself and others.

 Animal Safety Treat live or preserved animals or animal parts with care to avoid harming the animals or yourself. Wash your hands when you are finished with the activity.

 Plant Safety Handle plants only as directed by your teacher. If you are allergic to certain plants, tell your teacher; do not do an activity involving those plants. Avoid touching harmful plants such as poison ivy. Wash your hands when you are finished with the activity.

 Electric Shock To avoid electric shock, never use electrical equipment around water, or when the equipment is wet or your hands are wet. Be sure cords are untangled and cannot trip anyone. Unplug equipment not in use.

 Physical Safety When an experiment involves physical activity, avoid injuring yourself or others. Alert your teacher if there is any reason you should not participate.

 Disposal Dispose of chemicals and other laboratory materials safely. Follow the instructions from your teacher.

 Hand Washing Wash your hands thoroughly when finished with the activity. Use antibacterial soap and warm water. Rinse well.

 General Safety Awareness When this symbol appears, follow the instructions provided. When you are asked to develop your own procedure in a lab, have your teacher approve your plan before you go further.

Science Safety Rules

General Precautions

Follow all instructions. Never perform activities without the approval and supervision of your teacher. Do not engage in horseplay. Never eat or drink in the laboratory. Keep work areas clean and uncluttered.

Dress Code

Wear safety goggles whenever you work with chemicals, glassware, heat sources such as burners, or any substance that might get into your eyes. If you wear contact lenses, notify your teacher.

Wear a lab apron or coat whenever you work with corrosive chemicals or substances that can stain. Wear disposable plastic gloves when working with organisms and harmful chemicals. Tie back long hair. Remove or tie back any article of clothing or jewelry that can hang down and touch chemicals, flames, or equipment. Roll up long sleeves. Never wear open shoes or sandals.

First Aid

Report all accidents, injuries, or fires to your teacher, no matter how minor. Be aware of the location of the first-aid kit, emergency equipment such as the fire extinguisher and fire blanket, and the nearest telephone. Know whom to contact in an emergency.

Heating and Fire Safety

Keep all combustible materials away from flames. When heating a substance in a test tube, make sure that the mouth of the tube is not pointed at you or anyone else. Never heat a liquid in a closed container. Use an oven mitt to pick up a container that has been heated.

Using Chemicals Safely

Never put your face near the mouth of a container that holds chemicals. Never touch, taste, or smell a chemical unless your teacher tells you to.

Use only those chemicals needed in the activity. Keep all containers closed when chemicals are not being used. Pour all chemicals over the sink or a container, not over your work surface. Dispose of excess chemicals as instructed by your teacher.

Be extra careful when working with acids or bases. When mixing an acid and water, always pour the water into the container first and then add the acid to the water. Never pour water into an acid. Wash chemical spills and splashes immediately with plenty of water.

Using Glassware Safely

If glassware is broken or chipped, notify your teacher immediately. Never handle broken or chipped glass with your bare hands.

Never force glass tubing or thermometers into a rubber stopper or rubber tubing. Have your teacher insert the glass tubing or thermometer if required for an activity.

Using Sharp Instruments

Handle sharp instruments with extreme care. Never cut material toward you; cut away from you.

Animal and Plant Safety

Never perform experiments that cause pain, discomfort, or harm to animals. Only handle animals if absolutely necessary. If you know that you are allergic to certain plants, molds, or animals, tell your teacher before doing an activity in which these are used. Wash your hands thoroughly after any activity involving animals, animal parts, plants, plant parts, or soil.

During field work, wear long pants, long sleeves, socks, and closed shoes. Avoid poisonous plants and fungi as well as plants with thorns.

End-of-Experiment Rules

Unplug all electrical equipment. Clean up your work area. Dispose of waste materials as instructed by your teacher. Wash your hands after every experiment.

The microscope is an essential tool in the study of life science. It allows you to see things that are too small to be seen with the unaided eye.

You will probably use a compound microscope like the one you see here. The compound microscope has more than one lens that magnifies the object you view.

Typically, a compound microscope has one lens in the eyepiece, the part you look through. The eyepiece lens usually magnifies 10 ×. Any object you view through this lens would appear 10 times larger than it is.

The compound microscope may contain one or two other lenses called objective lenses. If there are two objective lenses, they are called the low-power and high-power objective lenses. The low-power objective lens usually magnifies 10 ×. The high-power objective lens usually magnifies 40 ×.

To calculate the total magnification with which you are viewing an object, multiply the magnification of the eyepiece lens by the magnification of the objective lens you are using. For example, the eyepiece's magnification of 10 × multiplied by the low-power objective's magnification of 10 × equals a total magnification of 100 ×.

Use the photo of the compound microscope to become familiar with the parts of the microscope and their functions.

The Parts of a Compound Microscope

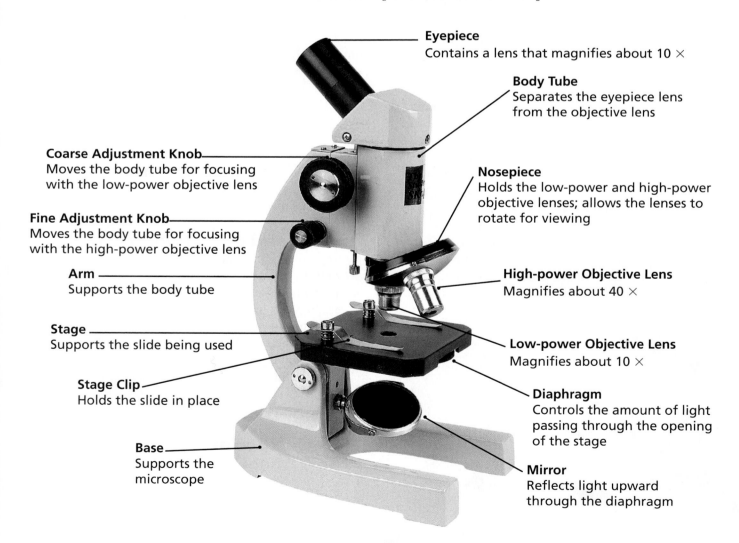

Eyepiece
Contains a lens that magnifies about 10 ×

Body Tube
Separates the eyepiece lens from the objective lens

Coarse Adjustment Knob
Moves the body tube for focusing with the low-power objective lens

Nosepiece
Holds the low-power and high-power objective lenses; allows the lenses to rotate for viewing

Fine Adjustment Knob
Moves the body tube for focusing with the high-power objective lens

Arm
Supports the body tube

High-power Objective Lens
Magnifies about 40 ×

Stage
Supports the slide being used

Low-power Objective Lens
Magnifies about 10 ×

Stage Clip
Holds the slide in place

Diaphragm
Controls the amount of light passing through the opening of the stage

Base
Supports the microscope

Mirror
Reflects light upward through the diaphragm

Using the Microscope

Use the following procedures when you are working with a microscope.

1. To carry the microscope, grasp the microscope's arm with one hand. Place your other hand under the base.
2. Place the microscope on a table with the arm toward you.
3. Turn the coarse adjustment knob to raise the body tube.
4. Revolve the nosepiece until the low-power objective lens clicks into place.
5. Adjust the diaphragm. While looking through the eyepiece, also adjust the mirror until you see a bright white circle of light. **CAUTION:** *Never use direct sunlight as a light source.*
6. Place a slide on the stage. Center the specimen over the opening on the stage. Use the stage clips to hold the slide in place. **CAUTION:** *Glass slides are fragile.*
7. Look at the stage from the side. Carefully turn the coarse adjustment knob to lower the body tube until the low-power objective almost touches the slide.
8. Looking through the eyepiece, very slowly turn the coarse adjustment knob until the specimen comes into focus.
9. To switch to the high-power objective lens, look at the microscope from the side. Carefully revolve the nosepiece until the high-power objective lens clicks into place. Make sure the lens does not hit the slide.
10. Looking through the eyepiece, turn the fine adjustment knob until the specimen comes into focus.

Making a Wet-Mount Slide

Use the following procedures to make a wet-mount slide of a specimen.

1. Obtain a clean microscope slide and a coverslip. **CAUTION:** *Glass slides and coverslips are fragile.*
2. Place the specimen on the slide. The specimen must be thin enough for light to pass through it.
3. Using a plastic dropper, place a drop of water on the specimen.
4. Gently place one edge of the coverslip against the slide so that it touches the edge of the water drop at a 45° angle. Slowly lower the coverslip over the specimen. If air bubbles are trapped beneath the coverslip, tap the coverslip gently with the eraser end of a pencil.
5. Remove any excess water at the edge of the coverslip with a paper towel.

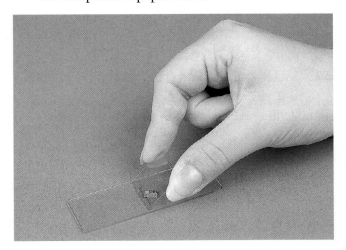

English and Spanish Glossary

active transport The movement of materials through a cell membrane using cellular energy. (p. 36)
transporte activo Movimiento de materiales a través de la membrana celular que usa energía de la célula.

adaptation A trait that helps an organism survive and reproduce. (p. 141)
adaptación Rasgo que ayuda a sobrevivir y a reproducirse a un organismo.

alleles The different forms of a gene. (p. 79)
alelos Diferentes formas de un gen.

amino acid A small molecule that is linked chemically to other amino acids to form proteins. (p. 28)
aminoácido Pequeña molécula que se une químicamente a otros aminoácidos para formar proteínas.

autotroph An organism that makes its own food. (p. 45)
autótrofo Organismo que produce su propio alimento.

branching tree A diagram that shows how scientists think different groups of organisms are related. (p. 152)
árbol ramificado Diagrama que muestra cómo piensan los científicos que se relacionan diferentes grupos de organismos.

cancer A disease in which some body cells grow and divide uncontrollably, damaging the parts of the body around them. (p. 65)
cáncer Enfermedad en la que algunas células del cuerpo crecen y se dividen sin control, dañando las partes del cuerpo que están a su alrededor.

carbohydrate Energy-rich organic compound, such as a sugar or a starch, that is made of the elements carbon, hydrogen, and oxygen. (p. 27)
carbohidrato Compuesto orgánico rico en energía, como azúcar o almidón, que está formado por carbono, hidrógeno y oxígeno.

carrier A person who has one recessive allele for a trait, but does not have the trait. (p. 115)
portador Persona que tiene un alelo recesivo para un determinado rasgo, pero que no tiene el rasgo.

cast A type of fossil that forms when a mold becomes filled in with minerals that then harden. (p. 156)
vaciado Tipo de fósil se forma cuando un molde se llena con minerales que luego se endurecen.

cell The basic unit of structure and function in living things. (p. 7)
célula Unidad básica de estructura y función de los seres vivos.

cell cycle The regular sequence of growth and division that cells undergo. (p. 56)
ciclo celular Secuencia regular de crecimiento y división de las células.

cell membrane A cell structure that controls which substances can enter or leave the cell. (p. 17)
membrana celular Estructura celular que controla qué sustancias pueden entrar y salir de la célula.

cell theory A widely accepted explanation of the relationship between cells and living things. (p. 10)
teoría celular Explicación ampliamente aceptada sobre la relación entre las células y los seres vivos.

cell wall A rigid layer of nonliving material that surrounds the cells of plants and some other organisms. (p. 17)
pared celular Capa rígida de material no vivo que rodea las células vegetales y de algunos organismos.

chemotherapy The use of drugs to treat diseases such as cancer. (p. 66)
quimioterapia Uso de medicamentos para tratar enfermedades como el cáncer.

chlorophyll A green pigment found in the chloroplasts of plants, algae, and some bacteria. (p. 46)
clorofila Pigmento verde que se encuentra en los cloroplastos de las plantas, algas y algunas bacterias.

chloroplast A structure in the cells of plants and some other organisms that captures energy from sunlight and uses it to produce food. (p. 22)
cloroplasto Estructura en las células vegetales y algunos otros organismos que captan la energía de la luz solar y la usan para producir alimento.

chromosome A doubled rod of condensed chromatin; contains DNA that carries genetic information. (p. 57)
cromosoma Doble bastón de cromatina condensada; contiene ADN que transporta información genética.

clone An organism that is genetically identical to the organism from which it was produced. (p. 125)
clon Organismo que es genéticamente idéntico al organismo del que proviene.

codominance A condition in which neither of two alleles of a gene is dominant or recessive. (p. 89)
codominancia Condición en la que ninguno de los dos alelos de un gen es dominante ni recesivo.

compound Two or more elements that are chemically combined. (p. 26)
compuesto Dos o más elementos que se combinan químicamente.

cytokinesis The final stage of the cell cycle, in which the cell's cytoplasm divides, distributing the organelles into each of the two new cells. (p. 60)
citocinesis Fase final del ciclo celular en la cual se divide el citoplasma de la célula y se distribuyen los organelos en cada una de las dos nuevas células.

cytoplasm The region between the cell membrane and the nucleus; in organisms without a nucleus, the region located inside the cell membrane. (p. 19)
citoplasma Región entre la membrana celular y el núcleo; en los organismos sin núcleo, la región ubicada dentro de la membrana celular.

D

diffusion The process by which molecules move from an area of higher concentration to an area of lower concentration. (p. 33)
difusión Proceso por el cual las moléculas se mueven de un área de mayor concentración a otra de menor concentración.

dominant allele An allele whose trait always shows up in the organism when the allele is present. (p. 79)
alelo dominante Alelo cuyo rasgo siempre se manifesta en el organismo, cuando el alelo está presente.

DNA Deoxyribonucleic acid; the genetic material that carries information about an organism and is passed from parent to offspring. (p.29)
ADN Ácido desoxirribonucleico; material genético que lleva información sobre un organismo y que se pasa de padres a hijos.

E

element Any substance that cannot be broken down into simpler substances. (p. 25)
elemento Cualquier sustancia que no puede descomponerse en sustancias más pequeñas.

endoplasmic reticulum A cell structure that forms a maze of passageways in which proteins and other materials are carried from one part of the cell to another. (p. 19)
retículo endoplasmático Estructura celular que forma un laberinto de pasajes por los que se transportan las proteínas y otros materiales de una parte de la célula a otra.

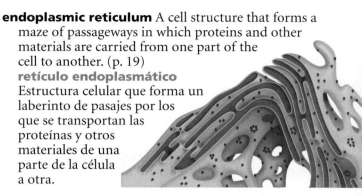

enzyme A type of protein that speeds up a chemical reaction in a living thing. (p. 28)
enzima Tipo de proteína que acelera la reacciones químicas en un ser vivo.

evolution The gradual change in a species over time. (p. 142)
evolución Cambio gradual de una especie a través del tiempo.

extinct Term used to indicate a species that does not have any living members. (p. 159)
extinto Término que se usa para indicar una especie que ya no tiene miembros vivos.

F

fermentation The process by which cells break down molecules to release energy without using oxygen. (p. 52)
fermentación Proceso por el cual las células descomponen las moléculas para liberar energía sin usar oxígeno.

fertilization the process in which an egg cell and a sperm cell join to form a new organism. (p. 77)
fecundación Proceso por el cual un óvulo y un espermatozoide se unen para formar un organismo nuevo.

fossil The preserved remains or traces of an organism that lived in the past. (p. 139)
fósil Restos o huellas preservados de un organismo que vivió en el pasado.

fossil record The millions of fossils that scientists have collected. (p. 158)
registro fósil Los millones de fósiles que han descubierto los científicos.

English and Spanish Glossary

gene The set of information that controls a trait; a segment of DNA on a chromosome that codes for a specific trait. (p. 79)
gen Conjunto de información que controla un rasgo; un segmento de ADN en un cromosoma el cual codifica un rasgo determinado.

gene therapy The insertion of working copies of a gene into the cells of a person with a genetic disorder in an attempt to correct the disorder. (p. 127)
terapia génica Inserción de copias activas de un gen en las células de una persona con un trastorno genético para intentar corregir dicho trastorno.

genetic disorder An abnormal condition that a person inherits through genes or chromosomes. (p. 118)
trastorno genético Condición anormal que hereda una persona a través de genes o cromosomas.

genetic engineering The transfer of a gene from the DNA of one organism into another organism, in order to produce an organism with desired traits. (p. 126)
ingeniería genética Transferencia de un gen desde el ADN de un organismo a otro, para producir un organismo con los rasgos deseados.

genetics The scientific study of heredity. (p. 76)
genética Ciencia que estudia la herencia.

genome All of the DNA in one cell of an organism. (p. 128)
genoma Todo el ADN de una célula de un organismo.

genotype An organism's genetic makeup, or allele combinations. (p. 88)
genotipo Composición genética de un organismo, es decir, las combinaciones de los alelos.

Golgi body A structure in a cell that receives proteins and other newly formed materials from the endoplasmic reticulum, packages them, and distributes them to other parts of the cell. (p. 22)
aparato de Golgi Estructura en la célula que recibe del retículo endoplasmático las proteínas y otros materiales recientemente formados, los empaqueta y los distribuye a otras partes de la célula.

gradualism The theory that evolution occurs slowly but steadily. (p. 163)
gradualismo Teoría que enuncia que la evolución ocurre lenta pero continuamente.

half-life The time it takes for half of the atoms in a radioactive element to break down. (p. 158)
vida media Tiempo que demoran en desintegrarse la mitad de los átomos de un elemento radioactivo.

heredity The passing of traits from parents to offspring. (p. 76)
herencia Transmisión de rasgos de padres a hijos.

heterotroph An organism that cannot make its own food. (p. 45)
heterótrofo Organismo que no puede producir su propio alimento.

heterozygous Having two different alleles for a trait. (p. 88)
heterocigoto Tener dos alelos diferentes para el mismo rasgo.

homologous structures Body parts that are structurally similar in related species; provide evidence that the structures were inherited from a common ancestor. (p. 150)
estructuras homólogas Partes del cuerpo que son estructuralmente similares entre las especies relacionadas; proveen evidencia de que las estructuras se heredaron de un antepasado común.

homozygous Having two identical alleles for a trait. (p. 88)
homocigoto Tener dos alelos idénticos para el mismo rasgo.

hybrid An organism that has two different alleles for a trait; an organism that is heterozygous for a particular trait. (p. 80)
híbrido Organismo que tiene dos alelos diferentes para un rasgo; un organismo que es heterocigoto para un rasgo en particular.

hybridization A selective breeding method in which two genetically different individuals are crossed. (p. 124)
hibridación Método de cruce selectivo en el cual se cruzan dos individuos genéticamente diferentes.

inbreeding A selective breeding method in which two individuals with identical or similar sets of alleles are crossed. (p. 124)
endogamia Método de cruce selectivo en el que se cruzan dos individuos con pares de alelos idénticos o semejantes.

interphase The stage of the cell cycle that takes place before cell division occurs. (p. 56)
interfase Fase del ciclo celular que ocurre antes de la división; durante esta fase la célula crece, copia su ADN y se prepara para la división.

karyotype A picture of all the chromosomes in a cell arranged in pairs. (p. 120)
cariotipo Imagen de todos los cromosomas de una célula, organizados en parejas.

lipid Energy-rich organic compound, such as a fat, oil, or wax, that is made of carbon, hydrogen, and oxygen. (p. 27)
lípido Compuesto orgánico rico en energía, como grasa, aceite y cera, formado por carbono, hidrógeno y oxígeno.

lysosome A small, round cell structure containing chemicals that break down large food particles into smaller ones. (p. 22)
lisosoma Pequeña estructura celular redonda que contiene sustancias químicas que descomponen las partículas de alimento grandes en otras más simples.

meiosis The process that occurs in the formation of sex cells (sperm and egg) by which the number of chromosomes is reduced by half. (p. 94)
meiosis Proceso que ocurre en la formación de las células sexuales (espermatozoide y óvulo) por el cual el número de cromosomas se reduce a la mitad.

messenger RNA RNA that copies the coded message from DNA in the nucleus and carries the message into the cytoplasm. (p. 99)
ARN mensajero ARN que copia el mensaje codificado del ADN en el núcleo y lo lleva al citoplasma.

microscope An instrument that makes small objects look larger. (p. 7)
microscopio Instrumento que hace que los objetos pequeños se vean más grandes.

mitochondria Rod-shaped cell structures that convert energy in food molecules to energy the cell can use to carry out its functions. (p. 19)
mitocondria Estructura celular con forma de bastón que transforma la energía de las moléculas de alimentos en energía que la célula puede usar para llevar a cabo sus funciones.

mitosis The stage of the cell cycle during which the cell's nucleus divides into two new nuclei and one copy of the DNA is distributed into each daughter cell. (p. 57)
mitosis Fase del ciclo celular durante la cual el núcleo de la célula se divide en dos nuevos nucleolos y se distribuye una copia del ADN a cada célula hija.

mold A type of fossil formed when a shell or other hard part of an organism dissolves, leaving an empty space in the shape of the part. (p. 156)
molde Tipo de fósil que se forma cuando la caparazón, concha u otra parte dura de un organismo enterrado se disuelve y deja un área hueca con la forma de esa parte.

multiple alleles Three or more forms of a gene that code for a single trait. (p. 112)
alelo múltiple Tres o más formas de un gen que codifican un solo rasgo.

mutation A change in a gene or chromosome. (p. 65)
mutación Cambio en un gen o cromosoma.

N

natural selection The process by which individuals that are better adapted to their environment are more likely to survive and reproduce than other members of the same species. (p. 143)
selección natural Proceso por el cual los individuos que se adaptan mejor a sus ambientes tienen más posibilidades de sobrevivir y reproducirse que otros miembros de la misma especie.

nucleic acid Very large organic molecule made of carbon, oxygen, hydrogen, nitrogen, and phosphorus, that contains the instructions cells need to carry out all the functions of life. (p. 29)
ácido nucléico Molécula orgánica muy grande compuesta de carbono, oxígeno, hidrógeno, nitrógeno y fósforo, que contiene las instrucciones que las células necesitan para realizar todas las funciones vitales.

English and Spanish Glossary

nucleus A cell structure that contains nucleic acids, the chemical instructions that direct all the cell's activities. (p. 18)
núcleo Estructura celular que contiene ácidos nucleicos, es decir, las instrucciones químicas que dirigen las actividades de la célula.

organelle A tiny cell structure that carries out a specific function within the cell. (p. 16)
organelo Diminuta estructura celular que realiza una función específica dentro de la célula.

osmosis The diffusion of water molecules through a selectively permeable membrane. (p. 34)
ósmosis Difusión de las moléculas de agua a través de una membrana con permeabilidad selectiva.

passive transport The movement of materials through a cell membrane without using energy. (p. 36)
transporte pasivo Movimiento de materiales a través de la membrana celular sin el uso de energía.

pedigree A chart or "family tree" that tracks which members of a family have a particular trait. (p. 119)
genealogía Tabla o "árbol genealógico" que muestra qué miembros de una familia tienen un rasgo en particular.

petrified fossil A fossil formed when minerals replace all or part of an organism. (p. 156)
fósil petrificado Fósil que se forma cuando los minerales reemplazan todo el organismo o parte de él.

phenotype An organism's physical appearance, or visible traits. (p. 88)
fenotipo Apariencia física de un organismo, es decir, los rasgos visibles.

photosynthesis The process by which plants and some other organisms capture the energy in sunlight and use it to make food. (p. 45)
fotosíntesis Proceso por el cual las plantas y otros organismos captan la energía de la luz solar y la usan para producir alimento.

pigment A colored chemical compound that absorbs light. (p. 46)
pigmento Compuesto químico de color que absorbe luz.

probability A number that describes how likely it is that an event will occur. (p. 84)
probabilidad Número que describe la posibilidad de que ocurra un suceso.

protein Large organic molecule made of carbon, hydrogen, oxygen, nitrogen, and sometimes sulfur. (p. 28)
proteína Molécula orgánica grande compuesta de carbono, hidrógeno, oxígeno, nitrógeno y, a veces, azufre.

punctuated equilibria The theory that species evolve during short periods of rapid change. (p. 163)
equilibrio puntuado Teoría que enuncia que las especies evolucionan durante períodos breves de cambios rápidos.

Punnett square A chart that shows all the possible combinations of alleles that can result from a genetic cross. (p. 86)
cuadrado de Punnett Tabla que muestra todas las combinaciones posibles de los alelos que pueden resultar de una cruza genética.

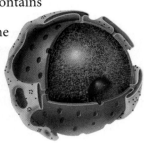

purebred The offspring of many generations that have the same traits. (p. 77)
raza pura Descendiente de muchas generaciones que tienen los mismos rasgos.

radioactive dating A technique used to determine the actual age of a fossil on the basis of the amount of a radioactive element it contains. (p. 158)
datación radiactiva Técnica que se usa para determinar la edad real de un fósil basándose en la cantidad de elementos radiactivos que contiene.

radioactive element An unstable element that breaks down into a different element. (p. 158)
elemento radiactivo Elemento inestable que se descompone en un elemento diferente.

recessive allele An allele that is masked when a dominant allele is present. (p. 79)
alelo recesivo Alelo que queda oculto cuando está presente un alelo dominante.

relative dating A technique used to determine which of two fossils is older. (p. 157)
datación relativa Técnica que se usa para determinar cuál de dos fósiles es más antiguo.

replication The process by which a cell makes a copy of the DNA in its nucleus. (p. 56)
replicación Proceso por el cual una célula copia el ADN en su núcleo.

respiration The process by which cells break down simple food molecules to release the energy they contain. (p. 50)
respiración Proceso por el cual las células descomponen moléculas simples de alimento para liberar la energía que contienen.

ribosome A small grain-like structure in the cytoplasm of a cell where proteins are made. (p.19)
ribosoma Estructura pequeña parecida a un grano en el citoplasma de una célula donde se fabrican las proteínas.

RNA Ribonucleic acid; a nucleic acid that plays an important role in the production of proteins. (p. 29)
ARN Ácido ribonucleico; ácido nucleico que juega un papel importante en la producción de proteínas.

scientific theory A well-tested concept that explains a wide range of observations. (p. 142)
teoría científica Concepto comprobado que explica una amplia gama de observaciones.

selective breeding The process of selecting a few organisms with desired traits to serve as parents of the next generation. (p. 124)
cruce selectivo Proceso de selección de algunos organismos con los rasgos deseados para que sirvan de como progenitores de la siguiente generación.

selectively permeable A property of cell membranes that allows some substances to pass through, while others cannot. (p. 32)
permeabilidad selectiva Propiedad de las membranas celulares que permite que algunas sustancias pasen y otras no.

sex chromosomes A pair of chromosomes carrying genes that determine whether a person is male or female. (p. 113)
cromosomas sexuales Par de cromosomas portadores de genes que determinan si una persona es macho o hembra.

sex-linked gene A gene that is carried on the X or Y chromosome. (p. 114)
gen ligado al sexo Gen portador del cromosoma X o Y.

species A group of similar organisms that can mate with each other and produce fertile offspring. (p. 139)
especie Grupo de organismos similares que pueden aparearse entre ellos y producir descendencia fértil.

stomata Small openings on the underside of a leaf through which oxygen and carbon dioxide can move. (p. 47)
estomas Pequeños orificios en la superficie inferior de la hoja a través de los cuales se intercambia oxígeno y dióxido de carbono.

trait A characteristic that an organism can pass on to its offspring through its genes. (p. 76)
rasgo Característica que un organismo puede transmitir a su descendencia a través de sus genes.

transfer RNA RNA in the cytoplasm that carries an amino acid to the ribosome and adds it to the growing protein chain. (p. 99)
ARN de transferencia ARN en el citoplasma que lleva un aminoácido al ribosoma y lo suma a la cadena proteínica que se está formando.

tumor A mass of abnormal cells that develops when cancerous cells divide and grow uncontrollably. (p. 65)
tumor Masa de células anormales que se desarrolla cuando las células cancerosas se dividen y crecen sin control.

vacuole A sac inside a cell that acts as a storage area. (p. 22)
vacuola Saco dentro de la célula que actúa como área de almacenamiento.

variation Any difference between individuals of the same species. (p. 143)
variación Cualquier diferencia entre individuos de la misma especie.

Index

Index

Index

Kaibab squirrel *153*
karyotype 120

laboratory safety 190–191
lactic acid fermentation 53
Leeuwenhoek, Anton van 9, 10
lenses, microscope 7
  magnification and 11–12
light microscope 7, 11–12
lipids 27
liter (L) 176
Lou Gehrig's Disease (ALS) 2
lung cancer 65, 67
lysosome 22

**magnification, microscope lenses
  and** 11–12
  compound microscope and 12
making models, skill of 175
manipulated variable 179
mass extinctions 162
mean 185
median 185
medicines, testing new 68–69
meiosis *94*–95, 145
  mutation during 102, 118
Mendel, Gregor 76–81
  discovery of genes and alleles
    79–81
  experiments of 76, 77–78, 86, 87
  as Father of Genetics 81
messenger RNA 99, 100–101
metaphase 57
meter (m) 176
microscope 7, 11–13, 196–197
  compound 7, 8, 12
  electron 13
  invention of 7
  light 7, 11–12
  magnification and lenses 11–12
  resolution 12
mitochondria *19*
  respiration in 51
mitosis 57
mode 185
mold (fossil) 156

molecules 26
  diffusion of **33**–34
monkey flowers 144
multiple alleles 112
**muscles, lactic acid fermentation
  in** 53
mutation 65, 102–103
  effects of 103, 118
  types of 102

naturalist, Darwin as 138
natural selection 143–145
  current evidence of 148
  overproduction and 143
nerve cell 23
nervous system 23
nitrogen bases in DNA 61
  of different species 151
  order of 98
  replication process and 62
nuclear envelope 18
nucleic acids 29
nucleolus 18
nucleus *18*
  absence of, in bacterial cell 24

observing, skill of 174
operational definition 179
organelles 16, 19–22
  chloroplasts **22,** 46, 47
  distribution to daughter cells, in
    cytokinesis 60
  endoplasmic reticulum *19*
  Golgi bodies 19, *22*
  lysosomes **22**
  mitochondria *19,* 51
  ribosomes 18, *19,* 99, 100
  vacuoles **22**
organic compounds 26
  carbohydrates **27**
  lipids **27**
  nucleic acids **29**
  proteins *28*
organisms 6
  cells in. *See* **cell**(s)
organs 23
organ systems 23
Origin of Species, The
  (Darwin) 143

osmosis 34–35
  effects of 35
  passive transport and **36**
**overproduction, natural selection
  and** 143
oxygen
  as product of photosynthesis 47
  respiration and 51

**parental generation (P
  generation)** 78
passive transport 36
**pea plants, Mendel's experiments
  with** 76, 77–78, 86, 87
pedigree *119*
percentage 85, **188**
**pesticide resistance, development
  of** 148
petrified fossils 156
phenotype *88*
  mutations affecting 102
phosphates 61
photosynthesis 44, **45**–48, 50
  comparing respiration and 52
  equation 48
  two stages of 46–48
pigments 46
pistil 77
plant cells 17–22
  cell wall of *17*
  cytokinesis in 60
  organelles in cytoplasm 19–22
  typical structures found in 20
plants
  adaptations to aid in
    reproduction 141
  cloning **125**
  containing starch 27
  genetically engineered 127
  photosynthesis by 44, **45**–48,
    50, 52
  stored energy in 48, 50
plasmids 126
pollination 77
  cross-pollination 77–78
  self-pollination 77, 78
**Precambrian Time (the
  Precambrian)** 159
precision 189
predicting, skill of 174
preserved remains, fossils of 156

Index ◆ 207

Index

Page numbers for key terms are printed in **boldface** type.
Page numbers for illustrations, maps, and charts are printed in *italics*.

Acknowledgments

Acknowledgment for page 172: From *James Herriot's Dog Stories* by James Herriot. Copyright © 1986 by the author and reprinted by permission of St. Martin's Press, LLC for US & reprinted by permission of Harold Ober Associated Incorporated for Canada.

Staff Credits

Diane Alimena, Scott Andrews, Jennifer Angel, Michele Angelucci, Laura Baselice, Carolyn Belanger, Barbara A. Bertell, Suzanne Biron, Peggy Bliss, Stephanie Bradley, James Brady, Anne M. Bray, Sarah M. Carroll, Kerry Cashman, Jonathan Cheney, Joshua D. Clapper, Lisa J. Clark, Bob Craton, Patricia Cully, Patricia M. Dambry, Kathy Dempsey, Leanne Esterly, Emily Ellen, Thomas Ferreira, Jonathan Fisher, Patricia Fromkin, Paul Gagnon, Kathy Gavilanes, Holly Gordon, Robert Graham, Ellen Granter, Diane Grossman, Barbara Hollingdale, Linda Johnson, Anne Jones, John Judge, Kevin Keane, Kelly Kelliher, Toby Klang, Sue Langan, Russ Lappa, Carolyn Lock, Rebecca Loveys, Constance J. McCarty, Carolyn B. McGuire, Ranida Touranont McKneally, Anne McLaughlin, Eve Melnechuk, Natania Mlawer, Janet Morris, Karyl Murray, Francine Neumann, Baljit Nijjar, Marie Opera, Jill Ort, Kim Ortell, Joan Paley, Dorothy Preston, Maureen Raymond, Laura Ross, Rashid Ross, Siri Schwartzman, Melissa Shustyk, Laurel Smith, Emily Soltanoff, Jennifer A. Teece, Elizabeth Torjussen, Amanda M. Watters, Merce Wilczek, Amy Winchester, Char Lyn Yeakley. **Additional Credits** Tara Alamilla, Louise Gachet, Allen Gold, Andrea Golden, Terence Hegarty, Etta Jacobs, Meg Montgomery, Stephanie Rogers, Kim Schmidt, Adam Teller, Joan Tobin.

Illustration

Art developed and produced by **Michelle Barbera:** 143–145; **Kerry Cashman:** 96, 106; **John Ceballos:** 30; **David Corrente:** 86–87; **John Edwards and Associates:** 10, 19t, 19b, 22, 33, 52, 87b, 152, 159; **Kevin Jones Associates:** 156–157; **Keith Kasnot:** 18; **Steve McEntee:** 35, 36, 61, 62, 99, 100–101; **Richard McMahon:** 46–47; **Karen Minot:** 45, 77, 78, 166; **Morgan-Cain & Associates:** 26, 58–59, 94–95; **J/B Woolsey Associates:** 40, 66–67, 72, 89, 126, 150; **XNR Productions:** 138–139. **All charts and graphs by Matt Mayerchak.**

Photography

Photo Research Paula Wehde

Cover Image top, David Madison/Getty Images, Inc.; **bottom,** Ian Walton/Getty Images, Inc.

Page vi, AP/Wide World Photos; **vii,** Richard Haynes; **viii,** E.R. Degginger/Color-Pic, Inc.; **x,** Rensselear Polytechnic Institute; **1l,** Angel E. Garcia (Los Alamos National Laboratory) and Jose N. Onuchic (University of California at San Diego); **1r,** Rensselear Polytechnic Institute; **2,** Bettmann/Corbis; **3,** Rensselear Polytechnic Institute.

Chapter 1

Pages 4–5, Dr. David E. Scott/Phototake; **5r,** Richard Haynes; **6t,** Richard Haynes; **6b,** McDonald Wildlife Photo, Inc./DRK Photo; **7t,** Photo Researchers, Inc.; **7b,** Richard Haynes; **8l,** FSU Research Foundation; **8m,** The Granger Collection; **8r,** Bettmann/Corbis; **9l,** Bettmann/Corbis; **9m,** Pascal Goetgheluck/SPL/Photo Researchers, Inc.; **9r,** Lawrence Migdale/Stock Boston; **10,** John Locke/Dembinsky Photo Associates; **11,** Getty Images, Inc.; **12t,** Photo Researchers, Inc.; **12bl,** Sinclair Stammers/SPL/Photo Researchers, Inc.; **12br,** SPL/Photo Researchers, Inc.; **13,** CRNI/SPL/Photo Researchers, Inc.; **14,** Richard Haynes; **16t,** Runk/Schoenberger/Grant Heilman Photography, Inc.;**16b,** Corbis; **17l,** Runk/Schoenberger/Grant Heilman Photography; **17r,** Mike Abbey/Visuals Unlimited; **18,** Alfred Paskieka/SPL/Photo Researchers, Inc.; **19t,** Bill Longcore/Photo Researchers, Inc.; **19b,** SPL/Photo Researchers, Inc.; **22,** Photo Researchers, Inc.; **23t,** Dr. David Scott/CRNI/Phototake; **23br,** Motta & S. Correr/SPL/Photo Researchers, Inc.; **23bl,** Eric V. Grave/Photo Researchers, Inc.; **24l,** Dr. Gary Gaugler/Photo Researchers, Inc.; **24m,** SNRI/Phototake; **24r,** Phototake; **25t,** Russ Lappa; **25b,** Jeffrey A. Scovil; **26,** Digital Vision/Getty Images, Inc.; **27t,** Japack Company/Corbis; **27m,** Andrew Syred/SPL/Photo Researchers, Inc.; **27bl,** Vittoriano Rastelli/Corbis; **27br,** Getty Images, Inc.; **28,** Scheidermeyer/OSF/Animals Animals/Earth Scenes; **31,** Richard Haynes; **32–33,** Damilo P. Donadomi/Bruce Coleman, Inc.; **35l,** Stanley Flegler/Visuals Unlimited; **35m,** David M. Phillips/Visuals Unlimited; **35r,** David M. Phillips/Visuals Unlimited; **37,** M. Abbey/Visuals Unlimited; **40,** Runk/ Schoenberger/Grant Heilman Photography.

Chapter 2

Pages 42–43, Michael J. Doolittle/The Image Works; **43r,** Russ Lappa; **44t,** Russ Lappa; **44–45b,** Todd Gustafson/Panoramic Images; **45 inset,** Stephen J. Krasemann/Photo Researchers, Inc.; **46,** Biophoto Associates/Photo Researchers, Inc.; **47,** Dr. Jeremy Burgess/SPL/Photo Researchers, Inc.; **48,** Superstock, Inc.; **49,** Royalty-Free/Corbis; **50l,** Stephen Dalton/Photo Researchers, Inc.; **50r,** Phil Dotson/Photo Researchers, Inc.; **53,** Richard Hutchins/PhotoEdit; **55t,** David Scharf/Peter Arnold, Inc.; **55b,** AP/Wide World Photos; **56–57t,** Royalty-Free/Corbis; **57b,** Biophoto Associates/Science Source/Photo Researchers, Inc.; **58–59 all,** M. Abbey/Photo Researchers, Inc.; **60,** Visuals Unlimited; **63,** Runk/Schoenberger/Grant Heilman Photography; **64t,** Richard Haynes; **64b,** Corbis; **65,** National Cancer Institute/SPL/Photo Researchers, Inc.; **68t,** Bettmann/Corbis; **68b,** Pallava Bagla/Corbis Sygma; **69t,** Royalty-Free/Corbis; **69b,** Gabe Palmer/Corbis; **70,** Royalty-Free/Corbis.

Chapter 3

Pages 74–75, Ron Kimball Studios; **75r,** Richard Haynes; **76t,** Getty Images, Inc.; **76bl,** Hulton Archive/Getty Images, Inc.; **76br,** Jerry Howard/Positive Images; **77,** Jerry Howard/Positive Images; **79,** Dorling Kindersley; **80 both,** Meinrad Faltner/Corbis; **81t,** David Young-Wolff/PhotoEdit; **81b,** Villanova University; **82tl,** Michael Newman/PhotoEdit; **82tml,** David Young-Wolff/PhotoEdit; **82tmr,** David Young-Wolff/PhotoEdit; **82tr,** David Young Wolff/PhotoEdit; **82bl,** Mary Kate Denny/PhotoEdit; **82bml,** Nicolas Russell/Getty Images, Inc.; **82bmr,** David Young-Wolff/PhotoEdit; **82br,** Corbis; **84t,** U.S. Mint/Omni-Photo Communications, Inc.; **84b,** David Young-Wolff/PhotoEdit; **85,** Jim Cummins/Getty Images, Inc.; **90,** Dorling Kindersley; **91t,** Dorling Kindersley; **91b,** Richard Haynes; **92,** Dennis Kunkel/Phototake; **93l,** Michael Abbey/Photo Researchers, Inc.; **93r,** E.R. Degginger/Color-Pic, Inc.; **97,** Adrian Warren/Last Refuge Ltd.; **103,** Dorling Kindersley; **104,** Adrian Warren/Last Refuge Ltd.

Chapter 4

Pages 108–109, Royalty-Free/Corbis; **109 inset,** Richard Haynes; **110b,** Michael Newman/PhotoEdit; **110t,** Richard Haynes; **111 grid, all,** David Young-Wolff/PhotoEdit; **111l,** Michael Newman/PhotoEdit; **111m,** David Urbina/PhotoEdit; **111r,** Everett Collection; **112,** Camille Tokerud/Getty Images, Inc.; **113l,** Biophoto Associates/Photo Researchers, Inc.; **113r,** Biophoto Associates/Photo Researchers, Inc.; **114l,** Corbis; **114r,** Michael Douma, Institute for Dynamic Educational Advancement; **116,** Amy Etra/PhotoEdit; **117b,** Jonathan Nourok/PhotoEdit; **117t,** CNRI/Photo Researchers, Inc.; **118 both,** Stanley Flegler/Visuals Unlimited; **119,** Craig Farraway; **121 both,** National Hemophilia Foundation; **122,** White Packert/Getty Images, Inc.; **123,** South West News Service; **124bl,** Foodpix; **124bm,** Photo Researchers, Inc.; **124br,** Foodpix; **124m,** Paul McCormick/Getty Images, Inc.; **124t,** Grant Heilman Photography, Inc.; **125,** Image Works; **127l,** 5-D and Segrest Farms/AP/Wide World Photos; **127r,** Animals Animals/Earth Scenes; **128,** Photo Researchers, Inc.; **129,** David Parker/Photo Researchers, Inc.; **130t,** Nathan Benn/Corbis; **130b,** Getty Images, Inc.; **131,** Andrew Brooks/Corbis; **132b,** Craig Farraway; **132t,** The Image Works.

Chapter 5

Pages 136–137, Tui De Roy/Minden Pictures; **137r,** Richard Haynes; **138t,** Portrait by George Richmond/Down House, Downe/Bridgeman Art Library; **138b,** Christopher Ralling; **138 frame,** Dorling Kindersley; **139 all,** Tui De Roy/Minden Pictures; **140t,** Photo Researchers, Inc.; **140b,** Jeremy Woodhouse/Masterfile; **141,** Dr. Jeremy Burgess/SPL/Photo Researchers, Inc.; **142t,** Barbara D. Livingston; **142m,** Barbara D. Livingston **142b,** AP/Wide World; **142 horseshoe,** Dorling Kindersley; **147,** Richard Haynes; **148t,** Richard Haynes; **148b,** Dorling Kindersley; **149 all,** Michael K. Richardson; **150l,** Photo Researchers, Inc.; **150m,** G. Alamany & E. Vicouns/Corbis; **150r,** Robert Pearcy; **151l,** Gary Milburn/Tom Stack & Associates, Inc.; **151r,** Betty K. Bruce/Animals Animals/Earth Scenes; **155t,** James L. Amos/Photo Researchers, Inc.; **155b,** AP/Wide World Photos; **157,** Peter Pavlovsky/Fossils.de; **162 all,** Douglas Henderson; **163,** Breck P. Kent; **164,** Photo Researchers, Inc.

Page 168b, Myrleen Ferguson Cate/PhotoEdit; **168t,** Bridgeman Art Library; **169,** Ron Kimball; **170 all except greyhound,** Corel Corp.; **170 greyhound,** Jack Daniels/Getty Images, Inc.; **171bl,** C. Jeanne White/Photo Researchers, Inc.; **171br,** Corel Corp.; **171m,** Corel Corp.; **171tl,** Corel Corp.; **171tr,** Dorling Kindersley; **172l,** G. K. & Vikki Hart/Getty Images, Inc.; **172r,** AP/Wide World Photos; **173,** Corbis; **174,** Tony Freeman/PhotoEdit; **175t,** Russ Lappa; **175m,** Richard Haynes; **175b,** Russ Lappa; **176,** Richard Haynes; **178,** Richard Haynes; **180,** Morton Beebe/Corbis; **181,** Richard Haynes; **183t,** Dorling Kinderlsey; **183b,** Richard Haynes; **185,** Image Stop/Phototake; **188,** Richard Haynes; **195,** Richard Haynes; **196,** Russ Lappa; **197 both,** Russ Lappa.